South–South Edu Humanitarianism

MW01493165

This ground-breaking book is one of the first to analyse the important phenomenon of South–South educational migration for refugees. It focuses particularly on South–South scholarship programmes in Cuba and Libya, which have granted free education to children, adolescents and young adults from two of the world's most protracted refugee situations: Sahrawis and Palestinians.

Through in-depth multi-sited fieldwork conducted with and about Sahrawi and Palestinian refugee-students in Cuba and Libya, and following their return to the desert-based Sahrawi refugee camps in Algeria and the urban Palestinian refugee camps in Lebanon, this highly pertinent study brings refugees' views and voices to the forefront and sheds a unique light on their understandings of self-sufficiency, humanitarianism and hospitality. It critically assesses the impact of diverse policies designed to maximise self-sufficiency and to reduce both brain drain and ongoing dependency upon Northern aid providers, exploring the extent to which South–South scholarship systems have challenged the power imbalances that typically characterise North to South development models.

Finally, this very timely study discusses the impact of the Arab Spring on Libya's support mechanisms for Sahrawi and Palestinian refugees, and considers the changing nature of Cuba's educational model in light of major ongoing political, ideological and economic shifts in the island state, asking whether there is a future for such alternative programmes and initiatives

This book will be a valuable resource for students, researchers and practitioners in the areas of migration studies, refugee studies, comparative education, development and humanitarian studies, international relations and regional studies (Latin America, Middle East and North Africa).

Elena Fiddian-Qasmiyeh is a Lecturer in Human Geography at University College London, UK.

Routledge Studies in Development, Mobilities and Migration

This series is dedicated to the growing and important area of mobilities and migration within Development Studies. It promotes innovative and interdisciplinary research targeted at a global readership.

The series welcomes submissions from established and junior authors on cutting-edge and high-level research on key topics that feature in global news and public debate.

These include the Arab Spring; famine in the Horn of Africa; riots; environmental migration; development-induced displacement and resettlement; livelihood transformations; people-trafficking; health and infectious diseases; employment; South–South migration; population growth; children's well-being; marriage and family; food security; the global financial crisis; drugs wars; and other contemporary crises.

South–South Educational Migration, Humanitarianism and Development

Views from the Caribbean,
North Africa and the Middle East

Elena Fiddian-Qasmiyeh

Routledge
Taylor & Francis Group

LONDON AND NEW YORK

First published 2015 by Routledge

2 Park Square, Milton Park, Abingdon, Oxfordshire OX14 4RN
711 Third Avenue, New York, NY 10017

Routledge is an imprint of the Taylor & Francis Group, an informa business

First issued in paperback 2017

British Library Cataloguing-in-Publication Data
A catalogue record for this book is available from the British Library

Library of Congress Cataloging-in-Publication Data
A catalog record for this book has been requested

ISBN: 978-0-415-81478-2 (hbk)
ISBN: 978-0-8153-7936-2 (pbk)

Typeset in Goudy
by HWA Text and Data Management, London

To Bissan-María and Yousif

'In a field where decentralised and historically-grounded studies remain rare, Fiddian-Qasmiyeh questions common assumptions about the nature, foundations, and lived experiences of humanitarian action. By documenting refugees' perceptions and pathways, she demonstrates that "alternative" models of support originating in the global South are neither utopias of solidarity nor mere political instruments. A challenging yet accessible insight into the complex identities, conflicting opportunities and paradoxical outcomes of humanitarian action.'

Eleanor Davey, University of Manchester, UK

'Fiddian-Qasmiyeh's excellent research opens our eyes to an important and neglected phenomenon: the transnational movement of refugees from one Southern state to another for educational purposes. Based on in-depth fieldwork, the author explains the politics underlying such movements and their social consequences, and unpacks the implications for how we think about humanitarianism and development. The book is accessible, well-written, and highly original.'

Alexander Betts, University of Oxford, UK

'This book draws attention to some of the most significant experiences of international migration today, those of Palestinian and Sahrawi refugee-migrant students, as they exercise agency over their own lives, pursuing ambitious education and employment goals in their camps in the MENA region and beyond. Their trials, tribulations and achievements are traced in minute detail from the perspective of individuals, families and (stateless) nations. This indispensible book also investigates the transnational education systems that have welcomed thousands of these and other refugees in Cuba and Libya. These modes of South–South co-operation and solidarity are largely unknown in the global North, and they are analysed here on the basis of extensive fieldwork in three continents. This book is a remarkable achievement, and it will remain an essential reference in the field.'

Alfredo Saad-Filho, University of London, UK

'Challenging canonical studies of Western-centric humanitarianism, this book unearths the neglected history of Southern-led interventions developed as a response to and in solidarity with Palestinian and Sahrawi refugees. Fiddian-Qasmiyeh carefully analyses the intersecting case studies of Palestinians and Sahrawis educated in Libya and Cuba, and traces their personal, professional and political experiences of returning as refugee-graduates to their home-camps in Lebanon and Algeria. Her thorough and critical assessment of Derrida and Agamben provides the critical foundations to centralise the agency of these refugees, and to further problematise the complex relationship between hospitality and hostility in these encounters.'

Sari Hanafi, American University of Beirut, Lebanon

Contents

Acknowledgements

This book is part of a broader comparative research project which examines the histories, modes of operation and implications of Southern-led responses to conflict-induced displacement. The book focuses specifically on initiatives revolving around South–South educational migration, drawing on the extensive research which I have conducted since 2001 with and about Middle Eastern and North African (MENA) refugees in countries both within and outside of the MENA region (including Algeria, Cuba, Lebanon, Libya, and Syria) – countries in the Global South which have provided different forms of humanitarian and development assistance to MENA refugee populations.

Between 2005 and 2010, this multi-sited research was funded by the Economic and Social Research Council (ESRC), and involved detailed ethnographic fieldwork in the Sahrawi refugee camps in Algeria, and in-depth analysis of Middle Eastern citizen and refugee students' experiences of studying in Cuba and Syria alike. In addition to thanking the ESRC for their support during the earlier stages of the research project, I am also grateful to the Fundación Fernando Ortiz in Havana, Cuba, which hosted me during my ESRC-funded Overseas Institutional Visit in 2006. Parts of the arguments developed in the following chapters have drawn significantly upon this research, and have appeared in earlier versions and other formats; I am grateful to the publishers for granting me permission to reproduce extracts from: 'Invisible Refugees and/or Overlapping Refugeedom? Protecting Sahrawis and Palestinians Displaced by the 2011 Libyan Uprising', *International Journal of Refugee Law* (2013) 24(2): 263–293; '"Paradoxes of Refugees" Educational Migration: Promoting self-sufficiency or renewing dependency?' *Comparative Education* (2011) 47(4): 433–447; 'Education, Migration and Internationalism: Situating Muslim Middle Eastern and North African students in Cuba', *The Journal of North African Studies* (2010) 15(2): 137–155; and 'Representing Sahrawi Refugees' "Educational Displacement" to Cuba: Self-sufficient agents or manipulated victims in conflict?' *Journal of Refugee Studies* (2009) 22(3): 323–350.

More recently, my interviews with and about Palestinian refugees who graduated from Cuba and Libya formed part of a study funded by the OUP Fell Fund between 2012 and 2014. Mohammad (Abu Iyad) and Mahmoud (Abu Ibrahim) provided detailed research assistance in the Palestinian refugee camps in Lebanon, for which I am immensely grateful. The OUP Fell Fund, the Oxford Department of International Development and the Refugee Studies Centre (University of Oxford), and the Policy Development and Evaluation Service of the United Nations High Commissioner for Refugees all provided invaluable support for an international workshop which I convened at the Refugee Studies Centre in October 2012, entitled South–South Humanitarianism in Contexts of Forced Displacement. I am grateful to these institutions for their support, and to the presenters and participants at the 2012 Workshop for their insightful contributions during and after the event.

At the Oxford Department of International Development, I would like to thank Julia Pacitto for her research assistance throughout the course of the project funded by the OUP Fell Fund, and Chloé Lewis and Georgia Cole for their help with the Workshop and the Workshop Report. Sections of Chapter 2 expand upon my concept paper for the Workshop and broader project, and the RSC Working Paper which Julia and I co-authored in 2012–2013 (*Writing the 'Other' into humanitarian discourse: Framing theory and practice in South–South humanitarian responses to forced displacement*, Working Paper No. 93). Chapter 2 in particular also benefited from the dynamic discussions at the 2012 South–South Humanitarianism Workshop in Oxford, and throughout the course of the Workshop hosted by Save the Children UK, in partnership with the Non-State Humanitarianism Network and the Humanitarian Policy Group, on *Between the Global and the Local in Humanitarian Action*, in April 2014.

At Routledge, I would like to thank Khanam Virjee, Charlotte Russell and Bethany Wright for their support and encouragement throughout all stages of this book project. Holly Knapp and Bramble Coppins also provided invaluable editorial assistance, for which I am grateful.

On a personal level, I am thankful to Gema Alcaide Cantero for having so lovingly looked after Bissan-María as I finalised this manuscript. None of this would have been possible without Yousif's patience, love and support for his family. As always, Yousif has pushed me to think and rethink, to write and rewrite, critically and carefully. Bisou and I are immensely fortunate – thank you.

Acronyms

ASEAN	Association of Southeast Asian Nations
DFLP	Democratic Front for the Liberation of Palestine
EFA	Education For All
GDP	gross domestic product
ICRC	International Committee of the Red Cross
INGO	international non-governmental organisation
LDC	least developed country
MENA	Middle East and North Africa
MINUSTAH	United Nations Stabilization Mission in Haiti
NGO	non-governmental organisation
NUSW	National Union of Sahrawi Women
OAU	Organization of African Unity
OCHA	Office for the Coordination of Humanitarian Affairs
OECD	Organisation for Economic Co-operation and Development
OPT	Occupied Palestinian Territories
PFLP	Popular Front for the Liberation of Palestine
PLO	Palestine Liberation Organization
Polisario Front	Popular Front for the Liberation of Saguiat el-Hamra and Rio de Oro
SADR	Sahrawi Arab Democratic Republic
SSC	Special Unit for South-South Cooperation of the United Nations Development Programme
UN	United Nations
UNCTAD	United Nations Conference on Trade and Development
UNDP	United Nations Development Programme
UNESCO	United Nations Educational, Scientific and Cultural Organization
UNFPA	United Nations Population Fund
UNHCR	United Nations High Commissioner for Refugees
UNICEF	United Nations Children's Fund
UNRWA	United Nations Relief and Works Agency for Palestine Refugees in the Near East

1 South–South educational migration and development

Introduction

Refugees often engage in multiple, and overlapping, forms of mobility and migration: far from being stagnant and dependent objects of humanitarian action who wait to be 'saved' by powerful Others,[1] Sahrawi and Palestinian refugees – amongst many others – have historically been highly mobile within and outside the Middle East and North Africa (MENA) for educational and employment purposes alike.

MENA refugees' access to Cuban and Libyan schools and universities are key examples of the ways in which transnational education systems have been created by, and in, the margins for other marginal(ised) populations: through such programmes, education has been provided by the Other for the Other, with providers and recipients alike being from, and of, the periphery.[2] In the context under analysis, the educational providers (two sovereign states) can be conceptualised as being positioned in the independent margin, providing support to members of the dependent margin: refugees who belong to territories and groups pending decolonisation and self-determination.

This book, therefore, examines the experiences of Sahrawi and Palestinian refugees during and after studying in Cuba and Libya both as a form of international educational migration, and as an example of South–South cooperation. In addition to, or precisely by, providing a different entry point to the analysis of the education-migration nexus from the perspective of non-aligned states, the Cuban and Libyan initiatives, as models of South–South cooperation, concurrently provide an 'alternative' to hegemonic responses to, and analyses of, forced migration.

These programmes have often offered an explicit challenge to mainstream theory, policy and practice vis-à-vis development and humanitarianism. Indeed, the policies and programmes advocated by Northern states and international organisations 'normatively privilege ... some forms of migration and/or development... [while] others [are] occluded through their invisibilisation' (Raghuram 2009: 108). To this I would add that these actors also 'normatively privilege' certain models of education, and certain student(s') bodies, to the detriment of Others. Through these (and other) mutually reinforcing processes, diverse forms of migration (such as refugee children's, adolescents' and young adults' migration to *access* education), planes and directionalities of migration ('horizontal' and South–South migration), or alternative conceptualisations of development and humantarianism (such as local, national or international self-sufficiency) have been marginalised from view. This book consequently places these marginalised subjects at the core of its analysis.

I start from the premise that not all international students, refugees and education systems are equally positioned, or have similar aims and expectations for the future. Indeed, if international student migration as a whole has remained under-examined (King and Raghuram 2013: 127), the experiences of hybrid figures such as 'refugee-student-migrants' have received even less academic attention, especially in the context of educational migration within the Global South, and in contexts which oppose, rather than reproduce, financially driven models of education.[3]

In particular, the book critically traces and examines the history and legacies of initiatives developed by two such states with a long history of supporting anti-colonial and liberation movements – Cuba and Libya – for two groups of long-standing Middle Eastern refugees. The first are Sahrawi refugees whose families are amongst the approximately 165,000 refugees currently in desert-based refugee camps in South-West Algeria; the Sahrawi are the United Nations High Commissioner for Refugees' second-most long-standing caseload, having been displaced in 1975 when the non-self-governing territory now known as the Western Sahara (formerly called the Spanish Sahara) was occupied by force by Morocco and Mauritania.[4] The second group are Palestinian refugees – the oldest protracted refugee situation in the world as a result of their expulsion, displacement and dispossession before, during and after the establishment of the state of Israel in 1948. An estimated 5 million Palestinians remain dispersed across the Middle East and in the broader diaspora outside of the MENA region, with this book focusing on those Palestinians who have migrated to Cuba or Libya from their urban refugee camp homes in Lebanon, a country which hosts approximately 455,000 Palestinians (UNRWA, 2014).

The comparative analysis developed in this book across these two refugee groups is highly relevant because '[t]he considerable literature on "refugee education" that has developed *overlooks the case of Palestinian refugees in host countries*' (Demirdjian 2012: 14, emphasis added). 'Overlooking' Palestinian refugees is habitual within Refugee and Forced Migration Studies due to academics', politicians' and policymakers' claims of Palestinian 'exceptionalism' (Kagan 2009; Akram 2014). In part, these claims to Palestinian exceptionalism are justified on the basis that although the United Nations High Commissioner for Refugees (UNHCR) is mandated to assist and protect 'refugees' around the world (including Sahrawi refugees), Palestinians are the only group of refugees excluded from the UNHCR's mandate since a separate United Nations (UN) agency – the United Nations Relief and Works Agency (UNRWA) – is ostensibly responsible for them (and their education) in five operational areas of the contemporary Middle East: Lebanon (the focus of this book), Syria, Jordan, Gaza and the West Bank. A related distinction is that although the 'international' definition of a 'refugee' is encompassed in the 1951 Geneva Convention on the Status of Refugees,[5] no such Convention definition exists for *Palestinian* refugees.[6]

If the provision of primary, secondary and tertiary level education for refugees is to be heralded – as international humanitarian agencies and Northern donors increasingly hold[7] – this leads us to interrogate why the programmes centralised in this book have been, at best, relegated to the margins of academic and policy analysis. Education may indeed now be recognised as a human right, and yet 'the ideology underpinning education and the organization, delivery and content of education is not neutral, and indeed can never be neutral because it always has political intention either for the domination of people or for their liberation' (Alzaroo and Lewando-Hundt 2003: 166). In this regard, both the Cuban and Libyan *national* education systems have been scrutinised on the basis of their ideological foundations and aims, often leading to their rejection of these as systems geared towards indoctrinating children and youth.[8] In contrast, the internationalist nature and implications of the Cuban education programme, and the Pan-Arabist reach of Libya's education system, have remained under-examined to date, especially vis-à-vis their relationship with, and influence upon, refugee groups from the Middle East and North Africa.

In effect, the Cuban and Libyan case studies clearly correspond to the broader networks 'of education systems under historical socialism' which are receiving increasing attention, 'particularly [due to] the provision of education for *citizens* of other, non-socialist, developing *countries* under the banner of international solidarity and as demonstrations of the superiority of socialist ideology' (Griffiths and Millei 2013: 165, emphasis added). As argued in this book, such systems reached not only *citizens* from developing *countries*, but also *refugee* children, adolescents and young adults associated with liberation movements struggling for the right to self-determination in the MENA region.[9]

This book demonstrates not only the importance of historically and geopolitically situating the experiences of refugees as international *students* but also of understanding the contours, experiences and impacts of educational *migration* as lived processes of (im)mobility, departure, arrival, emplacement and displacement. Furthermore, examining Cuba's and Libya's support for Sahrawi and Palestinian refugees through a *migratory* lens also enables us to develop an alternative analysis of dependency theories, which are traditionally understood to conceptualise migration as part of the exploitative capitalist system which leads to 'brain drain' (i.e. see de Haas 2008; King 2012: 17–18). This widespread interpretation of dependency theory effectively assumes that 'migration' is equal to 'labour migration', that movement will take place in a particular direction (from South to North) and that migration itself causes 'the development of underdevelopment' (Baran 1973). In contrast, a more nuanced relationship between migration and (under)development can be recognised if this equation between 'migration' and 'labour migration' from peripheral countries to the Northern core is disrupted.

Cuba's and Libya's state policies and worldviews have historically been heavily influenced by dependency theories, and yet certain configurations of *educational* migration have been seen by these states as a possible *solution* to underdevelopment and geopolitical marginalisation (also see Fiddian-Qasmiyeh 2010, 2011). A key question explored in the following chapters is, therefore, to what extent refugees' access to basic and further education in Southern states such as Cuba or Libya challenges, or reproduces, ties of dependency between refugees and their communities of origin on the one hand, and hegemonic states and institutions on the other.

Structure of the book

Following this introductory chapter, the history and broad aims of South–South cooperation are explored in Chapter 2, reflecting on its origin as an anti-colonial paradigm associated with the non-aligned movement, to the present day institutional mainstreaming of South–South initiatives by Northern states, and inter-governmental agencies including the United Nations Development Programme (UNDP) and UNHCR. The chapter argues that recognising the historical and ongoing significance of South–South cooperation enables us to (re)inscribe, rather than erase, Others from the multifaceted history of development and humanitarian action writ large.[10] Furthermore, it notes that in spite of increasing attention to South–South development initiatives – such as China's development projects across Sub-Saharan Africa and collaboration on South–South technology transfer – studies of South–South humanitarian responses to refugee situations are almost entirely absent from the literature. This long-standing gap in theoretical and conceptual engagement with Other models of responding to displacement and dispossession – including in the context of refugee education – is, therefore, filled in the subsequent chapters by focusing on how, why and to what effect Cuba and Libya have provided a free education to refugees from the Middle East and North Africa.

Turning to the first main case-study – Cuba's model of South–South cooperation with MENA refugees – Chapter 3 outlines the Cuban internationalist scholarship programme as a whole, before highlighting the ideological and political connections which have existed between Cuba and Arab socialist states and liberation movements since the 1950s, and the broad conditions which make Sahrawi and Palestinian students' educational migration to Cuba desirable or necessary. It then explores the experiences and expectations of a group of MENA students[11] who were studying in Cuba at the time of my research there in 2006.[12] The chapter thus traces students' accounts of material conditions in Cuba and at 'home', and of the nature of social relations with Cuban citizens and other MENA students, including with regards to religious identity and practice. It then concludes by turning to students' expectations for their own future upon graduation and the future of the programme itself, reflecting not only upon the transnational and trans-generational nature of the Cuban programme, but also on the extent to which Cuba's provision of scholarships for doubly and triply marginalised MENA refugees has created a space for what Qasmiyeh and I call the 'central margin' (Fiddian-Qasmiyeh 2010).

By presenting students' accounts of the educational migration programme through interviews conducted in Cuba, Chapter 3, therefore, offers one particular perspective of the scholarship system which is subsequently compared and contrasted with Sahrawi and Palestinian graduates' accounts of having studied in Cuba and having returned to their refugee camp homes – to the desert-based Sahrawi refugee camps in South-West Algeria (Chapter 4) and the urban Palestinian refugee camps across Lebanon (Chapter 5) respectively.

Chapter 4 examines the accounts of Sahrawi graduates in their home-camps in Algeria, arguing that although 'Cuba' is pivotal in Sahrawi refugees' imaginary landscapes and ideoscapes in the camps, a range of paradoxical outcomes have arisen from Sahrawi participation in this education programme. Hence, although a 'central margin' may have been created in Cuba, many graduates have experienced different forms of marginalisation and ostracism upon their return to the camps – female graduates in particular – while other graduates have placed themselves at the margins of the camps by undertaking onward labour migration to work as medical doctors in Spain, where their Cuban medical degrees are readily recognised. The chapter concludes by exploring the emerging ways in which different individuals and groups in the Sahrawi context evaluate these and other courses of action in relation to notions of 'self-sufficiency' and renewed dependence upon the North. In essence, the chapter contends that the Cuban scholarship system has reshaped and reinforced, rather than reduced, the Sahrawi refugee camps' dependence upon Northern aid providers, and yet Sahrawi refugees disagree as to whether these outcomes are considered to be a 'success' or a 'failure' in securing a 'better future' for Sahrawi individuals and families in the refugee camps and for the Sahrawi quest for self-determination more broadly.

An alternative perspective on the Cuban educational migration programme, and of 'self-sufficiency', is offered in Chapter 5 through a critical analysis of Palestinian graduates' narratives of gaining access to, studying in and returning from Cuba. Taking an explicitly comparative approach with the perspectives offered in Cuba and in the Sahrawi refugee camps, the chapter argues that Palestinian graduates in Lebanon have developed diverse discursive and practical strategies to distance themselves from Cuba's influence and legacy, including by centralising the roles played by Palestinian actors throughout all stages of their migration to and from Cuba. The chapter subsequently considers the ways in which Palestinian graduates retrospectively conceptualise the nature and impacts of the Cuban educational migration programme, through reference to identity, ideology, politics and humanitarianism. By placing Palestinian refugee graduates' reflections of the relationship between humanitarianism, politics and ideology at the forefront of the analysis, this chapter, therefore, fills a major gap in debates which consistently prioritise the perspectives of academics, policymakers and practitioners on programmes which are designed and implemented on refugees' behalf. If the discursive erasure of Cuba's legacy can be linked to graduates' fears that they might be perceived by external actors (and especially by UNRWA) to have been indoctrinated whilst studying in Cuba, the ongoing influence of Cuba's education programme is in many ways also the result of structural conditions, in this case local, national and international conditions which have (thus far) prevented Palestinian graduates from leaving the camps to work in Europe (as their Sahrawi counterparts have) or to work in Lebanese hospitals (due to the prohibition of Palestinians' employment as doctors in Lebanon). Consequently, Palestinian refugees continue to benefit from graduates' professional training in Cuba not only because they are committed to supporting their communities, but also because these graduates have limited alternatives. If the education programme has facilitated a high degree of Palestinian self-sufficiency in terms of medical professionals treating Palestinian patients in the camps, I conclude that this outcome can in many ways be considered to represent a form of what I refer to as 'circumstantial humanitarianism'.

Building upon the trans-regional, intergenerational and multi-directional links examined in Chapters 3, 4 and 5, Chapter 6 explores the changing nature and impact of Libya's support for Sahrawi and Palestinian refugees through initiatives, based upon Gaddafi's Pan-Arabist commitments, which are intimately linked to and yet significantly different from the Cuban internationalist education programme. In particular, this chapter examines the nature and implications of Libya's bifurcated approach to supporting Sahrawis on the one hand and Palestinians on the other. It starts by briefly tracing the history of Libya's structured support for Sahrawis, including through reference to Sahrawi graduates' experiences of having been allocated scholarships as young children through a bilateral agreement between the Polisario Front and the Libyan state. It then explores how, why and with what effect Gaddafi supported Palestinians' access to Libya's educational establishments through a range of intersecting mechanisms, including the provision of a small number of scholarships – primarily for individual Palestinians affiliated with particular factions to attend military colleges in Libya – but more broadly through the implementation of policies which facilitated the South–South migration of tens of thousands of Palestinians to Libya both as refugee-students but also as refugee-migrant workers.

In contrast with the formal scholarships institutionalised by Libya on behalf of Sahrawi refugees, Chapter 6 argues that Palestinians' migration to form part of Libya's transnational eduscape, as students and teachers alike, can best be conceptualised as a process of 'self-service', a term I use to capture the extent to which Palestinians were encouraged to 'help themselves' by migrating to Libya, but also to centralise the practical and political benefits which Libya itself accrued by virtue of Palestinians' presence in North Africa. A key question guiding the chapter is, therefore, the extent to which Libya's support for refugees' education can be conceptualised as a mode of South–South cooperation designed to promote the self-sufficiency of refugees, and/or is more readily identifiable as part of Gaddafi's Pan-Arabist ideology and regional aims. Ultimately, I argue that far from creating a 'central margin' via education, Libya's approach to Sahrawi refugees, but especially to Palestinians, can thus be conceptualised as a policy of *hostipitality* (following Derrida 2000) towards these refugees. This line of argumentation is developed through an analysis of discriminatory policies implemented sporadically by Gaddafi, and three major occasions when Sahrawi and Palestinian refugees alike faced mass expulsion from Libya – in the 1980s and 1990s when political relations between the Polisario and Gaddafi on the one hand and the Palestine Liberation Organization (PLO) and Gaddafi on the other were particularly fraught – and, more recently, as a result of the 2011 uprising in Libya. Through the notion of 'unintentional humanitarianism', the chapter argues that Libya's support for/to Sahrawi and Palestinian refugees was both accidental, rather than by design, and equally permeated with injury, disaster and renewed processes of displacement and dispossession.

By outlining the ambivalence of South–South programmes designed to support MENA refugees, and the tensions and violence which have led to expulsion at different geopolitical junctures, this chapter thereby provides the foundation to engage critically with the diverse opportunities and challenges which may emerge in South–South development/humanitarian initiatives which can, in turn, create and perpetuate, rather than reduce or eliminate, diverse forms of vulnerability and dependence.

Indeed, by viewing Cuba's and Libya's education programmes as processes of international migration, these chapters collectively also examine the fluid relationship(s) between voluntary and forced migration: as 'refugee-students' and 'refugee-graduates', the programmes' beneficiaries are simultaneously members of families who were forcibly displaced from their original homelands, and individuals who have left their home-camps to study abroad.[13] Eventually, these students also become 'refugee returnees' who return to their camp-based homes after a prolonged absence, and yet remain unable to repatriate to their occupied homelands. The complexity of overlapping forms of migration and displacement is further exemplified in the case of Sahrawi and Palestinian refugee-students who left their home-camps to study abroad and yet were forcibly displaced whilst studying in Libya, both in the context of the 2011 uprising, but also in earlier phases of the scholarship programme. The example of refugee-students in Libya explored in Chapter 6 thus demonstrates that, although policies are purposively developed by Southern states to support refugees across the South–South complex, initiatives designed under the remit of 'cooperation' may be characterised by instability and conflict on different levels, and can potentially lead to multiple and overlapping experiences of marginalisation, displacement and dispossession.

Drawing the book to a close, the concluding chapter rearticulates a set of continuities and discontinuities present in these intersecting models of South–South cooperation. It does so through an expanded interpretation of the notion of 'the exception': viewing the Cuban and Libyan cooperation models on the one hand, and the Palestinian and Sahrawi refugees on the other, as 'exceptional' initiatives and groups which transcend diverse expectations; in terms of Cuba and Libya 'making an exception' for Sahrawis and Palestinians through the institutionalisation of 'special treatment' (both in terms of rewards *and* punishments); and with reference to different actors 'taking exception to' the priorities and decisions of Southern states and refugee beneficiaries alike. The conclusion, therefore, assesses the extent to which these interconnected case studies may or may not provide a meaningful 'alternative' model for supporting long-term refugees, and the extent to which these or other forms of South–South intervention are, or potentially could be, founded upon reciprocity, the equalisation of power dynamics and 'solidarity'.

Notes

1 This widely held assumption has been actively critiqued, and ultimately rejected by scholars of Refugee and Forced Migration Studies since the 1980s, and especially since Harrell-Bond's classic, *Imposing Aid*, was published in 1986. Also see Fiddian-Qasmiyeh et al. (2014).

2 Although the world is witnessing 'a rapidly changing transnational eduscape' (Madge et al. 2014: 2), it is clearly the case that 'there is, and has always been, a complex multi-centred character of student mobility for international study at a variety of spatial scales, including south–south transfers and circulations between smaller regionally significant places' (ibid.: 12).

3 When research has examined the connection between education and migration, this has primarily taken place within the context of particular geographies, focusing on tertiary level educational migration as a subset of skilled migration occurring between or to Organisation for Economic Co-operation and Development (OECD) countries (Schapiro 2009). This primary focus on university students' migration to the Global North can be justified both in relation to the greater availability of statistical data in the OECD states, but also precisely due to the fact that these migrants are a major source of revenue for the North. It is only recently that academic research has started to examine international student migration and mobility in the context of the Global South.

4 For a detailed history of the conflict over the Western Sahara, see Fiddian-Qasmiyeh (2014).

5 An individual who 'owing to well-founded fear of being persecuted for reasons of race, religion, nationality, membership of a particular social group or political opinion, is outside the country of his [sic] nationality and is unable or, owing to such fear, is unwilling to avail himself [sic] of the protection of that country'.

6 Instead, *Palestine refugees* are defined for operational purposes by UNRWA (2009) as 'persons whose normal place of residence was Palestine during the period 1 June 1946 to 15 May 1948, and who lost both home and means of livelihood as a result of the 1948 conflict', in addition to their descendants.

7 For instance, see UNHCR (2007), Pinson et al. (2010), UNESCO (2011), Dermirdjian (2012) and Bartlett and Ghaffar-Kucher (2013).

8 Much more infrequently, such systems have been idealised, depending on the ideological and political commitments of the analyst in question. More generally, offering both Sahrawi and Palestinian refugees access to educational opportunities in Cuba and Libya is, in many regards, in line with Samoff's identification of one of the 'legacies of the educational agenda of socialist and "transition" states as having "expanded the education agenda" globally, such that education was widely understood as a human right' (Samoff 1991: 20, cited in Griffiths and Millei 2013: 164). Griffiths and Millei are quoting from Samoff's Introduction to the 1991 Special Issue on 'Education and Socialist (R)Evolution'.

9 The centrality of education to liberation movements is extensively documented: Madge et al. (2014: 13); also see Fiddian-Qasmiyeh (2014).

10 Pacitto and I have also developed this argument further (Pacitto and Fiddian-Qasmiyeh 2013).

11 Although there are many Christian Arab students in Cuba, Chapter 3 focuses specifically on the experiences and presence of Muslim Arab students in Cuba. It

thereby complements a newly emerging (Cuban and international) interest in documenting the historical and multifaceted nature of (forced and voluntary) immigration from the Middle East and North Africa to the island from the sixteenth century to the present (see Fiddian-Qasmiyeh forthcoming). I suggest that the presence of Muslim Arab youth in Cuba today can be understood as constituting a new form of migration – educational migration – which supersedes previous forms of connections between the Middle East and Cuba (also see Fiddian-Qasmiyeh 2010).

12 All interviews in Cuba were conducted in Spanish, while interviews in Algeria and Spain were conducted in both Spanish and in Modern Standard Arabic (*Fus-ha*). All quotations included throughout Chapters 3 and 4 are my own translations, unless noted elsewhere. The interviews conducted in Lebanon were, in turn, completed in the Palestinian dialect of Arabic, with all translations undertaken by the author in consultation with Yousif M. Qasmiyeh to ensure the accuracy of the translation.

13 In the case of children as young as six or eleven, whether these students have given their informed consent to participate in a programme is in and of itself a highly complex matter.

References

Akram, S. (2014) 'UNRWA and Forced Migration', in E. Fiddian-Qasmiyeh, G. Loescher, K. Long, and N. Sigona (eds) *The Oxford Handbook of Refugee and Forced Migration Studies*. Oxford: Oxford University Press, 227–240.

Alzaroo, S. and Lewando-Hundt, G. (2003) 'Education in the Context of Conflict and Instability: The Palestinian Case', *Social Policy and Administration*, 37(2): 165–180.

Baran, P. (1973) 'On the political economy of backwardness', in C.K. Wilber (ed.) *The Political Economy of Development and Underdevelopment*. New York: Random House, 82–93.

Bartlett, L. and Ghaffar-Kucher, A. (2013) 'Introduction: Refugees, Immigrants, and Education in the Global South – Lives in Motion', in L. Bartlett and A. Ghaffar-Kucher (eds) *Refugees, Immigrants, and Education in the Global South: Lives in Motion*. New York: Routledge, 1–21.

de Haas, H. (2008) *Migration and Development: A Theoretical Perspective*, International Migration Institute Working Paper No. 9. Oxford: International Migration Institute.

Demirdjian, L. (ed.) (2012) *Education, Refugees and Asylum Seekers: Education as a Humanitarian Response*, London: Continuum Publishing Corporation.

Derrida, J. (2000) 'Hostipitality', *Angelaki: Journal of the Theoretical Humanities*, 5(3): 3–18.

Fiddian-Qasmiyeh, E. (forthcoming) 'Embracing Transculturalism and Footnoting Islam in Accounts of Arab Migration to Cuba', *Interventions: International Journal of Postcolonial Studies*.

Fiddian-Qasmiyeh, E. (2014) *The Ideal Refugees: Gender, Islam and the Sahrawi Politics of Survival*. Syracuse, NY: Syracuse University Press.

Fiddian-Qasmiyeh, E. (2011) 'Paradoxes of Refugees' Educational Migration: Promoting Self-sufficiency or Renewing Dependency?' *Comparative Education*, 47(4): 433–447.

Fiddian-Qasmiyeh, E. (2010) 'Education, Migration and Internationalism: Situating Muslim Middle Eastern and North African students in Cuba', *The Journal of North African Studies*, 15(2): 137–155.

Fiddian-Qasmiyeh, E., Loescher, G., Long, K. and Sigona, N. (2014) 'Introduction: Refugee and Forced Migration Studies in Transition', in E. Fiddian-Qasmiyeh, G. Loescher, K. Long and N. Sigona (eds) *The Oxford Handbook of Refugee and Forced Migration Studies*. Oxford: Oxford University Press, 1–19.

Griffiths, T.G. and Millei, Z. (2013) 'Education in/for Socialism: Historical, Current and Future Perspectives', *Globalisation, Societies and Education*, 11(2): 161–169.

Harrell-Bond, B.E. (1986) *Imposing Aid: Emergency Assistance to Refugees*. Oxford: Oxford University Press.

Kagan, M. (2009) 'The (Relative) Decline of Palestinian Exceptionalism and its Consequences for Refugee Studies in the Middle East', *Journal of Refugee Studies*, 22(4): 417–438.

King, R. (2012) 'Theories and Typologies of Migration', Willy Brandt Series of Working Papers in International Migration and Ethnic Relations, 3/12. Malmö: Malmö Institute for Studies of Migration, Diversity and Welfare, Malmö University.

King, R. and Raghuram, P. (2013) 'International Student Migration: Mapping the Field and New Research Agendas', *Population, Space and Place*, 19(2): 127–137.

Madge, C., Raghuram, P. and Noxolo, P. (2014) 'Conceptualizing International Education: From International Student to International Study', *Progress in Human Geography*, 31 March, doi:10.1177/0309132514526442.

Pacitto, J. and Fiddian-Qasmiyeh, E. (2013) 'Writing the "Other" into Humanitarian Discourse: Framing Theory and Practice in South-South Humanitarian Responses to Forced Displacement', *RSC Working Paper No. 93*. Oxford: Refugee Studies Centre.

Pinson, H., Arnot, M. and Candappa, M. (2010). *Education, Asylum and the Non-citizen Child: The Politics of Compassion and Belonging*, London: Palgrave Macmillan.

Raghuram, P. (2009) 'Which Migration, What Development? Unsettling the Edifice of Migration and Development', *Population, Space and Place*, 45(2): 103–117.

Samoff, J. (1991) 'Socialist Education?' *Comparative Education Review*, 35(1): 1–22.

Schapiro, K.E. (2009) 'Migration and Educational Outcomes of Children', UNDP Human Development Research Paper 2009/57. New York: UNDP.

UNESCO (2011) *The Hidden Crisis: Armed Conflict and Education*. EFA Global Monitoring Report. Paris: UNESCO.

UNHCR (2007) *Tertiary Refugee Education: Impact and Achievements*. Geneva: UNHCR.

UNRWA (2014) 'Where We Work: Lebanon'. Available at http://www.unrwa.org/where-we-work/lebanon, last accessed 19/07/2014.

UNRWA (2009) 'Consolidated Eligibility and Registration Instructions'. Available at http://unispal.un.org/pdfs/UNRWA-CERI.pdf, last accessed 19/07/2014.

2 South–South cooperation

From dependency to self-sufficiency?

Introduction

South–South cooperation – understood here as encompassing a wide range of initiatives developed by Southern state and non-state actors in support of individuals, communities and peoples across the Global South – is of increasing interest to states, policymakers and academics alike (i.e. Bobiash 1992; Woods 2008; Six 2009; Mawdsley 2012). Hence, Northern states have recognised – arguably especially in light of the financial crises which have led to pressures on European and North American states' aid allocations – the extent to which Southern actors can 'share the burden' in funding and undertaking assistance and protection activities, and UN agencies are promoting South–South partnerships as a means of meeting the Millennium Development Goals and human development more broadly.

On an institutional level, this is demonstrated in the expansion and reconfiguration in 2004 of the 'Special Unit for South-South Cooperation of the United Nations Development Programme' (SSC), whose new name 'reflects the increased importance and expanded focus of cooperation among developing countries'.[1] Subsequently, the UNDP's 2013 Human Development Report – *The Rise of the South* – 'calls for new institutions which can facilitate regional integration and South–South cooperation', noting that 'Emerging powers in the developing world are already sources of innovative social and economic policies and are major trade, investment, and increasingly development cooperation partners for other developing countries' (2013: iv). Stating that Southern countries' 'experiences and South–South cooperation are equally an inspiration to development policy', the 2013 report 'offers very useful insights for our [i.e. UNDP's] future engagement in South–South cooperation' (ibid.).[2] UNDP summarises the report's 'headline story' as follows: 'The South needs the North, and increasingly the North needs the South' (ibid.: 2).

While the 2013 UNDP report noticeably fails to address South–South cooperation in the context of conflict-induced displacement, Southern states have often worked together to develop regional initiatives to protect refugees. This has especially been the case throughout the 2000s. For instance, the 2004 Mexico Declaration and Plan of Action to Strengthen International Protection of Refugees in Latin America, both reflects the long-standing history of, and the future commitment to, the development of Latin America's regional, South–South, cooperation regime for refugee protection (Harley 2014). In turn, the UNHCR has lobbied 'new' states to offer resettlement places to refugees unable to locally integrate in countries of first asylum, including through the Global Resettlement Solidarity Initiative launched in 2011 to address the protection needs of refugees displaced as a result of the uprisings and conflicts across North Africa (UNHCR 2011: 2) and subsequently throughout the Middle East.[3]

South–South cooperation as a whole is by no means a new phenomenon, and yet the mainstreaming of Southern-led initiatives by UN agencies and Northern states is paradoxical in many ways, especially since 'South–South cooperation for development' is historically associated with the Non-Aligned Movement, and anti-colonial and anti-imperialist struggles. The purposeful development of a South–South cooperation paradigm was, in essence, originally conceptualised as a necessary means of overcoming the exploitative nature of North–South relations in the era of decolonisation. In effect, South–South cooperation is one of the core aims of the Group of 77, an organisation that was established in 1964 by 77 'developing countries' at the first conference of the UN Conference on Trade and Development (UNCTAD). The Group of 77, which by 2014 has over 130 member states, 'is the largest intergovernmental organization of developing countries in the United Nations' and 'provides the means for the countries of the South to articulate and promote their collective *economic* interests and enhance their joint negotiating capacity on all major international *economic* issues within the United Nations system, and promote South-South cooperation for development'.[4]

Whilst recognising the difficulties in coherently defining which states (and, indeed, which non-state actors) are from and of the Global South (see below), a common worldview guiding the politics and policies of the original members of the Group of 77 throughout the 1960s and 1970s was *dependency theory*, which emphasised the economic, but also political and social, domination of the 'Third World' by the 'First World' (Ilda 1988: 383). The underlying premise pertaining to the ongoing hegemonic exploitation of former colonies by former colonial powers influenced, inter alia, the post-development debates of the 1990s and 2000s (also see Saul and Leys 2006). The post-development school is itself internally fragmented, including proponents of finding alternative *models* of development and those who espouse the need to develop an entirely new paradigm: an alternative *to* development (see Escobar 2006). In spite of this internal heterogeneity, post-development critics have as a whole maintained that 'development is a "neo-colonial" project that reproduces global inequalities and maintains the dominance of the South, through global capitalist expansion, by the North' (Kothari 2005: 48). Equally, one of the main critiques of the contemporary humanitarian regime is that Northern-dominated humanitarianism is a contemporary manifestation of colonial imperatives: '"humanitarianism' is *the* ideology of hegemonic states in the era of globalisation marked by the end of the Cold War and a growing North-South divide' (Chimni 2000: 3; also see Duffield 2001; Agier 2010). In light of the overwhelming influence of Northern actors and principles on the international humanitarian regime, Egeland notes that the regime is under threat of enduring opposition in many Southern contexts (2011: xviii).

As such, while many states and non-state actors across the Global South have actively engaged with Northern institutions, organisations and programmes, and have often aimed to become part of the 'international' development and humanitarian regime, others have expressed an overt opposition to Northern-led projects, developing not only a discourse of resistance and rejection, but also diverse strategies under the remit of South–South cooperation. Recognising the existence of such strategies across time and space ensures that we do not reproduce the oppositional and colonialist formulations which are inherent in much post-development literature, which frequently maintains, rather than disrupts, the notion that power originates from, and operates through, a unidirectional and intentional historical entity, that is, 'the West' (Brigg 2002). Acknowledging the historical and ongoing significance of South–South cooperation thereby enables us to (re) inscribe, rather than erase Others from the multifaceted history of development and humanitarian action writ large (also see Pacitto and Fiddian-Qasmiyeh 2013).[5]

As noted above, institutionalised platforms for South–South cooperation have historically emphasised the promotion of collective *economic* interests and *trade* as a means of advancing national economic development qua independence from former colonial and imperial powers. Nonetheless, South–South cooperation includes a widely diverse array of initiatives designed to advance human and national development, and to respond to disasters and conflicts across the Global South. These include programmes pertaining to health and education, as represented by the Cuban internationalist and the Libyan Pan-Arabist educational migration programmes explored in this book: enabling students from across the Global South to complete their secondary and tertiary level studies free of charge in cities including Havana and Santiago de Cuba, or Tripoli and Benghazi, has been conceptualised by the Southern state and non-state actors involved as a means of maximising national/local self-sufficiency and thereby reducing Southern actors' dependence upon Northern development and humanitarian assistance and professionals.

The reflection offered above vis-à-vis alternative modes and models of development *and* humanitarianism is particularly significant since there remains a relative paucity of research on South–South *humanitarian* responses, even when Southern-led *development* initiatives have enjoyed increasing attention by academics in recent years. This limited engagement with Southern humanitarianism is in part based on the widespread assumption by many academics and practitioners that 'although the idea of saving lives and relieving suffering is hardly a Western or Christian creation, modern humanitarianism's *origins are located in Western history and Christian thought*' (Barnett and Weiss 2008: 7, emphasis added; also see Fassin 2011: 1). Indeed, throughout the 2000s, numerous studies have examined the history, evolution and nature of humanitarianism, typically tracing the birth and origins of humanitarianism to the Enlightenment period, and more specifically to the activities and goals of Northern religious groups in the early-nineteenth century (i.e. Barnett and Weiss 2011; Wilson and Brown 2011; Barnett and Stein 2012). While repeatedly asserting humanitarianism's Northern origins, Barnett has nonetheless admitted that despite entitling his book *Empire of Humanity: A History of Humanitarianism*, the reader should note that 'Western bias is ahead. This is not a book on the history of *all forms of humanitarianism* around the world' (Barnett 2011: 15, emphasis added).

On the one hand, therefore, many academics recognise the existence of a multitude of humanitarianisms, including 'humanitarianisms of Europe, of Africa, of the global, and of the local' (Kennedy 2004: xv). On the other hand, humanitarian action not born of the Northern-dominated and highly institutionalised international regime has remained largely neglected in academia, or, as discussed below, has been rejected a priori as illegitimate courses of action which are not worthy of the humanitarian epithet (also see Pacitto and Fiddian-Qasmiyeh 2013). In particular, studies of South–South humanitarian responses in contexts of forced displacement are almost entirely absent from the literature; this book, therefore, fills a long-standing gap in theoretical and conceptual engagement with Other models of responding to displacement and dispossession by focusing on South–South educational migration programmes which aim to support long-standing refugees from the Middle East and North Africa.

A brief note on terminology

The terms 'Global North' and 'Global South' are used in this context in line with McEwan's suggestion that 'it is most useful to think of North/South as a *metaphorical* rather than a *geographical* distinction' (2009: 13). Whilst recognising the limitations of oppositional categorisations such as North/South, West/East, Developed/Developing, which fail to reflect the complexity and diversity of global realities,[6] the terms Global North/South nonetheless transcend the connotations of typologies such as 'First' and 'Third World', 'developed' or 'developing' which 'suggest both a hierarchy and a value judgment' (ibid.: 12), in addition to transcending the inherently *negative* framework implicit in the usage of the term '*non-*West' as the counterpoint to 'West'.

As noted above, over 130 states have *defined themselves* as belonging to the Group of 77 – a quintessential South–South platform – in spite of the diversity of their ideological and geopolitical positions in the contemporary world order, their vastly divergent gross domestic product (GDP) and per capita income, and their rankings in the Human Development Index.[7] Although self-definition may be one means of categorising states, conceptualising the Global South is arguably becoming increasingly complex in light of ongoing global transformations and the position of postcolonial states such as Brazil, China and India in the world economy, along with the global economic position of oil-producing Arab States, amongst others.

Focusing on postcolonial states with high GDPs facilitates an analysis of the role of such Southern states as 'new', 'emerging' or 'non-traditional' development and humanitarian *donors* – indeed, the role played by such states has now been widely acknowledged by academics and policymakers alike (Harmer and Cotterell 2009; Binder et al. 2010; Davey 2012).[8] In this regard, while their denomination as 'new' donors is often historically inaccurate,[9] Six nonetheless asserts that China, India and other postcolonial donors defy the Northern development model because they occupy a different place in the history of colonial and postcolonial relations (2009: 1108). As Pacitto and I have argued elsewhere, this assertion can, in turn, be extended to posit that the rise of postcolonial states as development donors demands a reconceptualisation of much dominant development theory, including post-development theories themselves, which (as noted above) often rely on colonialist and oppositional formulations in their analyses (Pacitto and Fiddian-Qasmiyeh 2013: 3). Postcolonial donor states, according to Six, occupy a 'dual position' in the aid world, with their historical and contemporary global position contesting the traditional dichotomy of Southern recipients and Northern donors (2009: 1110). However, even in light of a range of historical and interest-based solidarities which postcolonial states share with Southern and Eastern countries, it is equally the case that 'their political claim to speak "for the South" is problematic as their representativeness is increasingly questionable' (ibid.). The 'Southern' label nevertheless has the potential to give states, and also non-state actors, a degree of historical legitimacy, as it does not conjure the same neocolonial images as European or North American intervention (see Box 2.1). This historical legitimacy, according to Six, 'results in a distinct culture of South-South relations' (ibid.: 1113).

However, by focusing on the financial contributions of *high*-GDP Southern *donor* states, major gaps in understanding remain with reference to the nature and implications of responses developed by *low-* and *medium-*GDP states[10] on the one hand, and with regards to initiatives which transcend financial transfers and material donations on the other. Indeed, by developing educational migration programmes for citizens and refugees alike, states such as Cuba and Libya have in turn positioned themselves outside the traditional conceptualisation of 'donor states' per se. In providing educational opportunities to both citizens *and* refugees, these initiatives equally lead us to reconsider the meaning of, and relationship between, South–South cooperation for 'development' and South–South cooperation for 'humanitarianism'.

Defining humanitarianism and locating spaces for 'alternative' models of humanitarian cooperation?

The contemporary international humanitarian regime remains heavily influenced by the Red Cross movement, Northern international NGOs and the UN system (Davey 2012: 2). For many, the International Committee of the Red Cross's definition of humanitarianism is *the* definitive standard (Barnett and Weiss 2011: 9), with analysts considering that the seven organising principles established by the Red Cross/Red Crescent movement have become fundamental to the humanitarian movement (Ferris 2011: 11). In particular, Ferris holds

Box 2.1 The Brazil-Cuba-Haiti Tripartite Commission and the South-South Cooperation Project: a focus on Brazil's role in the response to Haiti's 2010 earthquake

After the 2010 Haitian earthquake, a major role was played by states across the Caribbean and Central and South America, including by Venezuela, Cuba and Brazil. In the immediate aftermath of the earthquake, Venezuela sent 400 personnel to establish camps for internally displaced people in five towns, and continued to provide material assistance and medical aid to affected persons on the island throughout 2010 and 2011 (Embassy of the Bolivian Republic of Venezuela to the U.S. 2012). In 2012, Venezuela subsequently pledged US$2.4 billion in aid to be delivered over six years and continues to support Haiti by sending doctors, building wells and offering agricultural support. In turn, Cuba contributed more than 350 members of its Henry Reeve Emergency Response Medical Brigade in addition to the 344 Cuban doctors already working in Haiti (see Box 2.2) (Kirk and Kirk 2010). Expanding its ongoing role as the leader of the UN Stabilization Mission in Haiti (MINUSTAH) since 2004, the Brazilian government participated in a health care initiative supported through the Brazil-Cuba-Haiti Tripartite Commission and the South-South Cooperation Project. The initiative, financially supported by Brazil while Cuba provides human resources and medical expertise (Gorry 2011), will provide vaccinations against measles, rubella and polio for over 2 million children in Haiti (Government of Brazil 2012).

Reflecting the abovementioned principles guiding South–South cooperation, the concept of 'mutual South-South understanding' has been consistently employed by the Brazilian government with reference to its actions in Haiti and elsewhere (Brancoli and Thomaz 2012). In 2011, for instance, President Dilma Rousseff of Brazil stated that 'We are ready to cooperate with our brother and sister countries in the developing world' (Rousseff 2011, cited in Brancoli and Thomaz 2012). Brazil's 'discourses of solidarity' (Brancoli and Thomaz 2012), reinforced through the use of the label 'Southern' as a specific identity marker, allow states such as Brazil to identify with a shared 'Southern' community based on certain perceived shared attributes. In this context, the invocation of the label 'Southern' by the Brazilian government also demonstrates the extent to which the label itself can hold political capital and can be used as an indicator of solidarity between post-colonial states.

In spite of such discursive affirmations of South–South solidarity, however, the relative position held by different Southern states is highlighted clearly by this example: Brazil, as an emerging economic and political force in the global arena, does not occupy the same global position as Haiti, one of the poorest states in the world with a recent history of political instability. The use of a solidarist rhetoric can, therefore, support the strategic objectives of relatively stronger states like Brazil, which is consolidating its relatively newly established authority in the global political sphere vis-à-vis other powerful global actors.

Adapted from Pacitto and Fiddian-Qasmiyeh (2013)

that four of these principles have become hallmarks of humanitarian assistance 'throughout the international community': humanity, impartiality, neutrality and independence (ibid.).[11]

The perspective of humanitarianism born out of these principles is 'that politics is a moral pollutant' (Barnett and Weiss 2008: 4). The strict dichotomy between morality and politics is robustly posited by the International Committee of the Red Cross (ICRC) and other Northern international organisations, and is considered to be central to the credibility of these organisations, and thus to their ability to function on the ground in often highly politicised conflict environments. There are those, however, who critique the assertion that humanitarianism should, and can, be separated from politics. The opposing position, therefore, asserts that it is impossible for humanitarian agencies to be apolitical (Barnett and Weiss 2008: 4).

As noted above, Northern-led humanitarian agencies in these settings are often viewed as agents of Northern domination, with Bitter maintaining that 'The Red Cross's principle of "universality" is sometimes impugned as a veil for neo-colonial power and a prolongation of religious missionary activity in a new form' (Bitter, 1994: 100–1, in Benthall and Bellion-Jourdan 2003: 58). Nonetheless, following the dominant institutional trend,[12] scholarly research on the history of humanitarianism has largely tended to focus on the actions and agendas of Northern agents and institutions, simultaneously overlooking the capacity for agency of Southern actors. Equally, unless forms of local capacity and action emanating from the South are expressed in the form of Northern-style institutions or in other recognisable ways, they have often been willingly ignored by outsiders (Juma and Suhrke 2002: 8).

Although Davey stresses that there is now a widespread acknowledgement of the significant role of 'new' donors and NGOs in the humanitarian enterprise, she nonetheless concedes that 'there is a fear that "non-Western" groups may not subscribe to the principles underpinning the formal system, and may have a misguided understanding of what it is to be "humanitarian"' (Davey 2012: 2). This fear, which reflects a position also posited by Ferris (2011), fails to consider the historical origins upon which the humanitarian label is founded or the extent to which common, formalised understandings of what constitutes 'humanitarian' responses are embedded within Northern practices and systems of knowledge. Slim's analysis of the oligopoly held by NGO humanitarians on the concept of humanitarian action as 'something they want everyone to value and enjoy but which only they are allowed to do' (Slim 2003, in Barnett and Weiss 2011: 14), and Haysom's critique of the predominance of what she refers to as the Northern 'relief elite' (2012), are especially pertinent in this regard. Whilst different actors have invoked the term 'humanitarian' across diverse spheres, the formal system's tendency to reject these diverse initiatives as 'political' or 'ideological', rather than 'humanitarian', is demonstrative of the institutional dominance and legitimisation of one particular vision of humanitarianism. Limiting the definition to such a narrow field of inquiry so as to exclude expressions of compassion that do not fall within the strictly delimited ICRC conception of 'humanitarian' is thus to pursue an agenda fraught with Northern bias.[13]

A prime opportunity, therefore, emerges to problematise Northern appropriations of the humanitarian label, and to enrich and expand popular understandings of the concept through engagement with responses to humanitarian crises located beyond the international organisational structure. As Reiff argues, '...every concept of humanitarianism, like every concept of what it means to be fully human, has a history and, more important, a historical context that we ignore at our peril' (2002: 67). In overlooking the values and experiences of actors and communities whose conception of 'humanitarian' action falls outside of the dominant Northern framework (Davey 2012: 4), we inevitably fail to grasp the complexity and contested nature of the term, and how it has evolved, and continues to evolve, over time and space.

At the same time as exploring the potential for Southern actors to 'appropriate' or 'share' the humanitarian label, the overwhelming focus on South–South *development* in existing academic and policy literature to the apparent detriment of South–South *humanitarianism*, can also arguably be explained through reference to the term 'South–South cooperation' itself: 'cooperation' has the potential to encompass both development *and* humanitarian initiatives. Furthermore, many members of the Group of 77 purposefully refrain from using terms such as 'humanitarian assistance' or 'aid donor' which are intimately related to the Northern-led regime (also see Greenhill and Prizzon 2012). This purposive distancing from mainstream/hegemonic terminology is one way of discursively affirming the unique approach taken by Southern actors, and is paralleled by the underlying principles motivating and framing South–South cooperation: mutual benefit, solidarity, reciprocity and non-interference in the national sovereignty of other states.[14] Inter alia, these underlying principles differentiate South–South cooperation from the 'traditional' Northern-led model of aid,[15] whilst simultaneously highlighting the roots of the discourses of solidarity and self-sufficiency which emerge in the case studies explored in the subsequent chapters.[16]

The joint principles of engaging in bilateral and multilateral cooperation between states in order to meet states' needs (as opposed to the needs of affected individuals) and of non-interference in order to protect national sovereignty, also have a practical implication in terms of the forms of assistance that Southern states will or will not offer in crisis scenarios: in essence, while South–South cooperation on national and regional levels has been extensively implemented in contexts of disaster relief, the role of South–South cooperation in situations of conflict-induced displacement is less visible and more under-researched.

With reference to the former, Southern states' and regional organisations' responses to specific humanitarian contexts such as the 2005 South-East Asian tsunami and the 2010 Haitian earthquake have been well documented (see Boxes 2.1 and 2.2).[17] The diverse motivations underpinning Southern responses to disasters have also been analysed, including with reference to specific forms of 'non-traditional' humanitarian action such as state-led Islamic faith-based humanitarianism (especially post-9/11),[18] and the principle of solidarity-based humanitarianism in Latin American responses to disaster-induced displacement (Moulin 2009; Fiddian-Qasmiyeh 2010, 2011a).

Box 2.2 Medical and educational internationalism: a focus on Cuba's model of cooperative relief

The Cuban state has sent over 42,000 Cuban workers to offer their services in 103 different countries, including over 30,000 health professionals, of whom 19,000 are medical physicians. For over 40 years, Cuban doctors have practised abroad, including in a wide range of displacement settings, and Cuban medical schools have concurrently trained non-Cuban students in Cuba itself (Kirk and Kirk 2010). Since the beginning of the Cuban Revolution in 1959, over 55,000 students including citizens, internally displaced persons and refugees from across 148 different countries have benefited from the Cuban scholarship programme, allowing them to pursue primary, secondary and/or tertiary education in Cuba (Martínez-Pérez 2012). A majority of non-Cuban students completing their tertiary studies in Cuba have focused on medical, nursing and dentistry degrees (Fiddian-Qasmiyeh 2010).

Cuba's strong medical presence in the wake of the 2010 Haitian earthquake builds upon a long history of Cuba's involvement in providing medical assistance across the Caribbean and Central America. 1998 was a particularly devastating, and important, year in this regard: that year, Hurricane Georges struck Haiti and Hurricane Mitch took over 30,000 lives across Central America. In response, Cuba immediately sent hundreds of Cuban doctors to the disaster-affected countries, but also agreed to train Caribbean and Central American doctors in Cuba. The latter would enable these doctors to return and substitute the Cuban doctors, and would simultaneously maximise their countries' professional self-sufficiency to respond to any future disasters.

To this effect, Cuba established the *Escuela Latino Americana de Medicina* (ELAM – the Latin American School of Medicine), with the first cohort of students commencing their studies in May 1999 (Huish and Kirk 2007); by 2010, Cuba had trained approximately 550 Haitian doctors (Kirk and Kirk 2010). As a result of extensive experience assisting disaster-affected populations in Central America, in late 1998 Cuba's Comprehensive Health Program was established to create sustainable models for the distribution of health professionals in remote and underserved areas to improve population health in dozens of countries, beginning with Central America (ibid.).

The beneficiaries of Cuba's medical assistance programme and its medical training programme have included diverse populations from contexts affected by disaster, but also conflict-induced displacement. For instance, 1,500 scholarships are now available for students from East Timor and Pakistan, countries that received Cuba's Henry Reeve disaster response brigade in 2005 (Huish and Kirk 2007). Amongst the beneficiaries of the broader Cuban scholarship programme are a range of refugee populations: 600 Sudanese 'lost boys' arrived in Cuba from Eritrean-based refugee camps in the 1980s (Ryer 2010; Finlay et al. 2011), with over 300 returning to the Republic of Southern Sudan upon independence in 2011; over 1,300 Namibian refugee-students left Cuba for their newly independent state in 1,990 (Hickling-Hudson 2004); and several thousand Palestinians and more than 4,000 Sahrawi refugees have returned to their refugee camps following graduation throughout the 1990s and 2000s, as examined in this book (see also Fiddian-Qasmiyeh 2010).

Disaster relief can be understood as a means of providing assistance to a disaster-affected *state* in order to strengthen that state's ability to offer assistance to its own citizens on its own territory, and yet delivering assistance in conflict situations in which the state is either involved as a belligerent party or has demonstrated no, or little, political will to offer protection to its population, could be understood as a breach of the principles of respect for national sovereignty and non-interference if such involvement does not take place at the explicit behest of the state itself. Although beyond the scope of this discussion, this distinction between the scenarios in which Southern states may feel it is appropriate or inappropriate to become involved has led to extensive criticisms by academics, policymakers and practitioners alike: by prioritising state sovereignty and the principle of non-intervention, such states effectively fail to denounce human rights violations committed by other states, including war crimes and crimes against humanity.

Arguably, however, these criticisms parallel the equally extensive debates regarding the moral dilemmas faced by international non-governmental organisations (INGOs): hence, while the ICRC has historically held the position that *not* denouncing human rights violations will ensure its ongoing access to populations in need of assistance, other organisations such as Amnesty International centralise the moral imperative of witnessing and denouncing such violations even if it leads to the expulsion of its staff. The politics of Southern actors' privileged access to a disaster-affected state that has simultaneously been involved in committing grave human rights abuses against its own citizens is evidenced clearly in the case of Myanmar (Box 2.3).

In spite of this state-centric approach to South–South cooperation, and the principle of non-interference, another key principle is of central significance to the current study: an anti-colonial commitment to support the overarching right to the self-determination of peoples. As explored in the remainder of this book, this commitment has led Libya and Cuba since the 1960s and 1970s to offer different forms of support to non-state interlocutors including the Popular Front for the Liberation of Saguiat el-Hamra and Rio de Oro (Polisario Front) and the PLO and its constituent factions as, respectively, the 'legitimate representatives' of the Sahrawi people and of the Palestinian people. While Cuba's and Libya's ideological positions and priorities are distinct (broadly reflecting internationalist and Pan-Arabist paradigms respectively – see Chapters 3 and 6), both states have expressed their solidarity for these particular liberation movements, and politics is consequently a central feature of the development and implementation of these models of cooperation.[19]

While the particularities of the Cuban and Libyan initiatives are explored in more detail in the subsequent chapters, offering free educational opportunities to Sahrawi children and youth and to Palestinian youth has historically been justified by the Cuban and Libyan states, and by the Polisario and PLO, as providing the means to maximise refugees' self-sufficiency and the foundations to establish and run the independent nation-states of Western Sahara and Palestine (Fiddian-Qasmiyeh 2010, 2011b). However, while these and other priorities are espoused by Cuba and Libya and by the Sahrawis' and Palestinians' political representatives,

Box 2.3 The politics of access: a focus on regional responses to the 2008 Myanmar cyclone and the persecution of Rohingya Muslims

In May 2008, a Category 4 cyclone hit Myanmar, affecting 2.4 million people and leaving an estimated 140,000 people dead or missing (Marr 2010). In the aftermath of the event, Myanmar's citizens contributed to the relief efforts by delivering emergency supplies to the cyclone-affected areas; local faith communities, monasteries and churches were pivotal to such grass roots community assistance, and aid organisations and NGOs already operating in the affected regions collected information on the damage and the needs of those affected. In contrast, NGOs and UN agencies that were not previously present in the affected areas were denied access, largely as a result of the tense relationship between Myanmar and many Northern states for almost 20 years.

The task, therefore, fell to the regional organisation, the Association of Southeast Asian Nations (ASEAN), to convince Myanmar (one of its member states) to provide access for relief efforts. Despite initial resistance to foreign involvement, Myanmar agreed on a mechanism led by ASEAN, upon assurances that assistance provided through ASEAN would not be 'politicised' (Marr 2010; also Cook 2010).

These events are a clear example of an instance in which Northern humanitarian organisations, despite their purportedly 'apolitical' and 'neutral' character, are often perceived as being inherently political and biased by other actors. ASEAN's success in negotiating and reaching an agreement with the government of Myanmar demonstrates the privileged position that Southern actors may hold in certain geopolitical contexts.

More recently, in 2012 the Organization of Islamic Countries was also granted access by the government of Myanmar to provide 'necessary assistance' to the Rohingya Muslim minority which continues to be displaced and persecuted in the West of the country (OIC 2012).

These examples thus demonstrate that Southern actors can hold a distinct place in the global humanitarian landscape. In an era where rhetoric around 'shrinking humanitarian space' is ever-present, the 'privileged access' which certain Southern states and organisations may be afforded requires further analysis.

Adapted from Pacitto and Fiddian-Qasmiyeh (2013)

a core issue explored in the subsequent chapters is how the education programme has been experienced and navigated by individuals and communities both in Cuba and in Libya and upon return to their home-camps (also see Fiddian-Qasmiyeh 2011b, 2012, 2013a, 2013b). This includes not only examining the diversity in the history and principles underpinning the Cuban and Libyan education programmes, but also exploring the extent to which beneficiaries themselves conceptualise and describe these initiatives as political, ideological and/or humanitarian in nature.

South–South cooperation through educational migration: refugees and the quest for 'a better future'

The notion of humanitarian action often invokes the image of immediate and life-saving assistance in times of conflict or natural disaster, with some analysts arguing that the word humanitarian has become synonymous with the 'provision of life saving assistance' (Ferris 2011: 16). However, humanitarian action can also be considered to consist of both 'an emergency branch that focuses on symptoms, and an alchemical branch that adds the ambition of removing root causes of suffering' (Barnett 2011: 10). To this, one can arguably add a cooperative element which aims to strengthen local and national capacity to *withstand* diverse forms of suffering, including through mechanisms designed to maximise self-sufficiency and 'a better future' (see below). Such an approach to capacity building is exemplified not only in the intersection between Cuba's medical and educational internationalism in its responses to disasters in the Caribbean and Latin America (see Box 2.2), but also in the prioritisation of providing primary, secondary and tertiary level educations to refugee children and youth.

It is widely recognised that 'refugees often see the education of their children as a principal way of ensuring a better future' (Dryden-Peterson 2003: 1). However, the means for providing such an education in contexts of protracted displacement, and views of what precisely would amount to a 'better future', are less consistently expressed by the different actors involved in planning for, and delivering, schooling to refugee children around the world. Refugee families and leaders may invest considerable amounts of otherwise scarce resources to establish schooling systems in refugee camps (Horst 2006: 13), even without international support, often viewing an education 'as a means of preserving their group's cultural, linguistic, and historical traditions' (Water and Leblanc 2005: 138). Such an investment in education in the face of immediate scarcity and uncertainty demonstrates the significance which individuals, families and collectivities might give to 'saving a way of life' over 'saving a life' per se (Allen and Turton 1996). Nevertheless, international organisations, UN relief agencies and both donor and host states have only relatively recently (primarily since the 1990s) accepted that schooling programmes should be amongst the internationally guaranteed services to be offered by humanitarian agencies (Water and Leblanc 2005: 135). Even since the 1990s, international actors have often heralded 'refugee education' for reasons and through means which may undermine local attempts to 'save a way of life', or may reflect the political priorities of donors as is arguably the case of the 'peace education' projects which prevail in many refugee contexts (see Verdirame and Harrell-Bond 2005: 258).[20]

It is clearly the case that 'irrespective of rhetoric to the contrary, planning for education is often done "for" refugees by external actors like the host country, UN relief agencies and NGOs, rather than "with" refugees' (Water and Leblanc 2005: 130). In contrast, this book explores two distinct transnational education programmes – Cuba's inter-regional internationalist programme, and Libya's Pan-Arabist intra-regional system – which have offered free primary, secondary and/or tertiary level education to (amongst other beneficiaries) members of two of the world's most protracted refugee groups: Sahrawi and Palestinian refugees.

In contrast with the trend for educational systems to be designed by external actors, the Cuban programme in particular has enabled these refugees' political representatives to play a key role in developing the curriculum, selecting the language, content and means of instruction of these refugee-students in Cuba.[21] In turn, the Libyan model of education has situated refugees from the MENA region not only as recipients (refugee-students) but also as providers, with Palestinians in particular acting as refugee-teachers for other Palestinian refugee youth as well as for Sahrawi refugee children and adolescents studying in the North African state. In direct contrast from what Water and Leblanc refer to as the 'awkward fit' of the provision of schooling 'into the "relief" model favoured by refugee assistance agencies' (2005: 135), these transnational education models reflect schemes which have been designed to facilitate longer-term development and refugees' self-sufficiency. Given infrastructural limitations in both the desert-based Sahrawi refugee camps in Algeria and in the urban Palestinian refugee camps in Lebanon, and these camps' dependence upon externally provided humanitarian and political aid, the potential to promote professional self-sufficiency in students' home-camps via educational migration is particularly significant in both of these refugee contexts.

In effect, the Cuban and Libyan educational migration programmes offer clear alternatives (and even a challenge) both to the way in which the education of foreign students is structured and managed elsewhere by states and institutions driven by capitalist priorities, and, simultaneously, to the way in which development and humanitarian assistance is offered to protracted refugee groups (Fiddian-Qasmiyeh 2010). As such, the Cuban and Libyan approaches to South–South cooperation through internationalist and Pan-Arabist paradigms respectively provide not only a challenge to the financially driven interest in foreign students, but also a counterpoint to dominant discourses and policies which situate humanitarian providers as the saviours of eternal victims in the Global South (also see Fiddian-Qasmiyeh 2014). In contrast to these hegemonic discourses and assumptions, the official rhetoric offered by the Cuban and Libyan states has positioned the scholarship systems as aiming to support beneficiaries (both as individual scholarship holders, and their communities or nations of origin) in achieving their own political goals, rather than aiming to save them through paternalistic assistance programmes.

This official state perspective may be understood as a welcome corrective to a premature demonisation or erasure of Other forms of humanitarian response, and yet far from idealising and prematurely celebrating this programme per se, by examining Cuba's and Libya's scholarship programmes from multiple perspectives – from the vantage points of MENA students in Cuba, and of Cuban- and Libyan-educated graduates in the Sahrawi refugee camps in Algeria and Palestinian camps in Lebanon – this book demonstrates the widely divergent views which may exist apropos the means to secure a 'better future'. As I demonstrate in this book, while the educational migration programmes are purposefully designed and projected to maximise refugees' self-sufficiency on a collective and national level, the implications of refugees' educational migration are paradoxical in nature.

Indeed, transcending the UN's definition of 'self-reliance' as 'providing… a professional qualification geared towards future employment' (UNHCR 2007: 7),[22] the following chapters critically examine diverse understandings of 'self-sufficiency', proposing that the relationship between higher education and self-sufficiency precisely depends upon whose definition of self-sufficiency (i.e. professional, economic, political, etc.), and which level of self-sufficiency (i.e. individual, collective and/or national) is prioritised, and why. By examining the experiences and impacts of Palestinian and Sahrawi students' educational migration to Cuba and Libya – including by investigating how age, gender and political affiliation have mediated students' access to the scholarship programmes and their experiences of studying abroad, but also of the ways in which individual and collective identities, combined with conditions in graduates' places of origin and broader geopolitical structures of inequality, have influenced graduates' experiences of their 'return' to their places of origin – this book, therefore, considers the wider implications of such South–South cooperation programmes vis-à-vis 'alternative' conceptualisations of development and humanitarianism alike.

Notes

1 The newly named SSC Unit replaces the UNDP's 'Special Unit for Technical Cooperation among Developing Countries' established in 1974. See http://ssc.undp. org/content/ssc/about/Background.html, last accessed 09/04/2014.

2 This future engagement in South–South cooperation includes UNDP's ongoing work with the Organisation for Economic Co-operation and Development's Development Assistance Committee to establish a new Global Partnership for Effective Development Cooperation through the UN Development Cooperation Forum (UNDP 2013: 108–109).

3 In addition to South–South resettlement (itself a form of South–South migration) being viewed as a viable durable solution to forced migration, South–South migration more broadly has been seen by UN agencies and both Northern and Southern states as a means of enhancing human development: for instance, the 2012 UNCTAD Least Developed Countries (LDCs) report focused on the development potential of South–South migration for LDCs specifically (UNCTAD 2012), and 2012 was also the first year that the Global Forum on Migration and Development discussed South–South migration per se (UNDP 2013: 107).

4 http://www.g77.org/doc/, last accessed 09/04/2014, emphasis added.

5 The erasure of such modes and models of resistance is represented, for instance, in Agier's critique of humanitarian projects, which he describes as 'the left hand of empire' (2010: 29). For Agier, the humanitarian regime forms part of a 'global police' which exercises control during crises in the Global South as part of an imperialist politics of 'containment' (2010: 29–30), characterising humanitarianism as a form of totalitarianism, in which a consensus is forged such that 'there is no longer any excess or outside party whose disruptive voice would threaten the consensus' (2010: 31). For a more expanded critique, see Pacitto and Fiddian-Qasmiyeh (2013).

6 While the prioritisation of elite southern beneficiaries reflects debates surrounding the existence of 'the North in the South' as explored in Chapters 4 and 5, it is worth

noting here that marginalised citizens within the Global North have also been viewed as potential beneficiaries of South–South cooperation, as evinced in Cuba's scholarships for African-American students, for instance.

7 See Bakewell (2009) for a critique of current conceptualisations of South–South migration.

8 The term 'non-traditional' donor can here be understood to differentiate between states which are (traditional) and are not (non-traditional) members of the OECD's Development Assistance Committee.

9 For instance, in their contributions to the 2014 Conference, 'Between the Global and the Local in Humanitarian Action', co-hosted by Save the Children, Humanitarian Policy Group and the Non-State Humanitarianism Network and sponsored by the Office for the Coordination of Humanitarian Affairs (OCHA), Caroline Reeves and Urvashi Aneja respectively documented the long history of financial, material and social support offered by Chinese and Indian state and non-state actors as a response to conflict and disasters on local, national and international levels.

10 Furthermore, although commentators have recognised the increasing contribution of non-governmental organisations (NGOs) and civil society movements from the Global South in the humanitarian sphere, with Egeland claiming that the growth in these civil society movements in Southern societies 'is probably the single most important trend in global efforts to combat poverty and conflict' (2011: xxi), the humanitarian responses initiated by Southern civil society networks and displaced populations themselves have also largely remained unexplored. This is the focus of my ongoing research into the roles of Southern local faith communities in humanitarian settings (Fiddian-Qasmiyeh 2011a; Fiddian-Qasmiyeh and Ager 2013; Fiddian-Qasmiyeh and Pacitto 2015) and into Southern civil society and refugees' responses to the displacement resulting from the Syrian conflict (also see http://www.rsc.ox.ac.uk/research/south-south-humanitarianism, last accessed 09/04/2014, and Pacitto and Fiddian-Qasmiyeh 2013).

11 The following paragraphs expand upon arguments made in Pacitto and Fiddian-Qasmiyeh (2013).

12 Haysom refers to this core number of Northern institutions as the 'relief elite' and argues that the oligopoly that these institutions hold on the 'humanitarian' label has practical, as well as theoretical, implications; these actors use the humanitarian principles as a rhetorical tool to assert themselves as a 'distinct market niche' (Haysom 2012, quoted in Pacitto 2012: 6).

13 In contrast, Fiori (2013: 5) notes that: 'In South East Asia, neutrality and impartiality have been seen as secondary to the principle of non-interference. In China, where the notion of the state as guarantor of the welfare of its people is grounded in Confucian tradition, the independence of humanitarian agencies from governments is not considered to be necessary, desirable, or possible. And in Latin America, support for those affected by conflict, extreme poverty and disaster has often been guided by a solidarity that precludes neutrality and impartiality.'

14 The principles of the G77 are closely linked to those of the Non-Aligned Movement, which, since 1994, have established a Joint Coordinating Committee; these include the Non-Aligned Movement's established aim of collective *self-reliance*, and principles that action should be motivated by solidarity, reciprocity, but also mutual respect for states' territorial integrity and sovereignty – including a commitment to non-aggression and non-interference in one another's internal affairs.

15 As noted by the High Level Forum on Aid Effectiveness (Busan Partnership for Effective Development Co-Operation 2011), 'the nature, modalities and responsibilities that apply to South–South co-operation differ from those that apply to North-South co-operation' (para. 2). The Forum further elaborated that the 'architecture for development co-operation has evolved from the North-South paradigm. Distinct from the traditional relationship between aid providers and

recipients, developing nations and a number of emerging economies have become important providers of South-South development co-operation' (para. 14) – South–South cooperation is thus conceptualised as a horizontal relationship, rather than the vertical/hierarchical axis characterising North–South relations.

16 A key concern explored in Chapter 5, in particular, is the extent to which the Cuban education programme is perceived as a 'humanitarian' initiative by the beneficiaries of this project themselves.

17 Such analyses include Benthall (2008), Cook (2010) and Al-Yahya and Fustier (2011).

18 For instance, see Ghandour (2003), Benthall and Bellion-Jourdan (2003) and Barakat and Zyck (2010).

19 As noted above, claims of impartial, apolitical universality in the international principles institutionalised by the ICRC can equally be interpreted and understood to be partial, politicised neo-imperialism. The Myanmar example outlined in Box 2.3 clearly demonstrates this. In effect, as Pacitto and I have argued elsewhere, politics pervades humanitarianism, and not just humanitarianism in the sense of the practices carried out by 'humanitarian' organisations; it is interwoven within the fibres of the epithet itself. It is this lexical politics that has for so long footnoted Other actors and Other modes of action in the study of humanitarianism (Pacitto and Fiddian-Qasmiyeh 2013).

20 UNHCR now asserts that refugees' higher education may contribute to what it refers to as 'self-reliance' and the quest for durable solutions (UNHCR 2007), and also to post-conflict nation-building (UNESCO 2011).

21 These are all identified as central features of refugee education by Horst (2006: 13).

22 UNHCR's evaluation of the 'impact' of the German-sponsored DAFI higher education programme on refugees' 'self-reliance' used structured questionnaires to assess graduates' professional and economic self-reliance, their contribution to the refugee community pending a durable solution, and to their country of origin upon repatriation (UNHCR 2007: 8). In contrast, by drawing on multi-sited ethnographic research, this book transcends the UNHCR's definition of self-reliance as 'providing [refugees] with a professional qualification geared towards future employment' (ibid.: 7), exploring diverse conceptualisations of self-sufficiency on different levels.

References

Agier, M. (2010) 'Humanity as an Identity and its Political Effects: A Note of Camps and Humanitarian Government', *Humanity*, 1(1): 29–45.

Al-Yahya, K. and Fustier, N. (2011) 'Saudi Arabia as a Humanitarian Donor: High Potential, Little Institutionalization', GPPi Research Paper No. 14. Berlin: GPPi.

Allen, T. and Turton, D. (1996) 'Introduction: In Search of Cool Ground', in T. Allen (ed.) *In Search of Cool Ground: War, Flight and Homecoming in Northeast Africa*. Geneva: UNRISD in association with James Currey, London and Africa World Press, Trenton, 1–22.

Bakewell, O. (2009) 'South-South Migration and Human Development: Reflections on African Experiences', Human Development Research Papers, Vol 15. New York: United Nations Development Programme.

Barakat, S. and Zyck, S.A. (2010) 'Gulf State Assistance to Conflict-Affected Environments'. Kuwait Programme on Development, Governance and Globalisation in the Gulf States, 10. London: London School of Economics and Political Science.

Barnett, M. (2011) *Empire of Humanity: A History of Humanitarianism*. New York: Cornell University Press.

Barnett, M. and Stein, J.G. (2012) *Sacred Aid: Faith and Humanitarianism*. Oxford: Oxford University Press.

Barnett, M. and Weiss, T.G. (2011) *Humanitarianism Contested: Where Angels Fear to Tread*. Oxford: Routledge.

Barnett, M. and Weiss, T.G. (2008) 'Humanitarianism: A Brief History of the Present', in M. Barnett and T.G. Weiss (eds) *Humanitarianism in Question: Politics, Power, Ethics*. New York: Cornell University Press, 1–48.

Benthall, J. (2008) 'Have Islamic Agencies a Privileged Access in Majority Muslim Areas? The Case of Post-tsunami Reconstruction in Aceh (Indonesia)', *Online Journal of Humanitarian Assistance*, www.jha.ac, posted 26 June.

Benthall, J. and Bellion-Jourdan, J. (2003) *The Charitable Crescent: Politics of Aid in the Muslim World*. London: I.B. Tauris.

Binder, A., Meier, C. and Steets, J. (2010) 'Humanitarian Assistance: Truly Universal? A Mapping Study of Non-Western donors', GPPi Research Paper Series, Global Public Policy Institute, 12: 1–41.

Bobiash, D. (1992) *South-South Aid: How Developing Countries Help Each Other*. Seitan: St Martin's Press.

Brancoli, F. and Thomaz, D. (2012) 'Controversial South-South Humanitarianism: Brazilian Performance in Haiti and towards Haitian Displacement'. Conference paper presented at the Workshop on South-South Humanitarianism in Contexts of Forced Displacement, Refugee Studies Centre, University of Oxford, 6 October 2012 (on file with authors).

Brigg, M. (2002) 'Post-development, Foucault and the Colonisation Metaphor', *Third World Quarterly*, 23(3): 421–436.

Busan Partnership for Effective Development Co-Operation (2011) Fourth High Level Forum on Aid Effectiveness, Busan, Republic of Korea, 29 November–1 December. Available at http://effectivecooperation.org/files/OUTCOME_DOCUMENT_-_FINAL_EN.pdf, last accessed 17/04/2014.

Chimni, B.S. (2000) 'Globalisation, Humanitarianism and the Erosion of Refugee Protection', Refugee Studies Centre Working Paper No. 3. Oxford: Refugee Studies Centre.

Cook, A. (2010) 'Positions of Responsibility: A Comparison of ASEAN and EU Approaches towards Myanmar', *International Politics*, 47(3–4): 433–449.

Davey, E. (2012) 'New Players through Old Lenses: Why History Matters in Engaging Southern Actors', HPG Policy Brief, 48, July.

Dryden-Peterson, S. (2003) 'Education of Refugees in Uganda: Relationships between Setting and Access', Refugee Law Project Working Paper No. 9, Uganda.

Duffield, M. (2001) *Global Governance and the New Wars: The Merging of Development and Security*. London: Zed Books.

Egeland, J. (2011) 'Foreword: Humanitarianism in the Crossfire', in M. Barnett and T.G. Weiss (eds), *Humanitarianism Contested: Where Angels Fear to Tread*. Oxford: Routledge.

Embassy of the Bolivia Republic of Venezuela to the U.S. (2012) 'Venezuela's Aid to Haiti: Two Years after the Earthquake'. Available at http://venezuela-us.org/live/wp-content/uploads/2009/12/01-10-2012-FS-Haiti.pdf, last accessed 14/10/014.

Escobar, A. (2006) 'Post-Development', in D. Clark (ed.) *The Elgar Companion to Development Studies*. Cheltenham: Edward Elgar Publishing, 447–451.

Fassin, D. (2011) *Humanitarian Reason: A Moral History of the Present*. Berkeley, CA: University of California Press.

Ferris, E. (2011) *The Politics of Protection: The Limits of Humanitarian Action*. Washington, DC: Brookings Institution Press.

Fiddian-Qasmiyeh, E. (2014) 'Transnational Abductions and Transnational Jurisdictions? The Politics of "Protecting" Female Muslim Refugees in Spain', *Gender, Place and Culture*, 21(2): 174–194.

Fiddian-Qasmiyeh, E. (2013a) 'The Inter-generational Politics of "Travelling Memories": Sahrawi Refugee Youth Remembering Home-land and Home-camp', *Journal of Intercultural Studies*, 34(6): 631–649.

Fiddian-Qasmiyeh, E. (2013b) 'Transnational Childhood and Adolescence: Mobilising Sahrawi Identity and Politics across Time And Space', *Journal of Ethnic and Racial Studies*, 36(5): 875–895.

Fiddian-Qasmiyeh, E. (2012) 'Invisible Refugees and/or Overlapping Refugeedom? Protecting Sahrawis and Palestinians Displaced by the 2011 Libyan Uprising', *International Journal of Refugee Law*, 24(2): 263–293.

Fiddian-Qasmiyeh, E. (ed.) (2011a) 'Faith-based Humanitarianism in Contexts of Forced Displacement', Special Issue of the *Journal of Refugee Studies*, 24(3): September.

Fiddian-Qasmiyeh, E. (2011b) 'Paradoxes of Refugees' Educational Migration: Promoting Self-sufficiency or Renewing Dependency?' *Comparative Education*, 47(4): 433–447.

Fiddian-Qasmiyeh, E. (2010) 'Education, Migration and Internationalism: Situating Muslim Middle Eastern and North African students in Cuba', *The Journal of North African Studies*, 15(2): 137–155.

Fiddian-Qasmiyeh, E. and Ager, A. (eds) (2013) 'Local Faith Communities and the Promotion of Resilience in Humanitarian Situations', RSC/JLI Working Paper 90, Oxford: Refugee Studies Centre, February.

Fiddian-Qasmiyeh, E. and Pacitto, J. (2015) 'Writing the Other into Humanitarianism: A Conversation between "South-South" and "faith-based" humanitarianisms', in Z. Sezgin and D. Dijkzeul (eds) *The New Humanitarian Actors and Their Principles*. New York: Routledge.

Finlay, J.L., Crutcher, R. and Drummond, N. (2011) '"Garang's Seeds": Influences of the Return of Sudanese-Canadian Refugee Physicians to Post-Conflict South Sudan', *Journal of Refugee Studies*, 24(1): 187–206.

Fiori, J. (2013) 'The Discourse of Western Humanitarianism', Humanitarian Affairs Think Tank Working Paper, October. Paris: IRIS/Save the Children.

Ghandour, A.-R. (2003) 'Islam, Humanitarianism and the West: Contest or Cooperation?' *Humanitarian Exchange*, 25: 14–17.

Gorry, C. (2011) 'Haiti One Year Later: Cuban Medical Team Draws on Experience and Partnerships', *MEDICC Review*, 13(1): 52–55.

Government of Brazil (2012) 'Brazil Supports Vaccination Campaign; Continues Humanitarian Efforts in Haiti'. Available at http://www.brasil.gov.br/para/press/press-releases/april-2012/brazil-supports-vaccination-campaign-continues-humanitarian-efforts-in-haiti/br_model1?set_language=en, last accessed 20/08/2012.

Greenhill, R. and Prizzon, A. (2012) 'Who Foots the Bill after 2015? What New Trends in Development Finance Mean for the Post-MDGs', ODI Working Paper 360. London: ODI.

Harley, T. (2014) 'Regional Cooperation and Refugee Protection in Latin America: A "South-South" Approach', *International Journal of Refugee Law*, 26(1): 22–47.

Harmer, A. and Cotterell, L. (2009) 'Diversity in Donorship: The Changing Landscape of Official Humanitarian Aid', HPG Research Report. Overseas Development Institute. London: ODI.

Haysom, S. (2012) 'Contemporary Humanitarian Action and the Role of Southern Actors: Key Trends and Debates'. Opening Lecture of the workshop on South–South Humanitarianism in Contexts of Forced Displacement, Refugee Studies Centre,

University of Oxford, 6 October. Podcast available at http://www.forcedmigration.org/podcasts-videos-photos/podcasts/workshop-south-south-humanitarianism, last accessed 13/06/2013.

Hickling-Hudson, A. (2004) 'South-South Collaboration: Cuban Teachers in Jamaica and Namibia', *Comparative Education*, 40(2): 289–311.

Horst, C. (2006) 'Introduction: Refugee Livelihoods', *Refugee Survey Quarterly*, 25(2): 1–22.

Huish, R. and Kirk, J.M. (2007) 'Cuban Medical Internationalism and the Development of the Latin American School of Medicine', *Latin American Perspectives*, 34(6): 77–92.

Ilda, K. (1988) 'Third World Solidarity: The Group of 77 in the UN General Assembly', *International Organization*, 42(2): 375–395.

Juma, M. and Suhrke, A. (2002) *Eroding Local Capacity: International Humanitarian Action in Africa*. Uppsala: Nordika Afrika Institutet.

Kennedy, D. (2004) *The Dark Sides of Virtue: Reassessing International Humanitarianism*. Woodstock: Princeton University Press.

Kirk, E.J. and Kirk, J.M. (2010) 'Cuban Medical Cooperation in Haiti: One of the World's Best-kept Secrets', *Cuban Studies*, 41(1): 166–172.

Kothari, U. (2005) 'From Colonial Administration to Development Studies: A Post-Colonial Critique of the History of Development Studies', in U. Kothari (ed.) *A Radical History of Development Studies: Individuals, Institutions and Ideologies*. New York: Zed.

McEwan, C. (2009) *Postcolonialism and Development*. Oxford: Routledge.

Marr, S. (2010) 'Compassion in Action: The Story of the ASEAN-led Coordination in Myanmar'. Jakarta: ASEAN.

Martínez-Pérez, F. (2012) 'Cuban Higher Education Scholarships for International Students: An Overview', in A.R Hickling-Hudson, J. Corona-González and R. Preston (eds) *The Capacity to Share: A Study of Cuba's International Cooperation in Educational Development*. New York: Palgrave Macmillan, 73–82.

Mawdsley, E. (2012). *From Recipients to Donors: The Emerging Powers and the Changing Development Landscape*. London: Zed Books.

Moulin, C. (2009) 'Borders of Solidarity: Life in Displacement in the Amazon Tri-Border Region', *Refuge*, 26(2): 41–54.

OIC (2012) 'Myanmar Approves Access for OIC Assistance in Arakan', 11 August. Available at http://www.oic-oci.org/topic_detail.asp?t_id=7080, last accessed 28/8/2012.

Pacitto, J. (2012) *Workshop Report: South-South Humanitarianism in Contexts of Forced Displacement*. Oxford: Refugee Studies Centre.

Pacitto, J. and Fiddian-Qasmiyeh, E. (2013) 'Writing the "Other" into Humanitarian Discourse: Framing Theory and Practice in South-South Humanitarian Responses to Forced Displacement', RSC Working Paper 93. Oxford: Refugee Studies Centre.

Reiff, D. (2002) *A Bed For The Night: Humanitarianism in Crisis*. London: Vintage.

Rousseff, D. (2011) 'Statement by H. E. Dilma Rousseff, President of the Federative Republic of Brazil, at the Opening of the General Debate of the 66th Session of the United Nations General Assembly'. Available at http://gadebate.un.org/sites/default/files/gastatements/66/BR_en_0.pdf, last accessed 01/08/2012.

Ryer, P. (2010) 'The Hyphen-Nation of Cuban-educated Africans: Rethinking the "1.5 Generation" Paradigm', *International Journal of Cuban Studies*, 2(1–2): 74–87.

Saul, J.S. and Leys, C. (2006) 'Dependency', in D. Clark (ed.) *The Elgar Companion to Development Studies*. Cheltenham: Edward Elgar Publishing, 111–115.

Six, C. (2009) 'The Rise of Postcolonial States as Donors: A Challenge to the Development Paradigm?' *Third World Quarterly*, 30(6): 1103–1121.

UNCTAD (2012) *Least Developed Countries Report 2012: Harnessing Remittances and Diaspora Knowledge to Build Productive Capacities*. Geneva: United Nations Conference on Trade and Development.

UNDP (2013) *2013 Human Development Report: The Rise of the South*. New York: UNDP.

UNESCO (2011) *The Hidden Crisis: Armed Conflict and Education*. EFA Global Monitoring Report. Paris: UNESCO.

UNHCR (2011) *Projected Global Resettlement Needs 2012*. Geneva: UNHCR.

UNHCR (2007) *Tertiary Refugee Education: Impact and Achievements*. Geneva: UNHCR.

Verdirame, G. and Harrell-Bond, B.E. (2005) *Rights In Exile: Janus-Faced Humanitarianism*. Oxford: Berghahn Books.

Water, T. and Leblanc, K. (2005) 'Refugees and Education: Mass Public Schooling without a Nation-State', *Comparative Education Review*, 49(2): 129–147.

Wilson, R. and Brown, R. (2011) 'Introduction', in R. Wilson and R. Brown (eds) *Humanitarianism and Suffering: The Mobilization of Empathy*. Cambridge: Cambridge University Press.

Woods, N. (2008) 'Whose aid? Whose Influence? China, Emerging Donors and the Silent Revolution In Development Assistance', *International Affairs*, 84(6): 1205–1221.

3 The Cuban–MENA educational migration nexus

Views from the Caribbean

Introduction

Since the beginning of the Cuban Revolution (1959), more than 55,000 students from over 148 countries have been granted full scholarships by the Cuban government, allowing them to pursue their secondary and/or tertiary education in the Caribbean island (Martínez-Pérez 2012). By the early 2000s, an estimated 16,500 international students had completed their professional university degrees there (Martín Sabina 2002; Fiddian-Qasmiyeh 2010); by 2008, over 30,000 international students had graduated from Cuban universities and 24,000 from vocational and technical courses of study; and in 2010 approximately 30,000 foreign students from 123 countries were enrolled in Cuban higher education establishments (Martínez-Pérez 2012: 75). Amongst these beneficiaries, thousands of young citizens and refugees born in the MENA have attended Cuban universities and other further education institutions, with many of these also having received their primary and/or secondary schooling in the Cuban *Isla de la Juventud* (Island of Youth).

The Cuban initiative to give full scholarships covering school and university fees as well as all accommodation, food and medical costs, to children and youth from around the world is one of the state's key internationalist programmes.[1] In addition to the broad support offered to Sub-Saharan African, Latin American, Middle Eastern and North African countries through this programme, the scholarships can be considered to be one way in which the Cuban state has assisted and/or influenced the struggles of various independence and anti-colonial movements since the 1970s, including those of the Palestinians and Sahrawi who are the focus of this book. By providing children and youth with access to formal secondary and tertiary education, the Cuban government has officially aimed to enable fully trained doctors, engineers, lawyers and teachers (amongst others) to return to their places of origin to serve their communities and ensure a high degree of national and local self-sufficiency, including in Palestinian and Sahrawi refugee camps. It has also (implicitly and often explicitly) hoped that through experiencing life in Cuba and participating in its particular education system, graduates will take 'socialist values' with them to their places of origin upon their return. In the case of students who have arrived from Arab socialist countries such as Syria and Yemen, for instance, this educational journey is in itself a continuation of the solidarity shared between these countries and Cuba on an ideological level. More broadly, however, and as I have argued elsewhere (Fiddian-Qasmiyeh 2010), one simple and yet essential approach to solidarity is embodied in the educational programmes run by the Cuban government despite the serious material limitations which Cuba faces due to the US embargo: what José Martí eloquently stated as '*compartir lo que tienes, no dar lo que te sobra*' ('to share what you have, not give what is left over').

The scholarship programme has attracted some attention from researchers interested in its role in Cuban foreign policy, with analysts attempting to discern Cuba's political and ideological rationale in giving these 'gifts' to non-Cuban students (Fernández 1988; on Cuba's 'educational diplomacy' see Richmond 1991). Such studies typically focus on macro-level institutional and political relations between states and political organisations from the 'second' and 'third' worlds, rather than engaging with the lived experiences of students during and following their studies on the island. Indeed, non-Cuban students' experiences of studying in the Cuban archipelago have received relatively little attention from academics in Havana or beyond. Notable (recent) exceptions are studies by Lehr (2008, 2012), Hickling-Hudson (2004, 2012) and Preston (2012), who have respectively documented the experiences of Cuban-educated students from Ghana, the English-speaking Caribbean and Namibia. Importantly, these authors, who have all contributed to Hickling-Hudson and colleagues' (2012a) edited collection entitled *The Capacity to Share* (a title inspired by Martí's philosophy referred to above), offer overwhelmingly positive accounts that are intimately connected to the Cuban state's official rhetoric regarding the scholarship programme. In particular, Martínez-Pérez reduces the 'main problems encountered in the programme' (2012: 74) to the following: the need to renovate student accommodation in Cuba; limited access to the Internet due to 'the blockade measures dictated by the US government' (ibid.: 80); and 'gaps in the educational levels of students entering the system' (ibid.). As such, although recent studies are to be welcomed for moving from the macro to the micro level, and for centralising students' perspectives of studying in Cuba and of returning to work in their home contexts, these authors simultaneously demonstrate the need to transcend either a premature demonisation *or* idealisation of the programme, and raise numerous questions regarding the nature and overarching outcomes of this mode of South–South cooperation.

Through research in Cuba (this chapter), Algeria (Chapter 4) and Lebanon (Chapter 5), these chapters, therefore, not only explore Cuba's scholarship programme for MENA students from a variety of geopolitical perspectives, but do so through a *critical* lens which analyses both the opportunities *and* challenges arising on individual, collective and national(ist) levels. In particular, these chapters examine a range of connections and ruptures between Cuba's official rhetoric and stated goals for the programme, and the often paradoxical impacts and implications of having studied in Cuba which have arisen following Sahrawi and Palestinian graduates' return to their refugee-camp homes.

Importantly, it must be stressed that I was only able to interview two young Sahrawi women during my fieldwork in 2006, whilst I was unable to meet any other MENA female students throughout my stay in Cuba. This chapter, therefore, primarily discusses the perspectives of a group of *male* MENA students regarding their experiences in Cuba, whilst noting that the gender ratio represented amongst the interviewees (eighteen males and two females) broadly reflects the fact that considerably fewer women than men from the MENA region currently study in Cuba. This is also consistent with the gender ratio of students from Sub-Saharan African countries, citizens and refugees alike: in spite of developing a recruitment process with guidance from Cuban technical advisors, Lehr's research vis-à-vis the Cuba–Ghana programme also revealed a consistent gender imbalance throughout the duration of the programme, which was 'heavily gender-skewed in favour of male students' (2012: 93); a gender imbalance also persisted amongst Angolan students, with Hatzky estimating that only 30 per cent of all students were female (2012: 151).[2] The gendered nature of the Cuban initiative, including with regards to access to, and participation in, the programme, but also regarding female and male graduates' experiences of return, are critically examined in the following chapters.

To get a perspective of the experiences of Sahrawi and Palestinian university students, along those of their MENA citizen counterparts, it is first important to briefly introduce the two main forms of scholarships which have historically been granted through bilateral agreements between Cuba and other states and organisations: school scholarships and tertiary education scholarships. The chapter then highlights the development of the scholarship programme since the 1970s, both with regards to changes in the national/regional origin of the international student body, and with reference to the shift away from providing secondary level schooling to prioritising the provision of higher education in specialist fields. Beyond the official rhetoric of 'solidarity', the chapter concurrently identifies and examines a range of motivations underpinning Cuba's scholarship agreements with different state and non-state actors, including MENA governments and liberation movements. The remainder of the chapter draws on MENA citizen- and refugee-students' narratives to examine their accounts of day-to-day life in Cuba and how they believed (from the vantage point of Cuba itself) that studying in Cuba had influenced their lives so far and would impact upon their futures.

Studying in La Isla de la Juventud

Formerly known as La Isla de Pinos, this small island's name was formally changed to La Isla de la Juventud (the Island of Youth) in 1978, coinciding with the celebration of the XI World Youth Festival. The transformation of this previously under-populated Cuban island into an *International Centre for Studies* revolutionised both the island's demography and its economic capacity, as students contributed to citric agricultural activities in the region (Alonso Valdés 1984). Indeed, post-Revolutionary Cuba identified education 'as a human right as well as a means of developing collective [national/ist] commitment and economic production capacity' (Hickling-Hudson et al. 2012b: 15). The first *Escuela Secundaria Básica en el Campo* (Secondary Basic Countryside School) in La Isla de la Juventud was created in 1971, with a total of 56 schools built there between 1959 and 1981 for secondary level Cuban and foreign students (Comité Estatal de Estadística 1982). Eight pre-university installations were also created in the same time period, ensuring that many of these students could access Cuban universities with the state's financial support.

With reference to the number of foreign children involved in this programme, 10,468 non-Cuban children took up school scholarships in 1982 alone, amounting to 37.7 per cent of the total number of students in La Isla de la Juventud (Alonso Valdés 1984). By 1988, foreign students numbered 13,098: 1,972 in primary schools, 9,151 in secondary schools, and 1,975 in pre-university centres (Richmond 1991). Offering scholarships at all levels of education was in particular essential for students arriving from countries (and refugee camps) with limited national educational infrastructure, and who would otherwise be unable to progress from basic to higher levels of education.

In addition to creating schools for both Cuban and non-Cuban students, one key initiative allowed some groups of non-Cuban children to study and live alongside their compatriots in nationality-based boarding schools. In August 1977, for instance, 1,200 Angolan children, 'among them many orphans or children of civil war refugees', arrived in the Island of Youth (Hatzky 2012: 151); by 1987, seven Angolan schools were educating 3,581 students, and 2,231 children were enrolled in four Mozambican schools on the island (Richmond 1991). In the case of Sahrawi refugees, one doctor who was completing her graduate medical studies in Havana at the time of our interview recounted:

> When I was 11 I travelled to Cuba with another 800 Sahrawi children from the refugee camps. There were three schools just for us in the Isla de la Juventud, but that year they had to open a fourth school because there were so many of us. I lived with about 100 Sahrawi girls who arrived with me, although there were 25 new girls who lived with the older girls in another student residence.

These nationality-based schools also received, in line with Cuban Ministerial resolutions, up to six non-Cuban teachers to provide a socially relevant education by covering the history, geography and language of the student's context of origin (Ministerio de Educación 1982b, Art. 35). These teachers accompanied the students when they travelled to Cuba, living with them, sharing responsibility for their care and 'helping the adolescents to preserve their linguistic and cultural identity' (UNHCR 2003), with a view to facilitating their reintegration into their context of origin following graduation.

Sahrawi refugees were the last group of non-Cuban children who continued to receive this sort of scholarship and schooling in La Isla de la Juventud, as the primary and secondary education programmes for children effectively ceased in the 2000s in order to prioritise resources and personnel to provide tertiary level training to an expanded student body. This decision to prioritise university level education, however, clearly has significant implications for children and youth from states and camps with limited primary and secondary education systems, who will neither be able to complete their basic nor their further education in Cuba.

Tertiary education in Cuba

It is estimated that more than 16,500 non-Cuban students obtained university degrees in Cuba between 1961 and the early 2000s (Martín Sabina 2002). In the 1990s alone it is calculated that approximately 4,000 graduates returned to their countries of origin (ibid.), with over 4,200 students being matriculated in tertiary education courses in the last year of that decade (UNESCO 1999). In 2001/2002, almost half of all foreign students in Cuba were studying courses supervised by the Ministry of Public Health: 2,020 were studying medicine, 71 dentistry and 22 nursing degrees, amounting to a total of 2,113 students (Ministerio de Salud Pública 2002).

Through these scholarships, the Cuban state has covered all tertiary students' university or polytechnic costs, providing all necessary study materials, clothes and uniforms, as well as housing them in student residences and catering for their nutritional and medical/dental needs, offering them a small stipend for additional expenses, and, upon graduation, sending them 'home' with books relevant to their area of expertise (as well as 10 kg excess baggage). In addition, the Cuban government has covered all national transportation costs, although students' states of origin have been responsible for their international travel. The major exception to this rule has arisen when Cuba has made scholarship agreements with non-state organisations or liberation movements including the Polisario Front/Sahrawi Arab Democratic Republic (SADR) and the PLO (Ministerio de Educación 1978, 1982a and 1982b). In the case of Sahrawi refugee-students, for instance, the Cuban state systematically paid for students' transport to and from the Algerian-based refugee camps from the late 1970s until 1994, when it requested that the UNHCR cover these costs due to the acute Cuban economic crisis which followed the collapse of the Soviet bloc.

Students' origins and Cuban motivations

The majority of students receiving scholarships to complete tertiary level degrees in Cuba between 1977 and the mid-1990s originated from countries across Sub-Saharan African (see Table 3.1). This was equally the case in terms of students in La Isla de la Juventud, with the Cuban government providing an education to large numbers of students from Angola, Congo, Ethiopia, Mozambique, Namibia and Sudan (amongst others), and hosting between 13,000 and 15,000 youth from across Sub-Saharan Africa throughout the 1980s (López Segrera 1988; Entralgo and González 1991; Richmond 1991; Dorsch, 2011; Finlay et al. 2011; Preston 2012). The reasons for Cuba supporting African countries through scholarships during

Table 3.1 Total number of 'African' and non-Cuban students in Cuban higher education (1977–1996)

	'African' students	Total non-Cuban students
1977	856	1411
1978	913	2031
1979	592	1691
1980	1114	2530
1981	1352	2887
1982	1335	2830
1983	1552	3178
1984	1836	3435
1985	1966	3161
1986	2687	4075
1987	2844	4143
1988	3345	4660
1989	2815	4057
1990	3040	5654
1991		5723
1992	3040	4811
1993		
1994		
1995		
1996		4243
1997		
1998		
1999		8220

Source: Derived from yearbooks produced by UNESCO (1990, 1994, 1999, 2004) and Comité Estatal de Estadística (1982 and 1991); and from Martínez Pérez (2012).

this time are too many to list here, but include those offered by Fidel Castro for supporting Angola:

> Many things link us to Angola: the common goal, shared interests, politics and ideology. But we are also connected by blood, blood in its double meaning: the blood of our ancestors and the blood that we've spilled together on the battlefields.
>
> (1979, cited in Hatzky 2012: 144)

Explanations for offering scholarships therefore range from a historical commitment to Africa due to the Cuban population's African heritage, to a desire to support African socialist states and anti-colonial and liberation movements (including Angola) which Cuba also often assisted militarily.

In light of more recent figures, however, it is equally evident that Cuba's focus has shifted away from Africa, and towards Latin America.[3] While 76 per cent of foreign students in Cuba in 1996–1997 were of African origin (UNESCO 1999),[4] by 2001/2002 they represented only 16.2 per cent of foreign students (Martín Sabina 2002). Conversely, the number of Latin American and Caribbean students increased almost tenfold in the same time period: although only 8.3 per cent of foreign students originated from South America in 1996–1997, over 78 per cent of the 11,000 foreign students receiving a Cuban education in 2001/2002 were from Latin America and the Caribbean (ibid.).

This reversal in students' place of origin is indicative of major changes in Cuba's political, diplomatic and material priorities, indicating the relevance of considering Cuba's motivations for the scholarship programme, in addition to, but also beyond, its official rhetoric of 'solidarity' and South–South cooperation.[5] As a Cuban university professor indicated during our interview, the increase in Latin American students is related to *la izquierdización* ('the Left-isation') of Latin America, associating this change with Cuba's ideological and political support for 'progressive' Leftist political parties. Further, however, Cuba's economic isolation due to the long-standing US embargo, and the need to confront the realities of the acute economic crisis faced from the 1990s onwards (known as the *Periodo Especial* – the Special Period) following the fall of the Communist Bloc, have been determining factors influencing the state's increasing focus on Latin America, and on countries such as Venezuela in particular. The scholarships currently granted by Cuba to Venezuelan and other Latin American students, paralleled by Cuban doctors completing internationalist medical placements in the region,[6] are a strategic necessity when we consider Cuba's increased material dependence on Venezuelan oil and other forms of technological assistance.[7]

However, while such strategic or functionalist analyses of Cuba's motivations for the scholarship programme may provide some insight into the nature of relations between Cuba and certain other states, such approaches appear less coherent when examining the cases of a range of students from the MENA region, including refugee-students.

MENA students in Cuba: motivations and necessities

Statistics regarding the number of Middle Eastern and North African students in Cuba are limited, although Alfaro Alfaro (2005) indicates that fourteen MENA countries sent students to Cuba between 1961 and 2002. Bilateral educational agreements include those which exist between Cuba and the following '*progre*' ('progressive' – the term used by López Segrera 1988) MENA states and organisations: Algeria, Lebanon,[8] the Sahrawi Arab Democratic Republic, the People's Democratic Republic of Yemen, the PLO (and its component factions – see Chapter 5) and Syria (Fernández 1988; López Segrera 1988).

Indeed, Cuba has created and maintained close connections with Arab socialist states in different ways since the Cuban Revolution: in addition to providing military support at times, the Cuban state has also sent both doctors and teachers on internationalist placements to many of these countries, as well as providing a free education to MENA students in Cuba itself via bilateral arrangements. These programmes of assistance have often overlapped, as indicated by one of the students I interviewed in Cuba: a Palestinian–Cuban doctor currently completing his medical specialisation in Cuba had been taught by Cuban doctors in a Yemeni university prior to arriving in Havana.

Beyond Cuba's multifaceted and complex *apoyo* (support) of liberation and anti-colonial movements, a significant motivating factor behind Cuba's scholarships for Arab students from the MENA region is the political connection between Arab and Cuban socialism in general. It is important to start by recognising the diversity of interpretations and developments of socialist thought and policy in different Arab countries, and that the birth of Arab socialism as a political philosophy preceded the Cuban Revolution by several decades (Said 1972).[9] Whilst sharing many elements, Ba'athism in Syria and Iraq from the 1940s onwards,[10] Nasserism in Egypt in the late 1950s and 1960s, Algeria's non-aligned/socialist perspectives since independence (1962), Gaddafi's fluctuating approaches in Libya from 1969 (see Chapter 6), the Marxist interpretations advocated by the People's Democratic Republic of Yemen (1970–1990), and the commitment to Marxism and communism amongst selected Palestinian factions such as the Popular Front for the Liberation of Palestine (PFLP) and the Democratic Front for the Liberation of Palestine (DFLP), are examples of a range of political, ideological and pragmatic approaches to socialism in the Arab world.[11] The differences encountered within the MENA region itself, and the discrepancies between the socialism of the Arab world and that espoused by Fidel Castro and his state, however, have not impeded Cuba from backing these MENA socialist states and liberation movements[12] in a number of ways since the Cuban Revolution of 1959, including through the South–South educational migration programme which is the main focus of the remainder of this book.

An ideological connection therefore (partially) underlies Cuba's decision to educate the citizens of Arab socialist states and refugees from non-self-governing MENA territories such as the Western Sahara and Palestine. This connection must furthermore be contextualised with reference to the Cuban state's position – held throughout the 1970s and 1980s and institutionalised through both the Ministries of Education and of Higher Education – that foreign students should benefit from a 'politico-ideological' education whilst in Cuba (Ministerio de Educación 1978, 1982a; Ministerio de la Educacion Superior 1980). In effect, the possible impact of Cuba's socialist ideology on these students has emerged as a vocal concern in popular, academic and policy responses to the scholarship programme. Indeed, following my return from conducting fieldwork in Cuba, I was regularly confronted with the claim (or assumption) that one of Cuba's main motivations in running the education programme must be to influence students' ideological inclinations, or, in essence, 'to brain-wash' or 'to indoctrinate them'.

However, in spite of – or perhaps precisely *because of* – the strength of these assumptions, students in Cuba and graduates in their home contexts alike dismissed the validity of these claims in different ways throughout our interviews.

I explore Palestinian graduates' critical accounts of the role of ideology throughout the course of their studies and claims of indoctrination in Chapter 5, and yet it is significant to note at this stage that my Cuba-based interviewees regularly, and largely spontaneously, distanced themselves from the notion that Cuban education might have had an ideological component per se. For instance, when I asked another student, a Sahrawi doctor, whether she felt that studying in Cuba might have influenced the way that she sees the world, she answered by stating that at university, as a medical student, she never had any overtly political classes. She indicated that the only 'socialist' approach she could remember having been taught was in a philosophy course which explained the Hippocratic Oath and its application in medicine.[13] In turn, in those instances where Cuban socialism was referred to by student interviewees in Cuba, such accounts often explicitly highlighted the differences between Arab socialism and Cuban socialism, with one Palestinian student explaining that, 'since materialism is by nature atheist, one cannot be a materialist socialist and a Muslim at the same time'. He stressed that, although he respects Cuban socialists, he feels that he cannot reconcile such an approach with his own religious identity and practice.[14]

While I explore the connection between the scholarship programme and ideology from the perspective of Palestinian graduates in Lebanon in greater detail in Chapter 5, at this stage I would hold that students were not 'imbued'[15] with or brainwashed by Cuban socialist values; rather, they developed a critical engagement with the ideologies and policies they encountered throughout their stay. This is perhaps particularly the case since all of the students whom I interviewed in Cuba were 'Muslim'[16] and originated either from Arab socialist states or were affiliated with Marxist/socialist groups – as a result, their engagement with Cuban socialism will have been directly influenced by their previous exposure to and critical understandings of socialist approaches in the MENA region.

Internationalist scholarships for MENA refugees

As indicated above, in addition to providing scholarships to MENA citizens, Cuba has a long history of supporting the Polisario Front/SADR and the PLO, both of which are members of the Non-Aligned Movement. Bearing in mind the legal and historical particularities of each case, Sahrawi and Palestinian students in Cuba belong to protracted refugee communities whose territories have been violently occupied by Morocco and Israel respectively, and whose struggles for independence are supported by Cuba for ideological and political reasons. The Cuban state has allocated scholarships to these groups of students since the very start of its internationalist education programme, providing a free education to Sahrawi refugees through the Sahrawi refugee camp-based government (the SADR) and the Polisario Front (the Sahrawi liberation movement), and to Palestinian students through bilateral agreements with the PLO.

Sahrawi–Cuban connections

Importantly, although a wide range of countries have offered scholarships to Sahrawi refugee-students (including Algeria, Libya, the former USSR, Qatar, Mexico and Venezuela), Cuba was one of the first countries to offer full scholarships to Sahrawi refugee children and youth in the late 1970s. These scholarships have formed part of a broader framework of Cuban support and solidarity for the Polisario Front, which has included sending hundreds of Cuban doctors on internationalist placements to the refugee camps, in addition to numerous visits by high-profile Cuban revolutionaries (e.g. Almeida Bosque in 1994).[17]

A brief overview of the number of Sahrawi students who have been granted scholarships will give an idea of the extent of the Cuban–MENA programme. The first generation of Sahrawi refugee youth was 'adopted' by Cuba in 1977, when twenty Sahrawi students were offered grants to study in the (secondary-level) *Escuela de Amistad Cuba–RASD* (School of Friendship Cuba–SADR) in the Isla de la Juventud, and then professional degrees in different Cuban universities (Petrich 2005). From 20 students in 1997, by 1995 UNHCR statistics specify that more than 1,400 Sahrawi refugee-students were based in Cuba, with over half of these having returned to the refugee camps over the following decade. Ten years later, 600 Sahrawi students remained in Cuba (ACN 2006), and Cuban and Sahrawi media reports calculate that the number of Sahrawis who have trained specifically as doctors in Cuba is approximately 300 (RHC 2002a, 2002b; SPS 2002). The total number of Sahrawi beneficiaries by the early 2000s was estimated to be well over 4,000 (Salazar 2002; García in San Martín 2005).

Unlike Cuba's relationship with Venezuelan and other Latin American states, one Sahrawi student reflected on her understanding of the basis of the connection between the SADR/Polisario Front and the Cuban government:

> When Cuba offered Sahrawi refugees a free education, Cuba was selfless in this respect, for what could the Polisario Front offer Cuba in return? Perhaps we will be able to repay their solidarity in the future, but for now, it is selfless.

While we cannot assume that Cuba was entirely 'selfless' when it gave scholarships to these young refugees, it could be posited that ideologically based motivations may have played a significantly more important role in the case of Sahrawi and Palestinian students than in the case of scholarships offered more recently to Latin American students.

On the one hand, neither the Palestinian nor the Sahrawi refugee-students themselves, nor their political representatives, are able to offer Cuba significant material or political support. In this sense, the support offered to these refugees and their political representatives appears to correspond to the latter mode of interaction referred to by Corona González et al. (2012: 46): the system 'operates as a philosophy of solidarity that can range from an equal partnership between countries able and willing to help each other, to a relationship whereby Cuba provides assistance expecting no return'.

Indeed, the scholarships extended to these refugee groups, and in particular to the Sahrawi, are necessary due to their almost total dependence on externally provided humanitarian aid and limited educational infrastructure in their places of origin. In the isolated Sahrawi refugee camps, for instance, although education has been prioritised since the camps' establishment in 1975–1976, there are only two secondary boarding schools, and no universities, for a total population of around 165,000 refugees – as such, the vast majority of Sahrawi refugee children and youth must study outside the camps if they are to study at all (see Chapter 4). In turn, until the mid-1990s, UNRWA only offered primary and intermediate[18] education for Palestinian refugees registered with the agency in Lebanon, since

> secondary education, a prerequisite for access to university, was [during the 1980s] never considered to be within UNRWA's temporary mandate. Until 1982, the PLO used to fill this gap by running secondary schools and by securing university scholarships in Lebanon and other sympathetic countries.
> (Abu-Habib 1996: 31)

In such situations, the education of refugee-students in Cuba allows for a relatively high degree of self-sufficiency in professional labour terms, which can be interpreted as embodying a fundamental Cuban socialist priority: to ensure that lesser-developed countries and communities are not reliant upon, and dominated by, Northern-run humanitarian aid and development industries.

It is, however, also worth noting that not insignificant numbers of Cuban-educated students have, upon their return to the refugee camps or their host countries, obtained important administrative, ministerial and diplomatic positions, as discussed in greater detail in the following chapters with reference to the experiences of Sahrawi and Palestinian graduates (also see Martínez-Pérez 2012: 78; Preston 2012: 134–135). If we accept that one motivation underlying the programme may be the hope that students will return with socialist principles to their places of origin, these individuals may indeed have the capacity to play a significant role in determining the political projects and orientation of their own political organisations in their respective refugee camps. In this regard, a small example of the potential to 'repay' Cuba in diplomatic and political terms is identifiable in a short article about Fatma Mahfoud, a Polisario representative based in Italy who studied psychology in Cuba. Fatma explains:

> Cuba is helping a lot of third world countries... The revolutionary government has opened up the Isle of Youth [sic], and each country has its own school on the island. I feel very strongly about this. It is unfair that in Western countries you never see any newspaper speak about this.
> (Cogga 2003)

By virtue of having studied in Cuba, and having obtained positions of relative power, graduates may thus be able to support the Cuban scholarship programme via what we may call a 'public relations' strategy.[19] However, the following chapters highlight that not all graduates replicate such public declarations of support for Cuba upon their return to their context of origin, whether to the Sahrawi or Palestinian refugee camps.

Palestinian–Cuban bonds

In terms of Cuba's potential motivations for allocating scholarships to Palestinian refugees specifically, most of the students interviewed in the island explained that the Cuban government has a long-standing commitment to the Palestinian struggle against Israeli occupation. This commitment is evident not only through many of Cuba's foreign policy decisions (including its history of voting in the UN – Díaz García 1991; Sánchez Porro 1994), through the official representation of many Palestinian factions and groups, in addition to the existence of a Palestinian Embassy, in Havana, but is also reflected in the history of the Palestinian scholarship programme.

In addition to Palestinian students from across the Middle East being able to apply for scholarships through the PLO and its component factions and groups (see Chapter 5), many of the students based in Cuba in the 2000s and 2010s are the children of Palestinians who themselves studied in Cuba during the 1970s and 1980s. Indeed, following a new agreement developed in the late 1990s, Palestinian students who married Cubans are automatically eligible to send their children to study their university degrees and graduate studies on the island, free of charge; Palestinian–Cuban children are, thereby, able to 'inherit' access to the Cuban education system. One doctor who was completing his medical specialisation in Cuba at the time of our interview reflected:

> My father studied in Havana in the 80s, and married my mother while he was here. We returned to the Middle East when I was about 4 or 5, but we never went back to Cuba… When I was old enough, my father suggested that I study in Havana, as he knew about the scholarships for Palestinian-Cuban children… I am happy, and grateful, to be able to study here, although it often seems that neither the Cuban government, nor we ourselves, are clear if we are considered to be Cubans or Palestinians here.

As in the case of Sahrawi refugee-students, infrastructural limitations, in addition to legal and economic barriers to accessing an education in Lebanon, Gaza, the West Bank and the Occupied Territories,[20] to a large extent underlie the necessity of the Cuban–Palestinian scholarship agreement. As a whole, Cuba's motivations in offering scholarships to Sahrawi children, adolescents and youth, and Palestinian youth appear to be less tangible than in the case of scholarships given to Latin American students, and rather more ideological and political in nature.

MENA students in Cuba: material conditions and social relations

The main focus of my interviews in Havana was to obtain further insight into MENA scholarship recipients' experiences of living in Cuba, about their impressions of Cuba itself and how they believed that studying in Cuba had influenced their lives and would impact upon their futures. In turn, I draw on my interviews with Sahrawi and Palestinian graduates in Algeria and Lebanon respectively to contrast these perceptions of the future with the medium- and longer-term impacts of the scholarship programme in Chapters 4 and 5.

Material conditions

When I asked the students about their arrival in Cuba, almost all of them reflected first and foremost on the harshness of living in the island and on the material difficulties they had faced, before turning to cultural or religious issues. This is simultaneously indicative of the long-standing nature of Cuba's economic situation, students' expectations regarding life on the island, and the differences in living conditions which they believe exist between Cuba and their places of origin.

A Syrian medical student, whose Cuban scholarship was at the time supplemented by the Syrian state, described his arrival in the island in the year 2000:

> I arrived in Cuba with another Syrian student, but he didn't stay for longer than a month. We had expected that having a Syrian scholarship would mean that we'd have really good conditions, but we weren't expecting the harshness and difficulties we faced here. Everything was difficult: the public transport, the accommodation, the food, and the cultural differences… He left after a few weeks. I've been here for five years and it's still hard.

He continued by stressing that conditions in the student residences were 'shocking', although he and many other students also highlighted that foreign students tend to be privileged by the system and are allocated to 'better' accommodation blocks than Cuban students. Indeed, in 1980 the Ministry of Further Education indicated that foreign students must be offered accommodation with 'adequate conditions' specifically due to the recognition that these hostels greatly influence students' impressions of life in Cuba (Ministerio de Educación Superior 1980).[21] More recently, in UNHCR's 2005 report on the protection situation of Sahrawi refugee adolescents studying in Cuba, the UN agency indicated that Sahrawi students 'enjoy equal educational opportunities as well as slightly more advantageous treatment in terms of material and health support provided in Cuban schools' (UNHCR 2005).[22]

Despite the material difficulties which currently characterise life in Cuba, and which have even led to several students renouncing a free university education in favour of a more comfortable life in their place of origin, material conditions in Cuba have nonetheless improved considerably since the 1990s, when Cubans and foreign students alike lived through the *Periodo Especial*. One female Sahrawi student's comments not only outline the extent of these difficulties, but also allow us to consider the differences and similarities which may exist between students' places of origin and Cuba:

> When we arrived [in 1988], the lack of food was one of the biggest shocks. There wasn't much food in the [Sahrawi] refugee camps, of course, but it was different there because we knew that our parents would always give us the best food, even if they went hungry themselves.

She continued:

> Here, when the Periodo Especial started, the [Cuban] government told us that the Cuban citizens, as well as the non-Cuban residents and students were hungry. They treated us all the same, sharing their rations with us, and promised that they would continue to support us. But they also stressed that if any of us wanted to return to the refugee camps, where more food was assured because of humanitarian aid, we could leave Havana and then continue with our studies later, when the situation in Cuba was better. Some children returned, but most of us stayed. We knew that our future depended on our education.

These students' descriptions of life in Cuba suggest that the physical structure of the city, alongside material and food scarcity, have impacted upon many foreign students greatly, with some of them having decided that living in the Caribbean island was 'too difficult' for them. Those who stayed may have become accustomed to the living conditions, but, as we shall discuss in greater detail below, food repeatedly emerged as a critical concern for students, especially those who did not eat pork for religious reasons. Further, when considering their experiences in Cuba, these students continually drew comparisons with their places of origin, and wished that things were easier in Cuba.

In the case of the Sahrawi students, it is perhaps paradoxical to note the frequency with which Sahrawi youth stated that material conditions in the refugee camps were 'better' than in Cuba in many respects, despite having been sent to study in Cuba due to the extremely limited educational infrastructure in the camps. Students' comments included: suggesting that there would have been a more reliable supply of food in the refugee camps than in Cuba during the *Periodo Especial*; indicating that there is greater availability of pharmaceutical ingredients to make medicine in the camps than in Cuba;[23] and noting there are cheaper telephone services (including mobile phones) in the refugee camps than on the island. Many of these students felt that it was 'strange' that a nation-state, such as Cuba, could have more material limitations than a refugee population which has been dependent on humanitarian aid for over three decades.

Social relations and religious identity/practice

While material conditions were mentioned first by most interviewees, social relations became the subsequent focus of most of my discussions. A central issue for most of the students interviewed was a recognition that Cuban approaches to social interactions and gender relations, as well as religious identity and practice, differ greatly from those characterising their places of origin.[24] It is worth stressing that while most of the students' places of origin are officially secular in nature, the majority of their populations are Muslim, with social, gender and religious matters being viewed accordingly.

I asked a Yemeni doctor who had studied in Havana for six years what he considered to be a 'typical' trajectory of a Muslim student arriving and studying in Cuba:

> His [sic] arrival is a massive shock. When he sees another Muslim drink, kiss a woman, or go dancing, he says 'You can't do that! What are you doing? It's *haram* [Islamically prohibited] to drink'. The student who's been here for longer will respond by saying 'It's normal here'. This leads to a change in the newly arrived student, who becomes not only tolerant but also enacts these forbidden activities.

He continued by suggesting that, after an initial shock and subsequent enactment of these 'forbidden activities',

> they will eventually develop a deeper understanding of Islam… As they grow older, they will mature, and will understand this and grow closer to Islam. They will see how life works in Cuba: relationships, marriage, divorce, child-rearing… and they will return [to Islam].

Many students did indeed reflect this pattern when they recounted their experiences of living in Cuba, although these explanations varied significantly since the period of time spent in Cuba by the different interviewees ranged from 2 months to 18 years.

One Palestinian student from the Occupied Territories recounted his own experience of living in Cuba for over 10 years:

> I admit that I became lost… I was lost spiritually, I used to go out drinking, dancing, and even ended up marrying a Cuban woman. But that didn't work, and we divorced. I gradually grew closer to Islam again and am now a fully practising Muslim. I am at peace with myself now.

For most of the students, they considered that doing 'some *haram* [Islamically prohibited] things' (in the present or past) did not mean that they were no longer Muslim. For two of the students interviewed, however, these transgressions were viewed very seriously, and they did everything in their power to, as they saw it, bring the younger students back to Islam. There was, therefore, a reasonably high degree of tension between some students regarding the precise meaning of Islamic religious identity and practice in Cuba. As the Syrian student who had lived in Cuba for five years at the time of our interview explained to me:

> I think that religion is a personal matter and you shouldn't be judged by others for how you behave. That is a matter between you and Allah. You also shouldn't judge others – if they want to drink, or have a relationship, that's the other person's choice. I think it's very problematic when others judge you, or when you believe you must behave in a certain way to be viewed in a positive light by others.

In addition to often radically different opinions on drinking alcohol, having relationships or 'going out dancing', the difficulty of finding *halal* (Islamically allowed) food in Cuba was also a major concern for many of the Havana-based students, especially those who prayed together on a regular basis. One group of students had negotiated special cooking rights with the management of their student hostel, enabling them to cook their own meals whenever pork products were used in canteen food. Given the centrality of pork in the Cuban diet, this, in essence, meant cooking for themselves almost every day, which, as a Syrian medical student stressed, 'can be draining after a 24-hour shift in the Accident and Emergency Department'.

The above discussion suggests that while some aspects of Cuba's permissive society may have initially been welcomed by visiting MENA students, a process of selection and rejection played a central role in students' approaches to their host society. Importantly, almost all students maintained a clear distinction between items they considered to be *haram*, and those they considered to be *halal*, even if they sometimes applied a liberal interpretation which allowed them to engage in some activities which they recognised would Islamically be classified as *haram*. Students often associated the process of selection and rejection with an increasing form of 'maturity', with students growing to understand the significance and implications of their actions with time. This clearly counters Altbach's assumption that students 'return home imbued with the norms and values of the host country', or that societies which may be labelled 'permissive' or 'liberal' will necessarily be welcomed by students (1989: 125).

As a brief aside, in order to contextualise MENA students' experiences of religious identity and practice in Cuba, it is worth stressing that Muslims in Cuba tend to be hidden from both social and academic view, with Cuban converts to Islam reportedly preferring to express their religious beliefs and practices in the private sphere (converts pray in informal meeting houses since there are no mosques in Cuba),[25] and with Cuban academics demonstrating little interest in examining the presence and experiences of Muslims in the island, either now or in the past.[26] As I discuss elsewhere, however, the connection between Arab Muslims and the Cuban archipelago is a long-standing one (going as far back as the sixteenth century), and Muslim populations – including those from North Africa and the Levant – have played a significant role in many aspects of Cuban life for many centuries despite Islam having been 'footnoted' in contemporary accounts of Arab migration to Cuba (Fiddian-Qasmiyeh forthcoming). The MENA students' presence in the island in this sense is not a 'novel' one, although most students interviewed were unaware of the history of Muslim Arab immigration to Cuba. What is certainly different is that, while individuals from North Africa and the Middle East had in the past primarily travelled to/via Cuba for political or economic reasons (either as slaves, as individuals escaping from religious and/or political persecution, or generally searching for a better life in the Americas), the more recent arrivals can be categorised as educational migrants (ibid.).

Education in Cuba and expectations (and fears) for the future

As noted above, the vast majority of students whom I interviewed in Cuba were studying courses related to medicine or dentistry, although others were studying degrees such as biology, pharmaceutical studies or accountancy. Their studies were very practical in nature, with medical and dentistry students spending most of their days, and many of their nights, working alongside qualified practitioners to obtain 'hands on' experience. Most stated that their courses were hard, whilst others suggested that non-Cuban students have 'special treatment' and, moreover, were rarely suspended or expelled if they performed poorly in exams. In addition, some students indicated that if their colleagues did not work hard, they might be transferred to less challenging courses. Others stressed that they had worked very hard and had been able to 'move up' the educational ladder, 'moving into' medical or dentistry studies and leaving their initial ('easier') subjects behind. As discussed in Chapter 5, the allocation of places to study prestigious subjects such as medicine was not always related to academic excellence, with Palestinian interviewees reporting that such subjects were often 'monopolised' by well-connected students.

Interviewees indicated that students' courses of study tended to be selected bearing in mind specific employment/existing priorities in their places of origin, with most expecting to return 'home', or, according to many of the MENA students interviewed in Cuba, 'maybe to another Muslim country [sic]', to work there. Therefore, experiences in Cuba, as well as expectations for the future, not only depended on the number of years they had spent on the island, but also on the students' legal statuses. The recognition that they would be able to find 'a good job' at home encouraged most of the Yemeni and Syrian students, whilst the Palestinian and Sahrawi refugee-students sometimes admitted that returning to their refugee camps or hosting countries was a less attractive prospect. For some of the refugee-students, the humanitarian, political and security situations 'at home', alongside their limited mobility rights as refugees, affected their plans and expectations for the future greatly. Torn between wanting to return to their place of origin to be with their families and to work for the benefit of their entire refugee community, they also considered the possibility of making the most of their professional capacities by working in a European country and sending remittances to their families in the camps.

Many students reflected on some potential difficulties of returning home which they anticipated they would face following graduation. Some of these were linguistic in nature, while others were more firmly framed in cultural terms. Most of the students had spent their first year in Cuba learning Spanish to fit into the Cuban education system: although the Sahrawi students had an advantage in the sense that Spanish is the second official language spoken in the refugee camps,[27] all students found it difficult to learn Spanish and complete their studies (including their exams) in their newly acquired second, or third, language. Bearing in mind that 'learning to work with the contradictory strains of languages *lived*, and languages *learned*, has the potential for a remarkable critical and creative impulse' (Bhabha 2006: x), a related difficulty was reflected upon by a Sahrawi medical student who said:

> It is ironic. As we don't have any universities in the refugee camps, Sahrawi youth have to study around the world, but they never study medicine in their own language! In Cuba we study in Spanish, in Algeria they study in French... I really don't know how I'll communicate with my patients in the camps.

Indeed, upon their return to their contexts of origin, all of the MENA students interviewed recognised that they would have to become accustomed to working in one of a range of Arabic dialects (see Chapters 4 and 5 on the roles of language upon return 'home'). In the case of Sahrawi students who studied in the Island of Youth from a young age, however, it is worth noting that these students are in general neither fluent in their mother tongue (Hassaniya Arabic) nor in Spanish. In fact, unlike most other MENA students who arrived as young adults in Cuba and, therefore, had a firm understanding of Modern Standard Arabic (*Fus-ha*) in addition to their national dialect, Sahrawi students who arrived as children indicated that their main 'language' in Cuba is what they have labelled *Arabañol* (= Árabe + Español), a hybrid combination of Hassaniya Arabic (the Sahrawi dialect) and Spanish.

In addition to the anticipated advantages of returning as professionals with university degrees, these students, therefore, also predicted that they would encounter a range of difficulties upon their return 'home'. These challenges transcended concerns about a shift in their work language, and rather related to major changes in all social settings, with one of the female Sahrawi students interviewed recognising that, having lived in Cuba for so long,

> I will have to adapt to life in the refugee camps when I return. I realise that it is I who will have to become accustomed to living there, not my family or the other camp residents who will have to accept what I have become in Cuba. I know that it will be hard.

Whilst perhaps being most pronounced for young women returning home (see Chapter 4), interviewees also noted that leaving Cuba and returning to the

Middle East and North Africa would, in most likelihood, be difficult at first for many male students. This was a concern which was vividly expressed by many of the students interviewed. One Palestinian student from the Occupied Palestinian Territories (OPT) wondered if he would be able to adapt to living in the OPT at all, and was considering applying for asylum in a third country so as to avoid having to encounter that major difficulty upon his return. Experiences of visiting 'home' during the holidays sometimes strengthened these fears: a male Sahrawi student who had recently returned for a short visit to the refugee camps admitted that he had found it difficult to know how to speak with different members of the community, how to engage with Sahrawi women, or to determine what would be considered appropriate or inappropriate for him to say to his mother, father or grandparents. From the vantage point of Cuba, he was concerned about his ability, or indeed desire, to adapt to conditions in the camps upon his graduation.

Reponses to a question regarding students' plans to marry and have children were also indicative of the significance of some problems students had experienced during their time in Cuba. The matter of finding a marriage partner was one issue that unmarried male students often felt ambivalent about, claiming that ideally there should be no difference between marrying a Cuban or an 'Arab' woman, but tending to favour the latter nonetheless. They stated that they did not believe that marrying a Muslim woman would necessarily be better than marrying a Christian (or secular) woman, although they did feel that a common cultural understanding would be important for rearing children in the future. One reason presented by several students for not marrying a Cuban woman is that the students do not want to remain in Cuba, and they know that Cuban women rarely want to move to the MENA region. They were concerned that if they had children with a Cuban woman, the mother would be responsible for raising these children, and they did not wish their children to be brought up in a non-Islamic fashion and in a non-Muslim environment.

Perhaps a more interesting discussion pertaining to children arose in answers to the question of whether students would want their own children to study in Cuba. Although all students were greatly appreciative of having been given the opportunity to study in Cuba free of charge, they admitted that their experiences would impact many of the decisions they might have to take as fathers.[28]

A Syrian medical student addressed this question ('Would you send your own child to study in Cuba in the future?') by drawing on a conversation he had during his summer holidays in Syria: 'I asked that exact question to a friend of mine who studied here in Cuba before. He said "No" to this question when I asked.'

Although my interviewee agreed with his friend's response, he recognised that there were a number of issues to be considered:

> In conclusion, I think that… no. I wouldn't send my own son or daughter here [to Cuba]. I know that sometimes a parent has to decide what's best for his [sic] child, and it might be good to send them here if they can gain something special. When I look back, I can see some good things, but also many difficult things that I have lived through. I just want to return to Syria.

On the other hand, however, it is worth stressing that the Cuban–Palestinian students' fathers had been in precisely this situation, as one medical student pointed out:

> My father was happy for me to come here now that I am 24, since he knows what Cuba's like. He wanted to be sure that I wouldn't let myself be carried away by the Cuban ways, and we know that, for younger students, it's harder not to be influenced, it's harder to resist the general flow of things. For the older students, it's easier to resist, although it's still difficult.

The issue of maturity and age was mentioned by a range of students, including Yemeni, Palestinian and Sahrawi students alike. A Sahrawi graduate answered the same question of whether he would send his child to study in Cuba as follows: 'When he's [sic] mature enough, and has reason… when he's mature enough, he can decide for himself what he wants to do.'

The students interviewed all agreed that arriving in Cuba at a young age is very challenging, generally explaining this in terms of requiring an in-depth understanding of Islam and pertinent cultural knowledge upon arrival (also see Fiddian-Qasmiyeh 2013). A Yemeni student framed this in terms of having the tools required to 'defend yourself' from certain aspects of Cuban society, while the Syrian student indicated that:

> If you're 17 or 18, you can get lost easily, but when you're older, your ideas are fixed, you won't be dragged along by others or change your mind. If you arrive when you're 11, you lived as an Arab for 11 years but then you become Cuban while you're here. You lose your Arabness. It's not good to come here so young.

Concluding remarks

> It was, gentlemen, after a long absence – seven years to be exact, during which time I was studying in Europe – that I returned to my people. I learnt much and much passed me by – but that's another story.
>
> (Salih 1969: 1)

This chapter has explored one side of a story, not the experiences of returning home 'after a long absence' (as examined in the following chapters), but rather some of the experiences of a group of Muslim MENA students during their 'long presence' in Cuba. By addressing some of the reasons behind these students' participation in this South–South educational migration programme, in addition to their impressions of life in the island, I have presented both commonalities and particularities shared by refugee and citizen students from the MENA region. Whilst sharing a common religious identity, the students' nationalities and legal statuses, as well as the political situations underpinning their places of origin, highlight not only the heterogeneity of the MENA region itself, but also the way in which individual and collective identities have inevitably influenced students' interpretations of living in Cuba during their participation in this model of South–South cooperation. Far from simply being 'imbued' with Cuban values, the Yemeni and Syrian citizens, like their Palestinian and Sahrawi refugee counterparts, constantly referred to their situations 'at home' (be this a desert-based refugee camp, urban refugee hosting context or state of citizenship) when evaluating their encounters with Cuban society and the Cuban system. In this sense, these interviewees allow us to better understand the ways in which participants view the Cuban international education programme itself, but also present us with a wealth of material on these students' perceptions of both of these locations (Cuba and 'home') and the relationship between Cuba and the MENA region.

The significance of long-standing connections between Cuba on the one hand and MENA liberation movements or Arab socialist states on the other, is, I suggest, simultaneously epitomised and paralleled by the trans-generational nature of Palestinian–Cuban students' experiences of following in their fathers' footsteps. While the majority of the students interviewed expressed reservations about sending their own children to study in Cuba in the future, and although concerns were also expressed regarding the future of Cuba's education programme following Fidel Castro's inevitable death, the potential for Cuba to welcome and educate a third generation of Palestinian students continued to be an imaginable reality for interviewees in Havana. The potential of such a transnational and trans-generational programme can be perceived as going beyond the benefits to individual students, or even the possible benefits offered to their communities or states.

As has been widely discussed within the postcolonial literatures, global systems have consistently been divided, interpreted and (mis)represented through the problematic centre/margin dichotomy, with the margin tending to correspond to the Other, in this case the 'developing'. While both Cuba and the Arab world are commonly conceptualised as the Other by mainstream European and North American state and non-state actors, and simultaneously as marginal and marginalised in political and economic terms, Cuba's South–South education programme provides us with another perspective on centre/margin relations. By situating marginal(ised) MENA youth, including doubly and triply displaced Palestinian and Sahrawi refugees, at the centre of their education programme, the politically and economically sidelined Cuban state has taken a step towards creating a space for what Qasmiyeh and I would call 'the central margin' (Fiddian-Qasmiyeh 2010). This space not only challenges existing centre/margin dichotomies (US/Cuba, for instance), but officially refuses to reproduce a similar dichotomous and unequal system within itself.

The following chapters now turn to the other side of the story – that of returning home 'to my people … after a long absence' (op. cit.) – to examine how Cuba's South–South educational migration programme is viewed from the perspective of the Sahrawi and Palestinian refugee camps in Algeria and Lebanon respectively, and whether the centralised margin has been maintained upon return or whether new processes of marginalisation and exclusion have taken place.

Notes

1 This internationalist approach paralleled Cuba's development of its national education system, which aimed to enable the 'deeply transformative process of social levelling' (Hickling-Hudson et al. 2012b: 15) necessary to establish a truly 'inclusive' model of education (Breidlid 2013), which would meet its official commitment for 'education for all' (well before the international Education For All (EFA) goals were established by United Nations Educational, Scientific and Cultural Organization (UNESCO), UNDP, United Nations Population Fund (UNFPA), United Nations Children's Fund (UNICEF) and the World Bank in 1990).

2 This is in contrast with the high proportion of female Latin American students, for instance, who have consistently participated in the programme – it is estimated that 50 per cent of all Latin American students completing their medical degrees in Havana in 2013 were female.

3 The opening of the *Escuela Latinoamericana de Medicina* (Latin American School of Medicine) in the late 1990s was one of the first steps embodying this shift – see Chapter 2.

4 The connection with African countries remains in place in different ways, however. For instance, some Cuban scholarships are now also offered to African students via UNESCO. In 2003, twelve African students benefited from this UNESCO–Cuban Fellowship Programme (Alfaro Alfaro 2005).

5 Also see Chapter 2 on Cuba's increasing role in providing medical training to Central American students following Hurricane Georges and Hurricane Mitch in 1998.

6 Teachers, as well as doctors, have completed international placements since the Cuban revolution began. In 1987, for instance, 125 teachers offered technical assistance to different countries, thereby, according to the Ministry of Education 'completing the internationalist characteristics of our Revolution' (Ministerio de Educación Superior 1987, my translation).

7 In the 1980s, Venezuela was forced to 'severely cut back on government funding for overseas study when [it]… encountered severe economic problems after the drop in oil prices' (Altbach 1989: 130).

8 Whilst categorised as a 'progressive' country by López Segrera (1988), Lebanon's ideological fabric, especially in light of the civil war which was at its peak in the 1980s, was of such a heterogeneous nature (including 'progressive' and 'anti-progressive' alliances) as to make such a classification highly contestable.

9 According to Said, whilst existing as a *concept* well before then (1972: 24), the term 'Arab socialism' was first used after the establishment of the Arab League (1945) to distinguish a 'political philosophy as distinct from Marxism as it was from other forms of socialism' (ibid.: 21–22).

10 Whilst still present in Iraq, the reader will be aware that the Iraqi Ba'ath party has been displaced from national politics by international events in the 2000s and 2010s.

11 For analyses documenting this diversity see the edited collections by Hanna and Gardner (1969), Karpat (1968) and Said (1972).

12 Importantly, Cuba has historically been a socialist reference point for many Arab states and Palestinian factions, both due to perceptions of the 'purity' of Cuba's socialism but also through the importance of Cuban revolutionary 'symbols', such as Castro and Guevara. For example, the relationship between the Cuban state and its revolutionary symbols on the one hand, and the PLO and the PLO's component Marxist and non-Marxist factions on the other, is examined in Chapter 5.

13 It is worth recalling that the majority of students I interviewed in Cuba were students of medicine or dentistry (as were approximately 50 per cent of all foreign students in the early 2000s (Ministerio de Salud Pública 2002) and 79.3 per cent of all overseas students in 2010 (Martínez Pérez 2012)). It could, therefore, be conjectured that students completing courses related to the humanities or politics will have had

greater explicit exposure to Cuba's socialist perspectives. More broadly, all students will have engaged with socialist values through their exposure to the Cuban society and system more broadly.

14 On the Islamic foundations of Arab socialism, and early Arab socialists' antagonistic relationship with Marxism, see Hanna and Gardner (1969) and Said (1972).

15 As per Altbach's conjecture (1989: 125) that international students 'return home imbued with the norms and values of the host country'.

16 Bearing in mind the diversity of its interpretations and implementations, personal and collective identification in relation to Islam was a central, and often ambivalent, element arising from the interviews conducted throughout the course of my research in Cuba, the Sahrawi refugee camps and the Palestinian refugee camps. Interviewees' multiple (re)presentations of religious identification reflect not only the heterogeneity of the category 'Muslim', but also the range of ways in which individuals define themselves and present themselves to others in different contexts. Thus interviewees often made precise references to the notion of religious practice and identity, ranging from non-committal descriptions of themselves as non-observant to a self-categorisation of being a 'bad Muslim'. For a more detailed discussion, see Fiddian-Qasmiyeh and Qasmiyeh (2010), Fiddian-Qasmiyeh (2013, 2014) and Qasmiyeh and Fiddian-Qasmiyeh (2013).

17 As argued in Chapter 4, through these and other modes of support, Cuba has come to be centrally positioned in the Sahrawi 'educational imagination'.

18 In the UNRWA system, primary level education consists of six years of study, followed by 4 years of intermediate study, and three years of secondary level schooling. As noted here, in Lebanon UNRWA only took on responsibility to provide Palestinians with secondary level schooling in the 1990s.

19 This corresponds with Corona González and colleagues' conclusion that through its overarching model of South–South cooperation, 'Cuba establishes an independent global profile of solidarity, which brings it political support from the majority of countries in the world [sic], thus providing a measure of protection from the implacable hostility of the United States government' (2012: 47; also see Hickling-Hudson 2012: 122).

20 Prior to the 2011 Arab Uprisings and the subsequent Syrian civil war, Syria and Jordan offered Palestinians access to state-run schools and universities, and some Palestinians were able to attend Lebanese educational institutions; as such, the university scholarships offered by Cuba to Palestinians hosted by those MENA states have offered *additional* opportunities to those already in place. The scholarships for these Palestinians, therefore, clearly embody Cuba's political commitment to the Palestinian cause, as much as providing essential educational opportunities per se.

21 My visits to a selection of student hostels around Cuba indicate that conditions vary depending on the location, with residences being 'better' outside Havana than in the city itself.

22 Responding to Moroccan claims that Sahrawi youth were abused in Cuba, UNHCR's 2005 report also highlighted that 'this scholarship programme meets the standards of treatment and care required by the 1989 Convention on the Rights of the Child', and that children are not abused (sexually or otherwise), militarily recruited or militarily trained in Cuba (see Fiddian-Qasmiyeh 2009).

23 These are limited in Havana due to the US embargo, whilst the camps receive materials through humanitarian projects.

24 As well as discussing their personal relationships with Islamic identity and practice, many of the interviewees commented on the way that Cubans approach, evaluate and critique Islam, as I discuss elsewhere (Fiddian-Qasmiyeh 2010).

25 There is a small 'tourist mosque' (which, in fact, is not a mosque but a prayer room) in the *Casa de los Árabes* (the House of the Arabs), a small museum based in the old part of Havana. This location is primarily frequented by Muslim ambassadors and visitors

to the island, rather than by either Muslim students or Cuban converts to Islam (see Fiddian-Qasmiyeh 2010, forthcoming).

26   There is a distinct absence of literature on this topic, with scant reference to Muslims throughout existing reports on Arab immigration to Cuba. In the island, the term 'Arab' is practically synonymous with 'Christian Arab' (i.e. Charon 1992; Perdomo Lorenzo 1992; Menéndez Paredes 1995, 1997, 1998, 1999, 2001; Departamento de Estudios Socioreligiosos 1998).

27   While Spanish is the second language taught in schools based in the Sahrawi refugee camps, and is the second official language in political terms, the majority of the Sahrawi students interviewed had left the camps at a relatively young age and had, therefore, not yet received in-depth Spanish language classes before arriving in Cuba. This explains their need for a year's Spanish language training before starting their formal studies.

28   The experiences of Cuban-educated *mothers* – including the internment of unmarried Cubaraui mothers in the Sahrawi refugee camps – are addressed in Chapter 4.

References

Abu-Habib, L. (1996) 'Education and the Palestinian refugees of Lebanon: A Lost Generation.' *Refugee Participation Network*, 21: 30–32.

Agencia Cubana de Noticias (ACN) (2006). 'Sahara: 30 años de exilio y lucha', *Agencia Cubana de Noticias*, 22 February. Available at http://www.rebelion.org/noticia.php?id=27171, last accessed 26/09/2006.

Alfaro Alfaro, C.E. (2005) *La colaboración educacional cubana con la UNESCO en la perspectiva de la Educación Para Todos*, MA thesis. Instituto Superior de Relaciones Internacionales, La Habana.

Alonso Valdés, C. (1984). *Población, migración internacional y desarrollo regional. Una experiencia Cubana: Isla de la Juventud.* Ponencia de Contribución: Seminario Internacional de Población y Nuevo Orden Económico Internacional. 3–5 July. La Habana.

Altbach, P.G. (1989) 'The New Internationalism: Foreign Students and Scholars', *Studies in Higher Education*, 14(2): 125–136.

Bhabha, H.K. (2006) *The Location of Culture.* 3rd ed. London: Routledge.

Breidlid, A. (2013) *Indigenous Knowledge and Development in the Global South.* London: Routledge.

Charon, E. (1992) 'El Asentamiento de Emigrantes Arabes en Monte (La Habana, Cuba), 1890–1930', *AWRAQ: Estudios sobre el mundo árabe islámico contemporáneo*, 8: 35–68.

Cogga, F. (2003) 'Saharawi Leader Tours New Zealand', *The Militant*, 23 June. Available at http://www.themilitant.com/2003/6721/672110.html, last accessed 14/10/2005.

Comité Estatal de Estadística (1991) *Anuario Estadístico de Cuba 1989.* La Habana: Comité Estatal de Estadística.

Comité Estatal de Estadística (1982) *Estudio demoeconómico Municipio Especial.* Isla de la Juventud. La Habana: Comité Estatal de Estadística.

Corona González, J., Hickling-Hudson, A. and Lehr, S. (2012) 'Challenging Educational Underdevelopment: The Cuban Solidarity Approach as a Mode of South-South Cooperation' in A.R. Hickling-Hudson, J. Corona-González and R. Preston (eds) *The Capacity to Share: A Study of Cuba's International Cooperation in Educational Development.* New York: Palgrave Macmillan, 35–52.

Departamento de Estudios Socioreligiosos (1998) *Panorama de la Religión en Cuba.* La Habana: Ed. Política.

Díaz García, W. (1991) *Cuba vota en la ONU contra la partición de Palestina*. La Habana: CEAMO.

Dorsch, H. (2011) 'Black or Red Atlantic? Mozambican Students in Cuba and Their Reintegration at Home', *Zeitschrift für Ethnologie*, 136: 289–310.

Entralgo, A. and González, D. (1991) 'Cuba et l'Afrique: quel avenir?' *Aujourd'hui l'Afrique*, 42: 16–19.

Fernández, D.J. (1988) *Cuba's Foreign Policy in the Middle East*. Boulder, CO: Westview Press.

Fiddian-Qasmiyeh, E. (forthcoming) 'Embracing Transculturalism and Footnoting Islam in Accounts of Arab Migration to Cuba', *Interventions: The Journal of Postcolonial Studies*.

Fiddian-Qasmiyeh, E. (2014) *The Ideal Refugees: Gender, Islam and the Sahrawi Politics of Survival*. Syracuse NY: Syracuse University Press.

Fiddian-Qasmiyeh, E. (2013) 'Inter-generational Negotiations of Religious Identity, Belief and Practice: Child, Youth and Adult Perspectives from Three Cities', in J. Garnett and A. Harris (eds) *Rescripting Religion in the City*. Farnham: Ashgate, 163–176.

Fiddian-Qasmiyeh, E. (2010) 'Education, Migration and Internationalism: Situating Muslim Middle Eastern and North African Students in Cuba', *The Journal of North African Studies*, 15(2): 137–155.

Fiddian-Qasmiyeh, E. (2009) 'Representing Sahrawi Refugees' 'Educational Displacement' to Cuba: Self-Sufficient Agents and/or Manipulated Victims in Conflict?' *Journal of Refugee Studies*, 22(3): 323–350.

Fiddian-Qasmiyeh, E. and Qasmiyeh, Y. (2010). 'Asylum-seekers and Refugees from the Middle East and North Africa: Negotiating Politics, Religion and Identity in the UK', *Journal of Refugee Studies*, 23(3): 294–314.

Finlay, J.L., Crutcher, R. and Drummond, N. (2011) "Garang's Seeds': Influences of the Return of Sudanese-Canadian Refugee Physicians to Post-Conflict South Sudan', *Journal of Refugee Studies*, 24(1): 187–206.

Hanna, S.A. and Gardner, G. (eds) (1969) *Arab Socialism: A Documentary Survey*. Leiden: Brill.

Hatzky, C. (2012) 'Cuba's Educational Mission in Africa: The Example of Angola', in A.R. Hickling-Hudson, J. Corona-González and R. Preston (eds) *The Capacity to Share: A Study of Cuba's International Cooperation in Educational Development*. New York: Palgrave Macmillan, 141–160.

Hickling-Hudson, A.R. (2012) 'Studying in Cuba, returning home to work: Experiences of graduates from the English-Speaking Caribbean', in A.R. Hickling-Hudson, J. Corona-González and R. Preston (eds) *The Capacity to Share: A Study of Cuba's International Cooperation in Educational Development*. New York: Palgrave Macmillan, 107–126.

Hickling-Hudson, A.R. (2004) 'South-south Collaboration: Cuban Teachers in Jamaica and Namibia', *Comparative Education*, 40(2): 289–311.

Hickling-Hudson, A.R., Corona-González, J. and Preston, R. (eds) (2012a) *The Capacity to Share: A Study of Cuba's International Cooperation in Educational Development*. New York: Palgrave Macmillan.

Hickling-Hudson, A.R., Corona-González, J., Lehr, S. and Majoli Viani, M. (2012b) 'The Cuban Revolution and Internationalism: Structuring Education and Health', in A.R. Hickling-Hudson, J. Corona-González and R. Preston (eds) *The Capacity to Share: A Study of Cuba's International Cooperation in Educational Development*. New York: Palgrave Macmillan, 13–34.

Karpat, K.H. (ed.) (1968). *Political and Social Thought in the Contemporary Middle East*. London: Pall Mall Press.

Lehr, S. (2012) 'The Children of the Isle of Youth: How Ghanaian Students Learned to Cope with "Anything in Life"', in A.R. Hickling-Hudson, J. Corona-González and R. Preston (eds) *The Capacity to Share: A Study of Cuba's International Cooperation in Educational Development*, New York: Palgrave Macmillan, 83–105.

Lehr, S. (2008) 'Ethical Dilemmas in Individual and Collective Rights-based Approaches to Tertiary Education Scholarships: The Cases of Canada and Cuba', *Comparative Education*, 44(4): 425–444.

López Segrera, F. (1988) *Cuba: Política Extranjera y Revolución (1959–1988)*. La Habana: Instituto Superior de Relaciones Internacionales.

Martín Sabina, E. (2002) *La Educación Superior en Cuba en la década del 90*. La Habana: Ed. Felix Varela.

Martínez-Pérez, F. (2012) 'Cuban Higher Education Scholarships for International Students: An Overview', in A.R. Hickling-Hudson, J. Corona-González and R. Preston (eds) *The Capacity to Share: A Study of Cuba's International Cooperation in Educational Development*. New York: Palgrave Macmillan, 73–82.

Menéndez Paredes, R. (2001) 'La Huella Árabe en Cuba', *Opus Habana*, 1: 26–35.

Menéndez Paredes, R. (1999) *Componentes Árabes en la Cultura Cubana*. La Habana: Ed. Bolaña.

Menéndez Paredes, R. (1998) '"La Ultima" Maronita', *Opus Habana*, 4: 53–55.

Menéndez Paredes, R. (1997) 'Monte de los Árabes', *Opus Habana*, 2: 7.

Menéndez Paredes, R. (1995) 'Un inmigrante árabe en la Casablanca Cubana', *El Árabe*, 45 (Nov/Dec): 2–5.

Ministerio de Educación (1982a) Reglamento para el recibimiento y atención de los becarios extranjeros en centros hasta el nivel medio y en los institutos superiores pedagógicos, Resolución Ministerial No. 480/82 (17. 11. 1982). La Habana: Ministerio de Educación.

Ministerio de Educación (1982b) Reglamento para el recibimiento y atención de los becarios extranjeros en centros del Municipio Especial Isla de la Juventud. La Habana: Ministerio de Educación.

Ministerio de Educación (1978). Règlement pour bousiers étrangers a Cuba, Resolución 145 (27.03.1978). La Habana: Ministerio de Educación.

Ministerio de Educación Superior (1987) *Reunión del Resumen del Curso Académico de 1986–1987*. La Habana: Ministerio de Educación Superior.

Ministerio de Educación Superior (1980) *Normas y Procedimientos para la Atención y Control de Becarios Extranjeros en Centros de Educación Superior*. La Habana: Ministerio de Educación Superior, Dirección de Relaciones Internacionales.

Ministerio de Salud Pública (2002) *Anuario Estadístico de Salud*. La Habana: Ministerio de Salud Pública.

Perdomo Lorenzo, G. (1992) *Aproximación al estudio de la inmigración Árabe en Cuba*. La Habana: Centro de Documentación e Información de la Unión Árabe de Cuba.

Petrich, B. (2005). 'Los avances de las saharahuíes ejemplo para el mundo árabe.' *La Jornada*, http://www.jornada.unam.mx/reportajes/2005/sahara/61/index.php, last accessed 18/08/2007.

Preston, R. (2012) 'Cuban Support for Namibian Education and Training', in A.R. Hickling-Hudson, J. Corona-González and R. Preston (eds) *The Capacity to Share: A Study of Cuba's International Cooperation in Educational Development*. New York: Palgrave Macmillan, 127–140.

Qasmiyeh, Y.M. and Fiddian-Qasmiyeh, E. (2013) 'Refugee Camps and Cities in Conversation', in J. Garnett and A. Harris (eds) *Migration and Religious Identity in the Modern Metropolis*. Farnham: Ashgate, 131–143.

Radio Habana Cuba (RHC) (2002a) *Una Visita Muy Provechosa, Dice Presidente Saharaui*, 31 January. Available at http://www.blythe.org/nytransfer-subs/2002-Caribbean-Vol-I/ Radio_Habana_Cuba-31_de_enero_2002, last accessed 29/10/2005.

Radio Habana Cuba (RHC) (2002b) *Presidente Saharaui Visita la Isla de la Juventud*, 24 January. Available at http://www.blythe.org/nytransfer-subs/2002-Caribbean-Vol-I/ Radio_Habana_Cuba-24_de_enero,_2002, last accessed 19/10/2005.

Richmond, M. (1991) 'Exporting the Education Revolution: The Cuban Project to Become a World Education Power', in H.M. Erisman and J.M. Kirk (eds) *Cuban Foreign Policy Confronts a New International Order*. Boulder, CO: Lynne Rienner.

Sahara Press Service (SPS) (2002) *Le President de la republique affirme que son sejour a Cuba aura 'une influence positive'*, 24 January. Available at http://www.spsrasd.info/sps-240102.html, last accessed 29/10/ 2005.

Said, A.M. (1972) *Arab Socialism*. London: Blandford Press.

Salazar, E. (2002) *Mandatario Saharaui Continua Viaje Por Cuba*. Radio Reloj, 25 January. Available at http://www.radioreloj.cu/noticiasdia2/notidia25-1-02.htm#2, last accessed 29/10/2005.

Salih, T. (1969) *Season of Migration to the North*. London: Penguin Books (Trans. D. Johnson-Davies).

San Martin, P. (2005) 'Nationalism, Identity and Citizenship in the Western Sahara', *Journal of North African Studies*, 10(3–4): 565–592.

Sánchez Porro, R. (1994) *Comunidades Árabes de Cuba*, unpublished manuscript. Habana: CEAMO Library.

UNESCO (2004) *Global Education Digest: Comparing Education Statistics across the World*. Montreal: UNESCO Institute for Statistics.

UNESCO (1999) *1999 Statistical Yearbook*. Paris: UNESCO.

UNESCO (1994) *1994 Statistical Yearbook*. Paris: UNESCO.

UNESCO (1990) *1990 Statistical Yearbook*. Paris: UNESCO.

UNHCR (2005) *Information Note: Western Saharan Refugee Students in Cuba*. September 2005. Geneva: UNHCR.

UNHCR (2003) *Summary Update of Machel Study: Follow-up Activities in 2001–2002*. Geneva: UNHCR Refugee Children Coordination Unit.

4 Paradoxes of educational migration to Cuba

Views from the Sahrawi refugee camps in Algeria

Introduction

The potential to promote self-sufficiency via educational migration is particularly significant in the Sahrawi context given infrastructural limitations in the Algerian-based refugee camps and the camps' dependence upon externally provided humanitarian and political aid. In effect, many Polisario representatives and SADR diplomats around the world, as well as camp-based SADR ministers, were educated in Cuba; so too were those former students who have taken on roles of great responsibility in administering the Sahrawi refugee camps and attending to prominent Spanish-speaking politicians, journalists and activists during their visits to the camps. However, although it is now widely recognised that 'refugees often see the education of their children as a principal way of ensuring a better future' (Dryden-Peterson 2003: 1 – see Chapters 1 and 2), the means for providing such an education, and views of what precisely would amount to a 'better future', are less consistently expressed by the different actors involved in planning for and delivering schooling to refugee children around the world. While both Cuba and the Polisario Front have endorsed the Cuban educational migration programme as a means of promoting Sahrawi self-sufficiency and 'preserving the group's cultural, linguistic, and historical traditions' (to quote Water and Leblanc 2005: 138), this chapter explores the multifaceted impacts and implications of the Cuban educational migration programme from the perspective of interviewees in the Sahrawi refugee camps themselves.

In particular, I argue that while Cuban educational migration has become a central part of Sahrawi refugee children's, youth's and adults' imaginary landscapes, and is purposefully designed and projected to maximise Sahrawi refugees' self-sufficiency, the implications of Sahrawi youth's participation in Cuba's South–South educational migration programme are paradoxical, ultimately reshaping and reinforcing, rather than reducing, the Sahrawi refugee camps' dependence upon Northern aid providers.

Furthermore, by drawing upon research with both male *and* female Sahrawi graduates in the Algerian-based Sahrawi refugee camps this chapter fills a major gap which emerged throughout my research in Cuba, where it was nearly impossible to identify female research/scholarship participants. By complementing the Cuba-based interviews with research conducted with youth in the 27 February Refugee Camp (commonly known as The Women's Camp) and in the camps' administrative core of Rabouni, I, therefore, highlight the extent to which gender has played a central role in access to, and experiences and perspectives of, this transnational education system. In so doing, the chapter provides critical insights into the medium- and longer-term implications of the Cuban education programme for Sahrawi refugees, and how 'development' can be conceptualised in such a desert-based refugee camp context.[1]

'Education for liberation' in the Sahrawi protracted refugee situation

In common with other liberation movements around the world, education emerged as a central feature of the anti-colonial movements which arose during the late colonial period (1960s and 1970s) in the territory currently known as the Western Sahara, and in particular of the main anti-colonial organisation which was born in May 1973: the Polisario Front.[2]

Extensive 'historical analyses highlight the constitutive role that international students have played in nationalist projects by becoming leaders and producing knowledges and policies that have shaped postcolonial spaces in the 20th century' (Madge et al. 2014: 13).[3] In the Sahrawi context, the first major urban-based anti-colonial movement in the territory (the Movement for the Liberation of Saguiat el-Hamra and Río de Oro) was established by Mohamed Sid Brahim Bassir (known as Bassiri) in 1968. Bassiri had studied in Casablanca, Cairo and Damascus (Hodges 1987: 48–49), and – influenced by the Pan-Arabist and socialist ideas of the Baathists while studying journalism in Syria (Hodges 1984: 153) – upon his return to the Spanish Sahara Bassiri taught the Qur'an and Arabic at Smara's mosque and started to recruit members for the liberation movement. Following Bassiri's permanent 'disappearance' in 1970 at a peaceful demonstration (Pazzanita and Hodges 1994), a new leader for the liberation movement emerged: El-Ouali Mustafa Sayed (known as Luali) had trained as a lawyer in Morocco and had reputedly read Fanon and Guevara in their first editions in Arabic (Damis 1983: 40).

As a result of Bassiri's, Luali's and other Polisario members' educational experiences, the liberation movement was thus influenced by the anti-colonial, socialist and non-aligned theories, frameworks and models that permeated the region at the time. While studying, these men had engaged with, and been impressed by, notions of Pan-Arabism and the activities of African and Middle Eastern liberation movements, especially the Palestinian Resistance (Hodges 1984: 158).

Upon the establishment of the Sahrawi refugee camps in South-West Algeria in 1975–1976, and following the Polisario's announcement of the birth of the camp-based SADR in February 1976, the Polisario developed its own constitution, camp-based police force (and prisons), army and parallel state and religious legal systems (the latter of which implements a Maliki interpretation of Islam). The vast majority of the earliest reports on the camps stressed the Polisario's 'participatory ideology' and 'democratic' organisation of the camps (e.g. Harrell-Bond 1981: 1–4; Black 1984: 1–2; Mowles 1986: 8–9). These further highlighted that the camps are 'models of efficient local government' (Brazier 1997: 14), whose members are elected in 'state' elections held during five-yearly National Conferences. The four main camps are headed by a *wāli* (governor) who is appointed by the 'head of state' (Shelley 2004: 183), with administrative and managerial functions completed by camp residents[4] employed by the Polisario/ SADR. This high degree of self-management has been widely commended by international observers, with the camps denominated 'the best run refugee camps in the world' (Brazier 1997: 14) and a 'success story' amidst a failing humanitarian system which creates 'dependency syndrome' amongst refugees (Harrell-Bond 1986; also Voutira and Harrell-Bond 2000: 66).

Indeed, the centrality given to education in this protracted refugee situation is an embodiment of the Polisario's aim for its 'nation-in-exile' to be wholly self-sufficient in the camps, but also in an independent Western Sahara if the long-awaited referendum for self-determination were to eventually take place.[5] As such, as soon as the camp-based Sahrawi Ministry of Education, Health and Social Affairs was created in 1976, its principal aims were twofold.

Firstly, the Ministry established a mixed, universal, obligatory and 'secular education system' in the camps, in order to 'constitute a modern society' (Gimeno-Martín and Laman 2005: 23) led by educated men and women who could ensure the self-sufficiency of 'the Sahrawi nation'. Schools were thus amongst the first structures to be built by the Polisario/SADR in the camps, and children and adults[6] alike benefited from the literacy campaigns run by the small number of individuals who had received an education during the colonial era (Fiddian-Qasmiyeh 2011). In addition to building crèches and primary schools, the need for secondary schools emerged, leading to the construction of two boarding schools[7] which offered an education to children from all of the camps, and maximised students' access to the small number of teachers.[8]

Secondly, the Ministry simultaneously requested that friendly countries welcome as many Sahrawi children and youths as possible to educate them abroad (Velloso de Santisteban 1993), in order to overcome the camps' infrastructural limitations and the total absence of higher education opportunities in or near the camps. As such, promoting self-sufficiency in the camps and the quest for national self-determination was intimately related to the development of a *trans*national education system which has historically been intimately tied to the principles of the Non-Aligned Movement and South–South cooperation (see Chapter 2). Although a wide range of countries have offered scholarships to Sahrawi students (including Algeria, Libya, the former USSR, Mexico and Venezuela), Cuba was one of the first countries to offer full scholarships to Sahrawi children and youths in the late 1970s as part of its broader programme of educational internationalism.[9]

Sahrawi reflections on educational migration to Cuba: a 'better future'?

Perhaps the clearest indication of the strength of the Cuban education programme in the Sahrawi refugee camps can be gleaned from the interviews which Crivello and I conducted with forty-six Sahrawi children aged between seven and twelve in 2005 (Crivello and Fiddian-Qasmiyeh 2010). These children's responses vis-à-vis their expectations for the future reveal the extent to which educational migration to Cuba is present in Sahrawi children's imaginary landscapes and provide the foundation for their imagined futures. Hence, sixteen children reported that their parents, siblings, uncle/aunt and/or cousins had studied in Cuba, with seven of these children directly expressing their desire to study in Cuba in the near-future:

> My mother studied in Cuba… I want to go to [study] in Cuba.
>
> (8-year-old boy)

> You have to study first in Cuba, and then become a doctor, because the doctors have to speak Spanish.
>
> (9-year-old boy)

> I want to be a doctor… [to do this] first you need to finish school, then you go to Cuba, like my aunt.
>
> (10-year-old girl)

> I'm going to Cuba this year if my parents let me… you have to study for 15 years there but I don't care, as long as I can study.
>
> (12-year-old boy)

These interview extracts demonstrate the importance which Sahrawi refugee children as young as eight give to educational migration directly as a result of their relatives' experiences, their recognition of the centrality of Cuban-educated doctors in the camps, and the particular association which children consequently make between Cuba, studying medicine and learning Spanish.

A large proportion of these Cuban-educated Sahrawi returnees currently occupy positions of authority in the camps, with one member of the Polisario Front's National Secretariat estimating that around 2,000 Sahrawi trained in Cuba occupy the most important political, social, administrative and professional roles in the refugee camps (Sayed quoted in ACN 2006). In addition to the centrality of Sahrawi doctors and nurses who studied in Cuba, the bearing of students' tertiary educations in the Caribbean island is particularly visible in those numerous cases when Sahrawi students of social science and humanities subjects completed undergraduate and postgraduate dissertations on the conflict over the Western Sahara (Fiddian-Qasmiyeh 2014). These students' time in Cuba provided them with the necessary political and linguistic training to work in Sahrawi institutions (Spanish is the official institutional language in medical settings in particular) and to represent the Sahrawi 'cause' in the camps and in SADR 'diplomatic missions' around the world. As the 'official face' of the Polisario and the main point of contact for the several thousand Spanish-speaking visitors (*solidarios*) who travel to the camps every year, these graduates in essence embody the benefits of Cuba's educational migration programme, demonstrating the high degree of professional self-sufficiency which parallels the camps' material dependence upon externally provided assistance (Fiddian-Qasmiyeh 2009, 2014).

Difficulties of return

Despite their prominence in the camps, however, most Sahrawi students and graduates of the Cuban education programme underscored a wide range of problems they had faced as a result of their educational migration to Cuba. With reference to their return 'home', interviewees pointed both to the anguish caused by such prolonged periods of separation during children's formative years, and to the linguistic, cultural and emotional difficulties faced upon their return (also see Fiddian-Qasmiyeh 2013a).

Recalling her childhood in Cuba, a young woman who was studying medicine in Havana at the time of our interview, and who had left the camps for Cuba aged eleven noted:

> I used to wake up in the middle of the night, thinking that I was in the camps, only to find that I was in the student residence, surrounded by other girls sleeping in bunk-beds, all squeezed together. I would cry myself to sleep. I can't explain how painful it was to be there, to know that my mother was alone, without me, in the camps...
>
> (Fatimetu, Havana, October 2006)

While longing to return to her mother and home-camp, and simultaneously feeling for/as her own mother, Fatimetu noted the emotionally fraught dimensions of her first visit 'home' after almost 10 years in Cuba:

> The first time I returned to the camp was in 1997, and no-one was expecting me. I arrived in the 27 February camp, which is where I knew that I lived. They left me in the camp, with a small suitcase full of university books. But I didn't remember where I lived, I hadn't been there for almost 10 years, so when I saw a woman outside of her *khaima* [tent], I asked if she knew X [mother's name]. She said yes, are you her daughter? When I said yes, she started ululating. I was so embarrassed! Other women started coming out of their tents and surrounded me and ululated until my mother arrived... I spent 23 days there, and then [I] returned to Cuba.

More personal, and more emotionally fraught, was her account of not only missing and longing for family and the camps, but of other students not remembering and recognising family members upon return:

Another [male] student who arrived with me, approached an old woman to ask if she knew X [his mother]. She said, yes, that's me! And he said, no, you can't be my mother! My mother's teeth are like this [sticking out] and yours don't do that, so you can't be my mother. She explained that she had had her teeth fixed many years ago, and that she was his mother. He was in shock. Can you imagine what that's like, not only for the children, but for the adults[10] to realise that *they don't even remember their own parents?*

(Emphasis added)

Indeed, paralleling the difficulties faced by innumerable immigrants around the world upon their return 'home', Tareq, a Sahrawi graduate who was employed by a European NGO in the refugee camps after spending 16 years in Cuba, stressed that:

When I returned to the camps [having left at the age of 11], I didn't know my family. I couldn't communicate with them… we were from two different worlds. I know certain Cuban families better than I know my own family. It's very hard – I even find it hard to spend time with them.

The challenges faced by Cuban graduates specifically as a result of their prolonged separation from their families in the camps[11] led a male Cuban-educated pharmacist to define 'Cuba' (i.e. the Cuban internationalist programme) as 'a social problem which took place…', and to refer to the experience as a 'sacrifice' characterised by 'cultural and social loss' (Rabouni, April 2007).

According to my interviewees in the camps, part of the 'social problem' experienced by these Sahrawi refugees as a result of their time in Cuba was the very creation of the new social group of *Cubarauis* (where 'Cubano' + 'Saharaui' = 'Cubaraui').[12] According to the above-cited pharmacist, these 'hybridised' Cubarauis not only have their own language (Arabañol – see Chapter 3) but also 'have another ideology, other thoughts, and when they arrive [in the camps] they're lost, they know nothing about life "here"' (interview, Rabouni, April 2007). Having left the refugee camps in their formative years, speaking broken Arabic and unaccustomed to the social and religious customs which permeate life in the camps, Cuban-graduates have experienced high levels of rejection upon their return 'home'.

Nonetheless, interviewees referred to a change taking place over time:

At first, people in the camps were reluctant to acknowledge and accept the *Cubarauis'* particularities, but increasingly we are being accepted in the camps. At first [in the early 1990s], there were 10 or 20 students who returned, but eventually there were thousands of young men and women who had returned from there [Cuba]. Now [people in the camps] see that the doctors, teachers, ministerial aides, etc. all studied in Cuba, they see that we work hard to keep the camps going, so [the refugee] society is more or less accepting of the students, and people still want to send their children to Cuba.

(Salman, NGO employee, 27 February Camp, April 2007)

Camp-based acceptance for Cuban-educated Sahrawi men has increased over time – especially given the extent to which the construction and maintenance of the SADR state project is so visibly tied to Sahrawi cooperation with Cuba – and yet the number of children leaving the camps to study in Cuba has decreased exponentially since the programme's inception. Indeed, despite Cuba continuing to be conceptualised as a location for education by many Sahrawi refugees and external observers (Fiddian-Qasmiyeh 2009), including the children cited above, the vast majority of the Cuban graduates whom I interviewed in Cuba and in the camps alike indicated that they would *not* send their own children to study there.[13] Notwithstanding the significance of this programme in 'creating' young cadres for the camps, the primary intersecting reasons given for this reluctance include the geographical, social and religious distances between Cuba and the Sahrawi camps.

In addition to these reasons, students' and graduates' hesitancy to send their own children to study in Cuba must be contextualised further through a gendered lens. Indeed, as noted in the previous chapter, when I asked MENA students in Cuba whether they would consider sending their children to Cuba in the future, the (primarily male) interviewees invariably responded with reference to the possibility of a *son* following in his father's footsteps. This raises key questions regarding the gendered nature of access to, and experiences of, Cuba's South–South educational migration programme: why were so few Sahrawi women studying in Cuba at the time of my research when female Cubarauis – including in particular female Cubaraui doctors – are hyper-visible and hyper-audible in the camps? Why did male interviewees in Havana and the Sahrawi refugee camps alike exclude the possibility of even imagining their *daughters* following in their footsteps to participate in the Cuban scholarship programme?

Gendered access and impacts

Cuban-educated female graduates are omnipresent throughout the Sahrawi camps, especially as female medical doctors and nurses but also working throughout the camps' social, cultural and political infrastructure, acting as bilingual guides for visitors to the camps, and participating visibly in the official parades which are regularly organised for *solidarios* (see Figure 4.1).

Given the centrality of *Cubaraui* women in the camps, I was particularly surprised to discover that there were only three Sahrawi women studying in Cuba at the time of my research in 2006 (all of whom were related to high-ranking members of the Polisario/SADR[14]). Indeed, throughout the 1980s hundreds of 10- to 11-year-old Sahrawi girls travelled to Cuba to complete their studies, and yet by the end of the 1980s female participation had decreased dramatically (see Table 4.1), for reasons, and with implications, explored in greater detail below.

Complementing the overview of experiences of the Cuban programme presented in Chapter 3, and overcoming the inherent gender bias resulting from the overwhelming proportion of male students interviewed in Havana, this chapter draws on detailed ethnographic observation of the experiences of

Figure 4.1 Female Cubaraui refugee doctors and nurses participating in a 'parade' held in Smara refugee camp for non-Sahrawi *solidario* visitors during the 2007 NUSW Conference (South-west Algeria, April 2007)

Table 4.1 Sahrawi students in Cuba (1977–2006)

Year	Sahrawi students in Cuba	Total female Sahrawis in Cuba
1977	20	
1978	n.d.	
1994	1,493	
1995	1,400+	± 200
1996	1,328	± 200
1997	1,099	
1998	963	140
1999	862	
2000	802	
2001	901	60
2002	878	27
2003	721	9
2004	719	
2005	597	
2006	600	3

Sources: UNHCR reports and Cuban statistical reports 1978–2007. Adapted from Fiddian-Qasmiyeh (2009).

and responses to Cubaraui women in the Sahrawi refugee camps, alongside a combination of interviews with two Cuban-educated Sahrawi women in Cuba and with over a dozen Cubaraui female graduates in the camps. These sources enrich our understanding of the gendered nature of experiences of the educational migration programme whilst in Cuba and upon return 'home', and also of the broader impacts and implications of this model of South–South cooperation in the medium and longer term.[15]

The presence and absence of Sahrawi refugee girls and women in Cuba

While Sahrawi families had originally agreed to send their sons and daughters to study in Cuba, in the mid- to late 1980s many demanded that their daughters return to the camps:

> Around adolescence, some families started to ask for their daughters to return to the camps. They would contact the [Sahrawi] embassy [in Havana] who would in turn contact the Cuban Ministry asking for their daughters to conclude their studies and leave Cuba. They did this, and girls started returning to the camps.
>
> (Khadija, Cuba, November 2006)

That girls should have been recalled by their parents upon reaching puberty is consistent with the concerns expressed by many of my (adult) interviewees in Algeria regarding the movement of pubescent and post-pubescent girls in certain areas of the camps (Fiddian-Qasmiyeh 2009, 2014). According to my research in the Sahrawi refugee camps, girls' movements there today continue to be increasingly limited as they develop physically and approach maturity, becoming young women who can be perceived to be *fatināt* (feminine plural, carriers of temptation and its related chaos). As they are progressively expected to observe certain religious practices (such as veiling and praying),[16] and to help their mothers with domestic tasks, combined with the possibility of marriage prospects emerging in the camps, parents may become more convinced of the need to recall their daughters at this stage.

At this time (around 1989), however, almost all families stopped sending their daughters to study in Cuba, although they continued to allow them to travel to those countries which were closer to the camps. This proximity was evaluated in geographical, linguistic, cultural and religious terms, with the largest number of girls travelling to Algerian towns and cities and the second largest group to Libyan centres. However, although girls continue to travel to and study in Algeria, and took up scholarships in Libya until the overthrow of Gaddafi in 2011 (see Chapter 6), the largest number of tertiary level scholarships offered to Sahrawis has always been through the Cuban state, with only a relatively small number of youth completing university degrees elsewhere.[17] As a result, by stopping girls from travelling to Cuba, their opportunities to access tertiary education outside the camps practically disappeared at this stage, although they were still eligible for vocational training in the camps.[18]

Such changes ultimately appear to be directly related to concepts of ideal female behaviour, and of female needs. Beyond claims that girls 'need' more 'things' than boys, as I was repeatedly told in interviews with Sahrawi youth in Cuba, Syria and in the camps, girls were also described as missing their families more than boys, and, therefore, finding the long-term separation from the camps harder to deal with. To this effect, one of the young women I interviewed in Cuba reflected that

> each year, one or two girls would return to the camps because they found it too hard to bear. The girls who stayed behind wondered how they could have done that. Maybe some of them dreamt of returning too, but I was determined to study, and to do that, I knew that I would have to stay in Cuba. It's too painful to even describe how I felt at that time.

Other interviewees suggested that it was the families themselves in the camps who found it harder to be separated from their daughters, with parents requesting their return from Cuba as puberty approached, while those with daughters still based in the camps decided to send them to study elsewhere.

Despite the additional answers offered, it is my conclusion that the latter is the main reason why Sahrawi girls effectively ceased to travel to Cuba. Although parents were largely unaware of the fact at the time, Cuban gender roles and relations are starkly different from those considered appropriate in the Sahrawi context, and young women returning from Cuba (unlike women who have studied in Algeria or Libya) have often faced stigmatisation from kin and community who were certain that the women had been 'bad girls' in Cuba (Fiddian 2002; Márquez 2005). This impression that *all* girls and young women had 'misbehaved' whilst abroad, no matter how they might have *actually* behaved, was derived from the experiences of what can only be called a minority: some of the older girls had entered into relationships and had become pregnant, facing serious consequences both in Cuba itself (being challenged by male students and political representatives alike) and when they were promptly returned to the camps to face their parents.[19]

Indicating the severity of their treatment upon return, three of my Cubaraui interviewees in the camps indicated that some of these young Cubaraui women were interned in the National Women's Prison (also referred to as the National Centre for Maternity Assistance), where women who have become pregnant out of wedlock have been sent since the camps were created.[20] Two of my interviewees, and one of Tortajada's sources (2003: 87), suggested that this was a 'good idea' since it was 'for their own safety', as they could face violent responses from their family and broader community as a result of their behaviour.

The reaction in the camps was clear: girls would no longer be sent to study in Cuba, and many parents requested that their daughters should return immediately, although some were able to finish their degrees before returning to the refugee camps. Of those who returned, and of those who might have travelled to Cuba under other circumstances, some continued studying in nearby (Muslim) Algeria and Libya, under close supervision by Sahrawi 'monitors'. And yet, as several Muslim Palestinian and Syrian students reflected during our interviews in Cuba, 'it is not surprising that girls who arrived at such a young age should act like the Cuban women who surrounded them. It's not really their fault.' Without adult Sahrawi female role models, the girls found it difficult to become 'traditional Sahrawi women', and, rather, they became 'Cubarauis'.[21]

Although the social experiences of Sahrawi male and female students were arguably similar in Cuba, the responses and discourses surrounding the 'outcomes' of these relationships are clearly gendered – as noted by Elejalde Villalon with reference to 'African' students in Cuba, 'they went to parties, had boyfriends and girlfriends, and sometimes this causes problems. They left some seeds in Cuba, and today there are quite a number of Cuban citizens with one African parent' (in Hickling-Hudson et al. 2012: 222) – the 'seeds' remaining in Cuba were as a whole born of Cuban women and non-Cuban men. These men have never faced the social stigma, ostracism and physical abuse encountered by their female Cubaraui counterparts.[22]

In addition to potentially facing incarceration, since their return to the camps, Cuban-educated young women have been perceived to be potential threats to the current social and political balance in the camps. Many parents and broader community members often consider that *las Cubarauis* have undermined the moral integrity of the camps through their activities in Cuba, while politicians have also recognised that Cuban graduates simultaneously have the capacity to challenge the representation of the camps to outsiders, and the status quo in the camps.

With the veteran members of the National Union of Sahrawi Women (NUSW) having monopolised the political scene in the camps since the 1970s and 1980s, Cuban-educated women have been granted roles which ensure that they are unable to directly challenge the power structures. On the one hand, their visibility to INGO workers and journalists grants them greater access to both material and social capital and networks, thereby leading both female and male Cuban graduates to recognise the benefits which arise from acting as the camps' 'ideal representatives', and what they could lose were they either to refute the images reproduced by camp managers during their engagements with non-Sahrawi interlocutors, or to directly challenge the legitimacy of the Polisario, SADR and/or NUSW. In addition to this element of 'self-policing', and as became apparent during the Fifth NUSW Congress held in the 27 February Camp in April 2007, the vast majority of Cuban-educated women are officially restricted to fulfilling their assigned roles as 'guides' and 'interpreters' in the camps, rather than being able to participate as conference delegates as many of them would wish (Fiddian-Qasmiyeh 2009, 2014).

Whilst arguably enjoying more freedom of movement around the camps than other Sahrawi refugee women, and accompanying visiting NGO representatives and journalists during their tours of the entire refugee setting, many of these young women are, for instance, unable to join these representative structures which continue as a whole to be run by the same women who are repeatedly re-elected to executive positions (Fiddian-Qasmiyeh 2014). Furthermore, even those young Cuban-educated women who work in the NUSW encounter major difficulties in travelling to and from work in the camps, and find their activities being judged by family members and neighbours alike.[23]

For instance, Mariam, a Cuban-educated woman in her early thirties employed in the offices of the NUSW in the 27 February Camp, lives in another one of the Sahrawi refugee camps, where she continues to look after her younger siblings. During our interview, she explained to me that to stay away from her home-camp, even if she were to stay with friends or family, would inevitably lead to people 'gossiping' about her, since, she concluded 'this society is a bit difficult' (27 February Camp, May 2007).

Having lived in Havana, Mariam, like other Cuban-educated women, found that her family and broader community are often prone to evaluate women's movements between camps negatively (especially the movements of female Cuban graduates), and she has thus acceded to commuting every day rather than live in the room provided by the NUSW. Kamila, another young female interviewee, had also studied in Cuba and was on sick leave from her job in one of the ministries in Rabouni (some 15 km from the 27 February Camp, and a 10–15 minute drive away) at the time of our interview in the camps. She admitted that she was considering not returning to her ministerial position in Rabouni, but rather to look for a job in her home-camp, since her family thought that it was 'not a good idea' for her to work so far away from home (27 February Camp, April 2007). A combination of familial and political pressure, therefore, works to keep Cubaraui refugee women in their place, following their period of educational migration in Cuba and their return to their refugee camp 'homes'.

While both male and female Cuban-educated Sahrawi youth experienced the pain of separation from parents and broader communities, longing to return to their families throughout their childhoods and adolescence only to encounter a wide range of social and linguistic challenges upon return, this section has demonstrated different ways in which gender has mediated experiences of accessing the programme and of returning to the camps. Importantly, although I have argued that Cubaraui women are 'kept in their place' through a combination of familial and political structures in the camps, and are at times even unable to continue working in their areas of professional expertise as a result, male graduates have faced different trajectories and experiences of movement and mobility.

Self-sufficiency or renewed dependency? Returning to the colonial past?

Cuba's educational policy has historically specified that scholarships will be provided only if students return to their locations of origins to ensure self-sufficiency (see Chapter 3). While all Cubaraui students have indeed returned to the camps following graduation, pressures to limit Cubaraui women's movement and mobility within the camps have not extended to male graduates, with increasing numbers of male Cubaraui youth leaving the refugee camps in search for work in Europe (especially to Spain).[24] In part, this trend for emigration is related to high levels of unemployment in the refugee camps, and the inability for most graduates to work in their own professions there. Concurrently, an expansion of paid jobs resulting from the arrival of foreign NGOs after the declaration of a ceasefire between Morocco and the Polisario in the early 1990s has also led to the phenomenon of emigration referred to by the Sahrawi Women's Union as 'a cancer devouring the Sahrawi [refugee] body' (Arabic document on file with author, author's translation). The emergence of opportunities for paid employment with NGOs in the camps (as opposed to 'voluntary' and unremunerated work for the Sahrawi 'state', as had previously been the case) has reinforced socio-economic inequalities between camp inhabitants. Many graduates who are unable to obtain a job with an NGO and/or a Polisario institution, and indeed many of those who have secured such positions, decide to leave the camps in order to send remittances to their families from Spain.

This trend, which is intrinsically gendered in nature, therefore appears to be related to the existence of a relatively large number of university graduates in a refugee camp setting characterised by a combination of minimal employment opportunities and a move towards a market economy following the arrival of European NGOs. However, it is arguably the medical training provided in the Spanish language by Cuba which is most significant in this respect: while the Cuban educational focus on training medical professionals was designed to ensure self-sufficiency and simultaneously to combat the legacies of colonialism, ever-increasing numbers of Cuban-trained doctors are leaving the camps to work for the Cubans' and Sahrawis' shared former colonial power: Spain.

Throughout this process, Cuba has become an intermediary between the camps and Spain, while the camps have themselves become a bridge which transports the bearers of Cuban education to its former coloniser. It is Cuba's extensively recognised excellence in medical training and practice which has led to Spain accepting medical degrees from Cuban universities with few bureaucratic complications, meaning that Spanish-speaking Cubaraui doctors are readily employed by private and public hospitals in Spain. Rather than lessening ties with former colonial powers, in this instance the Cuban education system has led to the inverse: the increased presence of Cubaraui doctors in Spain and decreasing numbers of doctors in the camps. The ultimate paradox resulting from this situation emerges when we recognise, as stressed by a Spanish doctor interviewed in the camps, that as Cubarauis leave the camps to work in Spain, increasing numbers of Spanish doctors will be required to travel to the camps via *comisiones médicas* (medical commissions), as hundreds of Spanish doctors currently do every year, to treat Sahrawi patients there.

The Sahrawi–Cuban case study therefore confirms the extent to which purposive attempts to maximise 'self-sufficiency' by minimising 'brain drain' within 'host' contexts may be contingent both upon conditions in locations of origin and broader structures of inequalities and opportunities (Skeldon 2008: 10–11).

On the one hand, both Palestinian and Sahrawi refugee interviewees in Havana consistently informed me that non-Cuban students are actively encouraged by the Cuban system to specialise in paediatrics, internal medicine, or gynaecology and obstetrics, as it is assumed that these will be the most necessary specialisations when they return to their places of origin; conversely, medical students have rarely been trained as surgeons, since Cuba understood that such a strategy could be counterproductive if these graduates were tempted to find well-paid jobs in the North, rather than staying to work in their community of origin. These strategies – which are absent in the context of the Libyan education system for Sahrawi and Palestinian refugees explored in Chapter 6 – are in line with the Cuban state's official stance, as summarised by Hickling-Hudson et al. (2012: 25), that graduates should return in order to

> offer services that favour the poor... [to] create a new culture of medical practice and an image of doctors in society grounded in humanitarianism. This new culture does not prioritize the selling of medical services and merchandise, but is based on the principle of relieving pain and saving lives, because human lives and health cannot be objects of trade.

In the Sahrawi refugee context, however, despite these and other approaches designed to encourage self-sufficiency and a 'brain gain' in students' communities of origin, structural conditions and Polisario's policies within the Sahrawi refugee camps have led to the increasing migration of skilled male Cubarauis to Spain.

This situation has been recognised not just by Cubarauis, the Polisario and Spanish observers, but also by the Cuban government itself. For example, Said, a specialist doctor who had returned to the camps only a few months before our interview, concluded that, in addition to Cuba's re-orientation towards Latin America since the mid-1990s (see Chapter 3), the main reason why 'Cuba no longer offers the massive number of training opportunities which it did in the past' is that the Polisario has mismanaged medically trained Cubarauis upon their return to the camps:

> If your population has increased at a normal rate, and if your policy is designed to cover primary health care, those doctors who graduated from Cuba between 1977 and today should be sufficient to cover your needs. And we know [in the refugee camps] that this is the case. It's very hard to demand [more scholarships] because Cuba [is] going to present all of the statistics... It's not [Cuba's] fault, it's [the Polisario's] fault.
>
> (Rabouni, April 2007)

As a result of these factors, Sahrawi youth are no longer sent to study in Cuba,[25] with the above-quoted Spanish and Sahrawi doctors concurring that the final Cubaraui doctor would have graduated from Cuba in 2012, embodying the end of Sahrawi refugee youth's participation in Cuba's South–South educational migration programme.

Conclusion

The Cuban–Sahrawi transnational education programme has come to symbolise Cuba in the refugee camps, and yet it has also come to be associated with long-term separation and loss on personal, familial and collective levels. Furthermore, despite the potential for Sahrawi refugees to build a 'better future' by engaging in educational migration specifically to ensure self-sufficiency in their Algerian-based refugee camps, this chapter has argued that Sahrawi refugees' educational mobility and migration have been fraught with ambiguities and, ultimately, paradoxes. In particular, high esteem for Cuban medical education has facilitated Spanish-speaking Cubaraui medical personnel's onward migration to Spain, where they work for the Cubans' and Sahrawi's common former colonial power. With increasing numbers of male Cubaraui doctors leaving the refugee camps to work in Spain, and fewer Sahrawi refugee-students graduating from Cuban universities as this South–South educational migration programme comes to a close, this therefore accentuates, rather than weakens ties of dependence upon Northern humanitarians.

An additional, counter-intuitive, outcome of the programme relates to the recognition that the increase in male Cubaraui out-migration has been paralleled by the majority of Cuban-educated women having stayed in the camps: most Sahrawi doctors in the camps are therefore Sahrawi women who studied in Cuba. As a result, Cubaraui women's roles in running core services in the camps are increasingly highly valued by other refugees who benefit from their medical care, and are celebrated by the Sahrawi political leadership in national parades. Indeed, beyond their professional activities in the camps, *Cubaraui* women have become key political symbols, embodying the Sahrawi's nationalist project of self-sufficiency on many levels, in spite of the major challenges which they have continued to face in the camps, and the limited educational opportunities which are available for Sahrawi girls and young women in the twenty-first century given the end of the Cuban–Sahrawi *and* the Libyan–Sahrawi scholarship programmes (see Chapter 6).

Despite purposive attempts to develop a South–South partnership that challenges the power imbalances which typically characterise Northern-led development and humanitarian initiatives, this chapter has demonstrated the extent to which participatory aid programmes may have unintended outcomes and unplanned longer term consequences for 'beneficiaries' and their communities of origin. On the one hand, having granted secondary and tertiary level scholarships to Sahrawi refugees since the late 1970s, Cuba has offered a clear alternative to the ways in which Northern donors conceptualise the provision of education to refugee children and youth (and, indeed, humanitarian assistance more broadly), explicitly advocating for a system which enhances self-sufficiency and self-management in the refugee camps. Influenced by Cuba's and Polisario's political and ideological priorities, the Sahrawi–Cuban scholarship system has historically been developed through an active dialogue with Polisario representatives. With the Polisario playing a key role in developing the curriculum and selecting the language, content and means of instruction for Sahrawi children and youth based in Cuba, this dialogue has illustrated the potential for refugee children and youth to receive a contextually relevant education both in their refugee camps and through transnational scholarship programmes.

However, divergent, and often conflicting, views may exist amongst aid recipients, political representatives, donors and international observers apropos the means to secure a 'better future' for a given refugee group, and, indeed, who (male or female, child or adult) should access opportunities to secure a 'better future'. In the context of international and local structures of inequalities and opportunities, including a combination of minimal employment opportunities and an emerging market economy in the refugee camps, a tension evidently exists between securing individual and family-based self-sufficiency through onward migration to Spain, and ensuring that the refugee camps are locally managed with minimal interventions from non-Sahrawi humanitarians. Whether the Cuban–Sahrawi scholarship system is considered to have been a success or failure is, therefore, dependent upon these diverse views vis-à-vis the present and the future, with retrospective evaluations of the transnational programme varying amongst diverse groups of Sahrawis, Cubarauis and non-Sahrawis alike. The longer-term implications of prioritising individual and family-based self-sufficiency appear to be clearer, since future generations of Sahrawi children and youth will no longer be able to complete their secondary and tertiary educations in Cuba. Although it remains to be seen whether Cuba will develop an alternative model for providing educational opportunities to Sahrawi refugees in their desert-based camps or elsewhere, Cuba's educational legacy will continue to play a significant role both in Sahrawi refugees' imaginary landscapes and in socio-political frameworks in the foreseeable future.

Notes

1 This chapter's focus on self-sufficiency qua development is complemented by the following chapter's examination of the ways in which Palestinian graduates conceptualise Cuba's education programme through the lens of 'humanitarianism'.

2 For a detailed history of the conflict over the Western Sahara, see Fiddian-Qasmiyeh (2014).

3 It is notable that the Western Sahara is still pending decolonisation, and is, therefore, not yet a 'postcolonial space'.

4 The total camp population is currently calculated by the UNHCR and the World Food Programme as being over 155,000 (Fiddian-Qasmiyeh 2014), with the UNHCR estimating in 2004 that 59 per cent of the refugee camp population was under the age of 18 (2004).

5 In the 1970s, education was also a means of 'socialising' the formerly nomadic population, which had to become accustomed to their enforced sedentarisation in the newly created refugee camps. This 'socialisation' ranged from campaigns regarding public health and hygiene in order to avoid epidemics, to the Polisario's determined attempt to eradicate the hierarchical tribal system in order to create a nation formed by equals. For a critique of the latter point, see Fiddian-Qasmiyeh (2014).

6 A range of 'national' (Polisario) vocational centres also offer professional training to young and adult refugees in the camps. These 'national' centres include the male-

dominated *Gazwane* which mainly provides computer, vocational and technical training courses; a co-educational nursing college; and a number of women's schools and centres which have been opened throughout the camps via foreign funding, primarily from the Euskadi (Basque Country) and other regional Spanish governments. The largest women's school continues to be based in the 27 February Camp (where the first Women's School was established), with boarding possibilities for women from all camps to be trained in a range of subjects such as computing, driving, weaving and languages.

7   By the mid-2000s, Sahrawi refugee children attended 29 primary schools and 25 pre-school centres in the camps (UNHCR 2006: 6), with some students eventually moving to a 'national' boarding school to complete their secondary studies. Although two boarding schools existed in the camps until the mid-2000s, only the 12th October Secondary School has been functioning since the major floods of 2006 destroyed the 9th June (Lower-secondary) School, dramatically limiting the number of students able to attend secondary school in the camps.

8   While the Polisario had initially relied upon externally provided materials (primarily from Algeria), by 1984 a 'national' syllabus had been developed by the Polisario (Perregaux 1990). As indicated by Cole and Kandiyoti, 'nations' can be created in many ways, 'including by setting up national school systems that impose a single linguistic standard and a cobbled-together "national" history' (2002: 195–196).

9   Sahrawi experiences of the Libya education programme are explored in Chapter 6.

10   In another piece, Crivello and I have argued that the Spanish summer hosting programme which allows Sahrawi children to leave the camps to spend two months living with Spanish host families have unintended consequences: 'In attempting to compensate for the Sahrawi community's inability to meet its youngest generations' needs in exile, the programme may further expose and emphasise this powerlessness' (Crivello and Fiddian-Qasmiyeh 2010: 111). By extension, the transnational educational migration programme – entailing children's separation from their parents for a much longer period of time – can also be understood as potentially undermining parents' agency as parents:

> There, they get what they want; they have refrigerators, fresh vegetables and fruits and they take what they want. Here, we have a different standard of living, so when they return, they look at us and look down on our tents which for them seem small. They start to see things very differently…they begin demanding things we cannot afford; sometimes we are forced to sell our rations to fulfil their demands.
>
> (49-year-old mother, Sahrawi refugee camps, cited in ibid.)

11   In many ways, it could be argued that Sahrawi children and youth were 'fostered' by Cuban families, and, more broadly, by the Cuban nation, during their studies on the island.

12   Other hybrid groups of Sahrawis who have graduated from educational establishments around the world include not only *La Tribu de los Cubanos* but also *La Tribu de Los Rusos*. I have argued elsewhere that these 'student-tribes' hold their own form of collective sub-memories, in part revolving around loss and separation from their families (Fiddian-Qasmiyeh 2013a).

13   In contrast, the Cuban–Palestinian scholarship programme is intergenerational in nature, as discussed in Chapters 3 and 5.

14   Regarding the broader implications of political/family background of Cuban-educated Sahrawi refugees see Fiddian-Qasmiyeh (2014); the role of *waSata* (nepotism) and family connections in the case of Palestinians educated in Cuba is examined in Chapter 5.

15   In contrast with the hyper-visibility of Sahrawi women educated in Cuba in the Sahrawi refugee camps, no female Palestinians were able to be interviewed in the refugee camps in Lebanon where the male graduates cited in Chapter 5 were

identified. Further research is therefore necessary to understand the experiences of Palestinian women educated in Cuba, although Palestinian men's accounts at least allow us to recognise the reality of female Palestinians' participation in the scholarship programme. The gendered nature of Sahrawi and Palestinian access to and participation in the Libyan education system is explored in greater detail in Chapter 6.

16 I discuss the relationship between the onset of puberty and religious obligations in the Sahrawi context in greater detail in Fiddian-Qasmiyeh (2014).

17 Only males were eligible to study in Syria prior to the Arab Spring, and although they can apply to study in Algeria, many fewer do so than had originally been planned in Cuba. For a comparative analysis of Sahrawi students' experiences of studying in Algeria, Cuba, Syria and Spain, see Fiddian-Qasmiyeh (2013b).

18 Access to vocational training was also offered to those girls and young women who had been studying in Libya and were 'repatriated' to the camps as a result of the violence and civil conflict which spread across North Africa in 2011 (see Chapter 6).

19 Notably, this appears to have coincided with similar experiences in the Cuba–Ghana scholarship programme: 'several pregnancies occurred among the Ghanaian female students, which led to a decision not to send any more girls to the Isle of Youth as of 1987, thus skewing the gender distribution even further' (Lehr 2012: 93).

20 This claim is also noted by Tortajada (2003: 87) and Caratini (2000: 448); on the 'centre' see Human Rights Watch (2008) and Fiddian-Qasmiyeh (2010).

21 The only response I received when I asked whether having Sahrawi women as role models in Cuba would have led to a different situation were shrugs.

22 The Sahrawi experience of return reveals that, although a small number of Cuban women returned to the Sahrawi refugee camps married to Sahrawi male graduates, children born of Cuban–Sahrawi unions have typically been 'erased' from the Sahrawi camps: these children have either physically remained in Cuba with their Cuban mothers (personal observations, Cuba, 2006), or have been removed from their mothers in the camps, especially in the case of Cubaraui women who returned from Cuba to give birth in the euphemistically named Maternity Assistance Centre (Fiddian-Qasmiyeh 2010, 2014).

23 The presence of Cuban-educated young women in the NUSW offices in the 27 February Camp is notable, as is their participation as employees in projects established and run jointly with non-Sahrawi NGOs. This is not to say that only those young women who studied in Cuba have obtained roles in the NUSW, since Fatma Mehdi, for instance, was educated in Libya, and I met several female employees who had trained in Algeria. At the same time, I suggest that the presence of Cuban-educated young women in ministries and union organisations is particularly important to the way in which the official discourse is received and evaluated by visitors to the camps.

24 This onward migration to Europe is rarely acknowledged in the few studies which aim to document graduates' experiences of return to their contexts of origin, with Martínez-Pérez, for instance, reporting that 'Lehr (2008) indicates that some of the students depart from the goal of practicing as professionals in their own countries, and take up jobs *in other countries of the Global South*. A also few [sic] pursue further studies at the graduate level in third countries' (2012: 77, emphasis added).

25 Whether this experience will influence Cuba's scholarship programmes for other refugee populations has yet to be determined.

References

Agencia Cubana de Noticias (ACN) (2006). 'Sahara: 30 años de exilio y lucha', *Agencia Cubana de Noticias*, 22 February. Available at http://www.rebelion.org/noticia. php?id=27171, last accessed 26/09/2006.

Black, R. (1984) *Helping Refugees to Help Themselves*. Unpublished work, RSC Grey Literature Collection, University of Oxford.

Brazier, C. (1997) 'Special Edition: War and Peace in Western Sahara', *The New Internationalist*, 297.

Caratini, S. (2000) 'Système de parenté sahraoui: L'impact de la révolution', *L'Homme* 154/155: 431–456.

Cole, J.R.I. and Kandiyoti, D. (2002) 'Nationalism and the Colonial Legacy in the Middle East and Central Asia: Introduction', *International Journal of Middle East Studies*, 34:189–203.

Crivello, G. and Fiddian-Qasmiyeh, E. (2010) 'The Ties that Bind: Sahrawi Children and the Mediation of Aid in Exile', in D. Chatty (ed.) *Deterritorialized Youth: Sahrawi and Afghan Refugees at the Margins of the Middle East*. Oxford: Berghahn Books, 85–118.

Damis, J. J. (1983) *Conflict in Northwest Africa: the Western Sahara Dispute*. Stanford, CA: Hoover Institution Press.

Dryden-Peterson, S. (2003) Education of Refugees in Uganda: Relationships between Setting And Access, Refugee Law Project Working Paper No. 9, Uganda.

Fiddian-Qasmiyeh, E. (2014) *The Ideal Refugees: Gender, Islam and the Sahrawi politics of Survival*. Syracuse, NY: Syracuse University Press.

Fiddian-Qasmiyeh, E. (2013a) 'The Inter-generational Politics of "Travelling Memories": Sahrawi Refugee Youth Remembering Home-land and Home-camp', *Journal of Intercultural Studies*, 34(6): 631–649.

Fiddian-Qasmiyeh, E. (2013b) 'Transnational Childhood and Adolescence: Mobilising Sahrawi Identity and Politics across Time and Space', *Journal of Ethnic and Racial Studies*, 36(5): 875–895.

Fiddian-Qasmiyeh, E. (2011) 'Paradoxes of Refugees' Educational Migration: Promoting self-sufficiency or renewing dependency?' *Comparative Education*, 47(4): 433–447.

Fiddian-Qasmiyeh, E. (2010) 'Concealing Violence against Women in the Sahrawi Refugee Camps: The Politicisation of Victimhood', in H. Bradby and G. Lewando-Hundt (eds) *Global Perspectives on War, Gender and Health: The Sociology and Anthropology of Suffering*. Farnham: Ashgate, 99–110.

Fiddian-Qasmiyeh, E. (2009) 'Representing Sahrawi Refugees' "Educational Displacement" to Cuba: Self-sufficient Agents and/or Manipulated Victims in Conflict?' *Journal of Refugee Studies*, 22(3): 323–350.

Fiddian, E. (2002) 'Promoting Sustainable Gender Roles during Exile: A Critical Analysis with Reference to the Sahrawi Refugee Camps'. Unpublished MSc thesis in Gender and Development, Development Studies Institute, London School of Economics and Political Science.

Gimeno-Martín, J.C. and Laman, M.A. (2005) *La Juventud Saharaui: Una Realidad. Preocupaciones y Expectativas*. RABUNI: UJSARIO-CJE-UAM.

Harrell-Bond, B.E. (1986) *Imposing Aid: Emergency Assistance to Refugees*. Oxford: Oxford University Press.

Harrell-Bond, B.E. (1981) *The Struggle for the Western Sahara*. Hanover, NH: American Universities Field Staff.

Hickling-Hudson, A., Corona González, J. and Preston, R. (eds) (2012) *The Capacity to Share: A Study of Cuba's International Cooperation in Educational Development*. New York: Palgrave Macmillan.

Hodges, T. (1984) *The Western Saharans*. London: Minority Rights Group.

Hodges, T. (1987) 'The Origins of Saharawi Nationalism', in R.I. Lawless and L. Monahan (eds) *War and Refugees: the Western Sahara conflict*. London: Pinter, 31–65.

Human Rights Watch (2008) *Human Rights in Western Sahara and in the Tindouf Refugee Camps: Morocco/Western Sahara/Algeria*. New York: HRW.

Lehr, S. (2012) 'The Children of the Isle of Youth: How Ghanaian Students Learned to Cope with "Anything in Life"', in A. Hickling-Hudson, J. Corona González and R. Preston (eds) *The Capacity to Share: A Study of Cuba's International Cooperation in Educational Development*. New York: Palgrave Macmillan, 83–105.

Madge, C., Raghuram, P. and Noxolo, P. (2014) 'Conceptualizing International Education: From international Student to International Study,' *Progress in Human Geography*, March 31, 2014, doi:10.1177/0309132514526442.

Márquez, A. (2005) *Las Cubarauis*. Azul Producciones. 48 mins.

Martínez-Pérez, F. (2012) 'Cuban Higher Education Scholarships for International Students: An Overview', in A. Hickling-Hudson, J. Corona González and R. Preston (eds) *The Capacity to Share: A Study of Cuba's International Cooperation in Educational Development*. New York: Palgrave Macmillan, 73–82.

Mowles, C. (1986) *Desk Officer's Report on Trip to the Sahrawi Refugee Camps near Tindouf, Southern Algeria, June 16–21, 1986*. Unpublished Oxfam report, RSC Grey Literature Collection, University of Oxford.

Pazzanita, A.G. and Hodges, T. (1994) *Historical Dictionary of Western Sahara*. Metuchen, NJ: Scarecrow Press.

Perregaux, C. (1990) *Femmes sahraouies, femmes du désert*. Paris: L'Harmattan.

Shelley, T. (2004) *Endgame in the Western Sahara: What Future for Africa's Last Colony*. London; New York: Zed Books in association with War on Want.

Skeldon, R. (2008) 'International Migration as a Tool in Development Policy: A Passing Phase?' *Population and Development Review*, 34(1): 1–18.

Tortajada Orriols, A. (2003) *Hijas de la arena*. Barcelona: Debolsillo.

UNHCR (2006) *Country Operations Plan. Executive Committee Summary. Country: Algeria. Planning Year: 2007*. Geneva: UNHCR.

UNHCR (2004) *Statistical Yearbook*. Geneva: UNHCR.

Velloso de Santisteban, A. (1993) *La educación en el Sahara Occidental*. Madrid: UNED.

Voutira, E. and Harrell-Bond, B.E. (2000) '"Successful" Refugee Settlement: Are Past Examples Relevant?' in M.M. Cernea and C. McDowell (eds) *Risks and Reconstruction: Experiences of Resettlers and Refugees*. Washington, DC: World Bank, 56–76.

Water, T. and Leblanc, K. (2005) 'Refugees and Education: Mass Public Schooling without a Nation-State', *Comparative Education Review*, 49(2): 129–147.

5 Solidarity, ideology and circumstantial humanitarianism

Views from the Palestinian refugee camps in Lebanon

Introduction

Unlike the Sahrawi children cited in Chapter 4, who have long dreamt of travelling to Cuba to become doctors,[1] most of the Cuban-educated Palestinians interviewed in their home-camps in Lebanon reflected that they had *not* chosen to travel to Cuba to pursue their studies. As noted by Ahmed and Mohammed, having completed their primary and secondary level educations at camp-based schools run by UNRWA and/or the PLO, or at subsidised Lebanese schools, their original preference had reportedly been to complete their university degrees in Lebanon.[2]

> I wanted to study in Lebanon, but I was not able to [pay the university fees and other costs] due to my family's financial situation. After completing my baccalaureate [in Tripoli, North Lebanon] I waited for two years until I received the scholarship to study in Cuba. In effect, *I chose Cuba because it was the only available option during that time*.
>
> (Ahmed, 57-year-old doctor running his own private medical clinic, Baddawi Camp; emphasis added)

> I was not able to start my university education then [when I completed my baccalaureate in Southern Lebanon] due to our social circumstances. I was finally granted a [full] scholarship in 1979, but *I didn't choose to study in Cuba: it was the only option which was offered to me*.
>
> (Mohammed, 56-year-old civil engineer employed by UNRWA, Beirut; emphais added)

With only one interviewee having expressed an explicit desire to study in Cuba, all other interviewees repeatedly indicated that studying in Cuba 'was the only option' available for them to pursue their university degrees as Palestinian refugees based in urban camps in Lebanon.

Drawing on interviews with Palestinians educated in Cuba and currently based in seven refugee camps across Lebanon, this chapter starts by examining the mechanisms through which Palestinians from Lebanon gained access to

Cuba's scholarship programme. In so doing, it highlights the extent to which many Palestinian graduates have developed discursive and practical strategies to distance themselves from Cuba's influence and legacy: in effect, Cuba has often being marginalised in their accounts, while the roles played by Palestinian actors (in particular Palestinian factions and, to a lesser extent, the PLO) have been consolidated therein. The chapter subsequently examines the ways in which Palestinian graduates have understood the motivations, nature and impacts of Cuba's scholarship system through reference to identity, ideology, politics and humanitarianism. By centralising Palestinian refugees' own perspectives on this South–South programme, and the extent to which they consider that it can or should be conceptualised as a 'humanitarian' programme, this chapter, therefore, complements *academic* and *policy* debates regarding the desirability and/or tensions of 'alternative' forms of development and humanitarianism (Chapter 2).

The remainder of the chapter then situates these Palestinian graduates' accounts of returning to widely dispersed urban camps in Lebanon which have been denominated as 'islands of insecurity' fought over by competing armed factions (Sayigh 2000), in relation to the descriptions offered by Sahrawi graduates upon their return to their geographically isolated and yet refugee-run desert-based home-camps, depicted as 'the best run refugee camps in the world' (Brazier 1997, cited in Chapter 4).[3] Through a comparison of Palestinians' and Sahrawis' views of Cuba's educational migration programme, the chapter therefore highlights the importance of identities and identifications on the one hand, and of structural conditions in refugee graduates' home-camps and host country on the other, to understanding the complex dynamics which underpin access to, as well as the multifaceted experiences and outcomes of, the scholarship programme on both individual and collective levels.

In all, studying in Cuba has offered Palestinian graduates, like their Sahrawi counterparts, professional employment and often significant political positions in the Palestinian camps, enabling them to contribute to the well-being of their communities of origin as doctors, engineers and teachers. However, the programme is ultimately paradoxical in nature, although in different ways to those evidenced in the Sahrawi case study: rather than engaging in onward labour migration to their former colonial power as Cubaraui graduates do when they travel to work in Spain (Chapter 4), many Palestinian graduates' professional success in their home-camps has ultimately been dependent upon their publicly 'blurring bonds' with Cuba (following Alba 2005). This has effectively meant that graduates erase their experiences of having studied in Cuba in order to work with UNRWA, the overarching administrator of medical, educational and infrastructural services in these urban refugee camps. In other instances, even when graduates have 'brightened bonds' (ibid.) with Cuba to strengthen their political capital and opportunities for personal and familial development, graduates' attempts to develop a 'better future' (Dryden-Peterson 2003: 1, cited in Chapter 4) do not necessarily align with Cuba's official aim for graduates to enhance the self-sufficiency of their communities of origin.

The analysis developed in this chapter must be viewed in light of the vast majority of the interviewees approached for this part of the study having been initially reluctant, and indeed suspicious, of discussing their experiences of having studied in Cuba. Unlike the hyper-visibility (and hyper-audibility) of Cubaraui graduates in public spaces throughout the Sahrawi refugee camps, where graduates are interlocutors with foreign visitors and researchers in the camps, it was very difficult to identify Palestinian graduates to invite them to participate in this part of the project. Many graduates, it emerged, had explicitly distanced themselves from Cuba, and their educational trajectories were, therefore, not commonly known to their colleagues and, in many instances, to their neighbours and even established acquaintances. In particular, it transpired that graduates were concerned about the impact that contributing to this research project might have on their current jobs, and, specifically, on their contracts as UNRWA employees. Interviewees were especially concerned that UNRWA as an institution might be wary of the ideological influence which studying in Cuba could have had on graduates, and that this might lead to difficulties working in UNRWA. This was most notably the case for the graduates who are not affiliated with the Palestinian–Cuban Union (examined below) established in 1990 by Palestinians who had graduated from Cuban institutions. The fact that some Palestinians *have* publicly and politically aligned themselves with the Cuban scholarship programme through this union, while others have rendered this a private experience to be kept out of the public sphere, is pertinent not only in methodological terms (given the difficulties which arose in attempting to identify potential interviewees),[4] but also with reference to the politics of identification and the politics of participating in 'alternative' humanitarian programmes more broadly.

The politics of 'choosing' Cuba?

Many Palestinian graduates' concerns about revealing their Cuban *alma mater*, combined with declarations to the effect that they had not *really* wished to study in Cuba, are in distinct contrast with the ways in which Palestinian interviewees in Cuba, and Sahrawis in Cuba and Algeria, repeatedly and very publicly expressed their gratitude to the Cuban state for having offered them an opportunity to complete their tertiary education. Indeed, Palestinian graduates in Lebanon even presented the allocation of scholarships itself as a Palestinian, rather than as a Cuban, phenomenon.[5] Comparing these graduates' accounts of the scholarships to those offered by Sahrawi children and youth further underscores this active distancing of Cuba.

Two key accounts regarding the centrality of Palestinian mediators emerged in this regard. First, Abdullah – a 44-year-old teacher based in UNRWA's Siblin Training Centre in Saidon – declared that he had benefited from a 'Free education offered by the PLO, the sole representative of the Palestinians in Palestine and the diaspora'. This teacher, therefore, simultaneously centralised the PLO as the legitimate representative of the Palestinian people, and asserted that it had been the *PLO*, rather than *Cuba*, which had allocated scholarships to Palestinian refugees. Such statements effectively distance the graduate Self from Cuba whilst realigning the Self with the official Palestinian national cause.

In spite of one graduate claiming that the allocation of scholarships was based solely on grades and not based on politics and ideology, the most significant account offered by the interviewees was that 'political affiliation played an important role' (Mustafa, 55-year-old doctor at UNRWA clinic, Baddawi Camp). This reference to political affiliation transcends the depiction of the PLO as Palestinians' official mediator in Cuba and in the broader international arena, by drawing attention to the roles played in Lebanon by the heterogeneous Palestinian factions which have formed part of and/or challenged the PLO since the 1970s.

Indeed, in his reflection on the factors which determined the allocation of scholarships, Mohammad noted that: 'As for *the Palestinian factions, through which these scholarships were made available*, politics and ideology did indeed play an important role in allowing young Palestinians to access such schemes' (emphasis added). This 56-year-old civil engineer thereby asserts that Palestinian factions with a particular political and ideological connection with Cuba made these scholarships available to Palestinian students. Other graduates also repeatedly asserted that it was 'normal to have such strong *bonds* between the Cuban state *and the Palestinian factions...*' (Khalil, 54-year-old electronic engineer, Beiruti camp), and that, beyond the scholarship programme, 'Cuba played an important political role through its *bond* with many *Palestinian factions* and also socialist Arab regimes' (Mustafa).[6]

Indeed, the heterogeneity of political and ideological positions held by the factions which allocated scholarships to Palestinians reflects the diversity of positions which exist both within the Palestinian camps and further afield. This heterogeneity is particularly significant when contrasted with the accounts offered by the Sahrawi refugees whom I interviewed in Havana and in Algeria, who only referred to students' and graduates' political affiliation and commitment to the Polisario Front. In part, this can be explained due to the Polisario's position as the Sahrawis' sole official political representatives on the international and local (camp-based) levels until self-determination is achieved (as enshrined in Article 31 of the Constitution of the Sahrawi Arab Democratic Republic, 2003), but it can also arguably be traced to the students' age at the time of leaving their home-camps to travel to Cuba. As a result of their common starting point as children separated from their families and brought up in Sahrawi boarding schools in Cuba's Isla de la Juventud, and in light of the smaller range of alternative ideological interpretations available in the Sahrawi camps, Sahrawi students in Cuba formed strong political affiliations with the 'official discourses' presented by Polisario/SADR and Cuba both vis-à-vis the conflict over Western Sahara, and the scholarship programme itself (Fiddian-Qasmiyeh 2010, 2013a, 2013b; Chapter 3 and 4). These children also established strong emotional connections with other members of the Sahrawi cohort in Cuba, which ultimately resulted in the formation of the hybrid Cubaraui identity discussed in Chapter 4 (also see Fiddian-Qasmiyeh 2009, 2014).

In contrast to this, Abdullah denominated the continued significance of factional affiliation as being at the root of the fragmentation of the Palestinian student body in Cuba:

The main disadvantage revolves around the Palestinians' inability to engage with each other in Cuba given that the majority belonged to competing factions within the PLO umbrella and they carried their political and ideological understandings to Cuba.

Although the establishment of multiple Marxist Palestinian factions in the 1970s may have offered a degree of commonality amongst many students in Cuba in overarching ideological terms,[7] factional and political affiliations were also considered to be unacceptable by those students who did not benefit from what one interviewee – Marwan, a 46-year-old shopkeeper based in North Lebanon – referred to as the underlying 'corruption' of the scholarship system.

In particular, Palestinians who were part of Fatah were reportedly prioritised and preferred over other Palestinian students, with the former even being allocated pocket money. Marwan – who was highly critical of the entire scholarship programme – continued by noting that, even within Fatah, there was a notable hierarchy with respect to the opportunities offered to different students according to the individual's relationship to the Fatah leadership, whether as relatives or friends. In some cases, it emerged that students with concrete political affiliations had access to an even wider range of options, as reflected in Khalil's revelation that he had in fact been 'offered several scholarships from different countries [including the former USSR]' and had, therefore, been able to select the most favourable educational package available to them. Although the majority of students had not 'chosen' Cuba, Khalil indicated that 'I chose the Cuban scholarship because of my love for this country, and also because I believe in the Cuban struggle.' Notably, this interviewee not only revealed the range of options available to him before travelling to Cuba, but also publicly announced his commitment to the ideological stance shared both by his faction and by the Palestinian–Cuban Union of which he has been an active member since his return to Lebanon (see below).

In this regard, a common feature emerging across the Sahrawi and Palestinian interviews was the significance of *waSata* (nepotism, or connections) in both the allocation of scholarships and in the opportunities offered upon arrival in Cuba. This is in spite of the major differences that exist between the Polisario's role as a centralised hegemonic political institution mediating between Sahrawi refugees and Cuba, and the fragmented factions which have facilitated scholarships for Palestinian refugees.

In particular, political and familial identity appears to have at least partly determined the subject of study in which Palestinian students could enrol. Unlike the remaining students, seven graduates (four doctors, two engineers and one sonographer) indicated that they had chosen their own subjects of study, including Khalil, who had both 'chosen' Cuba over the other scholarships offered to him, and had also been free to choose which subject (in his case, engineering) he wished to enrol in at university. In contrast, Younis noted that

> I didn't determine my field of study, it was decided on my behalf by the PLO. Becoming a lab technician was the only available option for me because

some well-connected Palestinians monopolized the more important subjects [i.e. medicine and engineering].

(45-year-old laboratory technician employed by
UNRWA in Baddawi Camp)

This raises a number of questions: first, if there was indeed a quota of places for Palestinians to study specific subjects, and, if so, how these subjects were selected by the Cuban government; second, whether the Cuban government was aware of the ways in which the PLO and the diverse factions allocated subjects of study – Younis believed not.

Indeed, the PLO was in effect both Cuba's main interlocutor and the overarching administrator of the programme, in spite of only one graduate, Abdullah, having indicated that he had accessed the scholarship programme directly via the PLO, while all of the other graduates stressed that this had occurred through their connections with specific factions. The PLO's position as Cuba's main interlocutor for the programme is consistent with Cuba's long-standing recognition of the PLO as the only legitimate representative of the Palestinian people (Dominguez 1989: 129–130). In this regard, whilst fully aware of the existence of diverse Palestinian factions – many of which continue to have representational offices in Havana, in addition to the Palestinian Embassy itself – it could be argued that *Cuba* did not ultimately differentiate between factions based on their ideological understandings: students affiliated with Fatah, the PFLP, the DFLP, the Arab Front and the Liberation Front all received scholarships to study in Cuba from the mid-1970s onwards.[8]

It could, therefore, be argued that the PLO viewed the scholarship programme as a way to homogenise the experiences of otherwise ideologically fragmented and geographically dispersed Palestinians by presenting itself as offering equal opportunities across all factions, and all of the contexts hosting Palestinians in the region (Lebanon, Jordan, Syria and the OPT). In turn, however, factions such as the DFLP endorsed the programme and appropriated it as their own, using the scholarships as a means to enhance membership of their factions at a critical time (as discussed in further detail below).

Such strategies, however, ultimately failed on at least two, apparently paradoxical, levels: factional identities continued to fragment the Palestinian student body on a daily basis, and many students witnessed the extent to which they were not prioritised in the 'corrupt' allocation of places or subjects by the PLO and its factions, being seen as 'ordinary members' rather than the children or friends of officials. As a result, their experiences of studying in Cuba consequently led many Palestinians to ultimately question their identities and their position in 'their' factions, with different effects.

Cuba as a space for formation, transformation or consolidation?

As noted earlier, many Palestinian graduates were reluctant to speak about their experiences of studying in Cuba due to their fear that they might be *perceived* as having been unduly influenced (i.e. indoctrinated) by Cuba's ideological frameworks. Nonetheless, as interviews developed, a number of apparent inconsistencies emerged between this initial reluctance and the effective erasure of Cuba's role as the allocator of scholarships on the one hand, and, on the other, both the warmth with which many interviewees eventually spoke about the Cuban revolutionary project and their criticisms of 'their' factions following their return to their home-camps. In effect, graduates' accounts of the impact which studying in Cuba had on them in professional, social, political and ideological terms can be broadly divided into three intersecting processes: *formation, transformation* or *consolidation.*

The clearest accounts of Cuba's formative influence on graduates pertained to students' professional development in the main subjects offered via the scholarship system, while exposure to different people and different ways of life to those which students had encountered as children and young men in Lebanon, emerged as a significant experience on both a social and a political level for Abdel-Wahid, Ibrahim and Abdullah. Professional and personal development in Cuba, in turn, often led to graduates becoming increasingly engaged on socio-political levels. Ahmed, for instance, referred to the process of studying in Cuba as having 'crystallised my vision' and as prompting him to 'become more responsible', while Abdel-Wahid reflected that his time in Cuba 'enabled me to become a social being'.

Ahmed's and Abdel-Wahid's representations, therefore, simultaneously suggest that studying in Cuba offered them a formative experience whilst, or precisely *by, changing* their outlook (from blurred to clear 'vision') and approach (from lesser to greater 'responsibility'), and even facilitating the process for them to *become* 'social beings'. Indeed, in direct contrast with MENA students' and graduates' assertions that the Cuban education programme neither had an ideological *component* nor an ideological *impact* (as cited in Chapter 3), clear connections emerged between many Palestinians' depictions of the Cuban education programme as being both *formative* and *transformative* in nature.

For instance, a Palestinian doctor currently working in an UNRWA clinic in Baddawi Camp recognised that although he had studied medicine, 'I also studied Political Economy, courses on capitalism, socialism and scientific communism, all of which are courses pertaining to Marxist thought'. For some graduates, such as Marwan, the ideological component of the education system amounted to attempts to *forcibly* transform the scholarship recipients' opinions and commitments (also see Breidlid 2013). Marwan had in fact left Cuba before completing his degree and, therefore, had both disengaged from and rejected the ideological nature of the scholarship system in the 1990s. He reflected that:

I felt that the Cuban education system was trying too hard to promote the Communist understanding of things. At the time, there was no separation between education and indoctrination, which was mainly ideological in nature. The two were strongly and intimately intertwined... In fact, communism and socialism were discussed everywhere: in coffee shops, in meetings, everywhere. Everyone during that time [the *Periodo Especial*] in Cuba was discussing these [communism and socialism]. Even the cup of coffee['s heart] was beating with Communist beliefs.

Abdul-Wahid also recognised that 'Cuba lives the revolution on a daily basis, and this is clearly manifested in their educational programmes, at schools and universities', and yet Hamdi argued that that although 'Cuba was a Marxist state, I did not feel that this was imposed upon me as an individual'.

Indeed, Hamdi immediately followed his assertion that Marxist thought was not 'imposed' upon him as a student with the clarification that 'Politically, the majority of the Palestinian students in Cuba were part of the PLO, as it was the umbrella for all of the Palestinian factions'.[9] Equally, other graduates reflected that there was no such indoctrination, precisely because 'During that time, there was a strong *bond* between the Palestinian Left and Cuba, and *an entire Palestinian generation was influenced by revolutionary symbols* such as Che Guevara and Fidel Castro' (Ibrahim, 53-year-old doctor, Baddawi Camp, emphasis added).

These graduates asserted that having already been influenced by Cuba's ideological underpinnings before arriving in Cuba (or, rather, with Palestine being an established part of the broader internationalist imaginary shared by non-aligned actors at the time – Khalili 2007: 96–97), it was precisely the pre-existing connection between Cuba and the Palestinian Left which had simultaneously led to the scholarship programme itself, and enabled Palestinians to build strong relationships with their Cuban counterparts. As Abdel-Wahid argued: 'Because Palestinians were influenced by the Cuban revolutionary experience, and also by its icons and symbols, we had very strong and special relationships with Cubans – some of these relationships were political, and some were ideological.' These connections included, according to Hamdi and 43-year-old lab technician Nimr, common views with regards to justice and freedom on international(ist) levels.

In spite of these apparently paradoxical declarations of attempted indoctrination on the one hand, and the continuation, or even consolidation, of pre-existing revolutionary connections on the other, two key interconnected points emerge at this stage: first, a small number of students accepted that their experience of studying in Cuba *had* transformed their understandings of the meaning of revolution, and of their political convictions more broadly. Second, however, viewing these accounts of transformation alongside the abovementioned assertions that Cuba had merely provided a space for the *consolidation* of students' ideological and political commitments, leads us to ask why many Palestinian graduates appeared, at different stages of their interviews, to minimise the perception of Cuba's influence on their political development. I return to this latter point in greater detail below.

With reference to the first point, for instance, Hamdi indicated that learning Spanish 'allowed me to know more about the cultures of the other. This also gave me the opportunity to consolidate my convictions.' Furthermore, Mohammad referred to Cuba as offering 'a very special educational experience which allowed me to crystallise my ideas – it allowed me to understand the Cuban society more, and to acquaint myself with commonalities in political understanding'.

Importantly, although the MENA students interviewed in Havana and interviewees in the Sahrawi camps suggested that Sahrawi children had been unduly influenced by their experiences of studying in Cuba because they had been *too young* at the time of their arrival, Ahmed offered a different perspective on the notion of age and political maturity:

> I was 20 when I left for Cuba, and I didn't consider myself to be politically mature in the sense that I didn't yet have the tools to talk about my cause. It was through the Cuban experience and its relationship with most international liberation movements, that I gained revolutionary awareness.

He continued by referring to the 'crystallisation' (also a term used by Ahmed and Mohammad, cited above) of his political awareness as a form of increasing responsibility: 'I became more responsible through reading and interacting with other cultures, and also by studying the university's compulsory educational materials… this experience has helped to crystallise our understanding, it enabled us to develop an alternative outlook'.

While fears of indoctrination have pervaded many academic and foreign policy discussions of Cuba's education programme, with such externally held assumptions in turn leading many graduates to fear that they might be *perceived* as having been indoctrinated, I argue that living and studying in Cuba provided the foundations for graduates' capacities and opinions, practices and beliefs to be variously formed, transformed and consolidated to different degrees.

The recognition of a distinction between Cuba's official aims and the individual and collective outcomes of the education process concurrently leads us to interrogate the ways in which Palestinian graduates retrospectively conceptualise the educational migration programme with reference to its underlying motivations, nature and implications.

Cuba's scholarship programme: ideology and humanitarianism intertwined

Although interviewees in Cuba and in the Sahrawi refugee camps repeatedly asserted the humanitarian nature of the Cuban scholarship programme, precisely what this denomination of 'humanitarianism' might mean, and how compatible it could be given the ideological and political links highlighted by Palestinian graduates in Lebanon, requires further discussion.

As noted in Chapter 2, the contemporary international humanitarian regime is habitually equated with the principles of humanity, impartiality, neutrality and independence (Ferris 2011: 11), and a strict separation is firmly upheld by Northern humanitarian institutions between morality and politics. However, many critics reject the assertion that humanitarianism can ever be separated from politics, since '"humanitarianism" is *the* ideology of hegemonic states in the era of globalisation' (Chimni 2000: 3). Recognising the extent to which the Northern-led and Northern-dominated humanitarian regime is deeply implicated in, and reproduces, 'the *ideology* of hegemonic [Northern] states' is particularly significant since many (Northern) academics, policymakers and practitioners reject the right of Southern-led initiatives to be denominated 'humanitarian' in nature on the basis that such projects and programmes are motivated by ideological and/or faith-based principles, rather than 'universal' humanitarian principles.

While long-standing academic and policy debates have addressed the relationship between humanitarianism, politics and ideology, few studies to date have examined the ways in which refugee beneficiaries – as opposed to academics, policymakers and practitioners – conceptualise the programmes which are designed and implemented 'on their behalf'. The following discussion addresses this gap precisely by centralising Palestinian graduates' reflections on the Cuban scholarship programme and the extent to which they conceptualise ideological connections as being compatible with humanitarian motivations and outcomes.

Graduates repeatedly referred to 'ideology', 'politics', 'humanitarianism' and 'human values' when describing the Cuban scholarship programme, and yet, while they maintained that Cuba's programme for Palestinian refugees is 'humanitarian' in nature, graduates offered different perspectives regarding the *balance* between these different dimensions, implicitly and at times explicitly noting the ways in which these overlap or are in tension. Importantly, these recurrent concepts are to be contrasted with the prevalent terminology and frames of reference arising in Sahrawis' accounts of the Cuban programme, which can perhaps be traced to the continued significance of Spanish – the language learned and lived (following Bhabha 2006: x) in Cuba – amongst Cubarauis living in the Sahrawi refugee camps, where Spanish is the official language of the major Sahrawi medical institutions. As such, in our interviews and in informal conversations, Cubarauis consistently used the Spanish-language term *solidaridad* (solidarity) to define both the nature of the connection between the Sahrawi people and Cuba, and the nature of the scholarship programme; they also regularly cited Cuban revolutionary figures such as José Martí and Fidel Castro. In contrast, no such quotes were offered by Palestinian graduates, even if the significance of Fidel Castro and Ché Guevara was noted by many (op. cit.).

Explaining his understanding of the basis of the scholarship programme for Palestinians, Abdullah elaborated that this was: 'mainly prompted because Cuban politics is based upon human values and mutual respect, and in particular upon socialism, which used to be very prominent in the Arab world during that time'. In turn, referring to the common visions uniting both parties and facilitating Cuba's scholarship programme for Palestinian refugees, Hamdi posited that 'Certain ideological and political commonalities *contributed* to this collaboration between the Cuban government and the PLO. *However*, the humanitarian *factor* was present in these negotiations' (emphasis added).

These accounts reflect the extent to which ideology *and* humanitarianism are both recognised as playing a key role in the scholarship programme, and yet Hamdi's usage of the term '*however*', and his reference to 'the humanitarian *factor*', demonstrate an awareness that a tension may be perceived to exist between ideology/politics and humanitarian motivations. Indeed, rather than describing the programme *as* a humanitarian programme per se, eight of the interviewees offered remarkably similar humanitarian 'qualifiers': the Cuban education programme is described as having 'a humanitarian *component*' (Marwan), 'a humanitarian *dimension*' (Younis), a 'humanitarian *aspect*' (Saadi[10]), and 'humanitarian *ingredients*' (Abdel-Wahid); while other interviewees argued that it is 'a *mainly* humanitarian system' (Nimr) which 'carr[ies] humanitarian *elements*' (Hamdi) and 'shares its humanitarian *message* in spite of the embargo [against Cuba]' (Ibrahim).

As exemplified by these qualifiers, the Palestinian beneficiaries of this programme themselves recognise that humanitarianism was not the sole determining justification for the initiative, but rather that it formed part of the broader Cuban revolution and a particular mode of expressing support for other liberation movements, including the Palestinian cause. In terms of weighting these different motivating and experiential elements, Mohammed argued that the 'humanitarian aspect *outweighs* the ideological one', emphasising the 'programme's strong humanitarian aspect'.

In turn, Ahmed and Nimr declared that the Cuban scholarships were offered 'without conditions or conditionalities' and without 'blackmailing Palestinians to educate them'. These references are particularly relevant when viewed alongside critiques of neoliberal development programmes and strategies which have often been characterised by 'tied aid' or diverse economic, socio-political and gendered conditionalities which require beneficiaries to comply with Northern-dominated priorities vis-à-vis 'good governance' – all of which are, in effect, politically and/or ideologically driven.

Concurrently, Khalil argued that the programme is 'humanitarian *if used correctly*', thereby drawing attention to the extent to which the nature of the programme transcends either Cuba's or the PLO's underlying motivating factors per se, and is, rather, characterised both by the way in which the programme has been implemented since the 1970s, and its longer-term impacts. With reference to the former, claims regarding the absence of conditionalities on Cuba's behalf must be viewed alongside the extent to which Palestinians could only access the scholarships if they were affiliated with specific Palestinian factions (as highlighted above): can the programme be 'truly' humanitarian if individual participation has historically been contingent upon an official declaration of ideological commonality with a Leftist Palestinian faction and/or the Cuban internationalist project?

With universality, neutrality and impartiality being three of the core 'international' humanitarian principles, a tension is apparent from the perspective of 'the Northern relief elite' who arguably monopolise the epithet humanitarian (Haysom, cited in Pacitto and Fiddian-Qasmiyeh 2013: 6). Indeed, although Jose Marti's humanitarian principle to '*compartir lo que tienes, no dar lo que te sobra*' ('to share what you have, not what is left over') has historically guided many of the Cuban state's revolutionary programmes on national(ist) and international(ist) levels, precisely *who* Cuba should share *with* (on a collective) has often been geopolitically framed.[11] Whilst designed to overcome the historical legacy of diverse exclusionary processes in Cuba, the programme could itself be conceptualised as being guided by an ideological commitment to inclusion with exclusionary underpinnings. On many levels, therefore, Breidlid (2013: 162) is correct in noting that

> Such inclusiveness is in any case never complete. The imposition of a hegemonic discourse leaves people out, primarily on ideological grounds. Ideological repression means that everybody who questions the regime in a fundamental way is basically left out in the dark. There is a creation of boundaries between Self and Other that leaves very little room for fundamental critique.

However, the existence of a hegemonic discourse, and demands for students to publicly assert their affiliation to an official ideological stance, whether this refers to Cuban or Palestinian discourses, should not necessarily be equated with the exclusion of individuals and groups who do not share particular opinions and beliefs. In the case explored in this chapter, a distinction can, therefore, perhaps be usefully made between the *collective* basis of scholarships primarily being offered to groups and nations with political and ideological bonds to Cuba's revolutionary project,[12] and the extent to which *individual* Palestinian students have arguably negotiated the Cuban system and the factional system alike to maximise their personal, professional and political development. To achieve the latter, individuals have developed official performances of ideological loyalty to access and complete their university studies in Cuba, whilst ultimately maintaining or developing political and ideological opinions, and critiques, of their own.

With reference to the broader *outcomes* of the programme, is it sufficient to announce, as seven Palestinian graduates did, that the project was 'humanitarian' in nature precisely because the beneficiaries of the scheme were *refugees*, and the overarching aim was to achieve professional self-sufficiency in *refugee* camps? In effect, as explored in the preceding chapter, Cuba's programme might appear to fall under the remit of a developmental approach, rather than being 'purely' humanitarian in nature, precisely due to the official aim of maximising self-sufficiency as opposed to addressing immediate basic needs in an emergency phase (with the latter more readily falling under the remit of 'humanitarian' assistance). Nonetheless, Cuba's aim to enhance refugees' self-sufficiency corresponds to the UNHCR's well-established Development Assistance to Refugees approach, and programmes supporting medium- and long-term capacity building are particularly common in protracted refugee situations. At the same time, it could be argued that the distinction between humanitarianism and development is immaterial given that the rhetoric of solidarity underpins *all* of Cuba's internationalist projects, whether in contexts of war or peace, and, furthermore, since Cuba has offered scholarships not only to refugees but also to *citizens* from across the Global South.

Related to the programme's reach to citizens and refugees alike, and simultaneously to the nature of the connection between humanitarianism and politics, Younis drew attention to another pivotal dimension: 'although the educational system had a humanitarian *dimension*, I don't think it is possible to separate *the human being* from politics'.

Cuba's political (in essence, socialist) commitment to the 'human being' was reasserted throughout the interviews, with Saadi, for instance, referring to Cuba's prioritisation of the 'relationship between a human being and a fellow human being', and Khalil explaining that Cuba had adopted 'the cause of the human being, and that's why it supported Palestinians in their struggle'. While critiques of Northern-led human rights discourses have been widespread, and such critiques have often paralleled or influenced critical analyses of humanitarianism (see Chapter 2), in their responses Palestinian graduates invoked an alternative approach to supporting the rights of human beings. Conceptualising Cuba's commitment to human beings as being inherently connected to politics, graduates, by extension, also highlighted that politics cannot be separated from approaches geared towards supporting humanity, whether external analysts consider that such approaches should be labelled 'development' or 'humanitarianism'. Whilst absent from the terminology used by Palestinian graduates, it can be argued that the notion of *solidarity* centralised in Cubaraui (and Cuban) accounts captures precisely these dimensions of Cuba's internationalist approach.

Ser humano: citizens, refugees and revolutionaries

In light of references to Cuba's support for 'the cause of the human being', how Palestinians felt that they were treated throughout the course of their studies in Cuba is also highly significant. All but one of the Palestinian interviewees stated that they had received 'special treatment' (to quote Marwan), with this 'special treatment' being conceptualised by interviewees through three (political and legally loaded) frames of reference: Palestinians as citizens, refugees and revolutionaries.

First, in line with the broadly egalitarian socialist perspective characterising the Cuban Revolution and its commitment to international cooperation (Hickling-Hudson et al. 2012: 1), eight interviewees indicated that they were 'treated as citizens' during their studies in the island. Younis, Nimr and Mustafa used this phrase exactly, while Abdullah clarified further by stating that Palestinian students were 'treated the way Cuban citizens were treated', and four other interviewees (Marwan, Saadi, Abdel-Wahid and Ibrahim) used elative adjectives to indicate that they were treated as '*real* citizens', '*more than* citizens', as '*first class* citizens' and as '*complete* citizens'. These elative terms combine superlative and comparative functions, bestowing authenticity on the legal and political term 'citizen'.

The trope of being treated as supra-citizens overlapped with the second category which interviewees indicated were commonly invoked by Cubans, and which is particularly notable when considering the role of humanitarianism and ideology in the context of this scholarship programme. Hence, Hamdi stressed that

> *Although we were treated as citizens*, Cubans were nonetheless fully aware that *we were also refugees*. We were treated the same way that our fellow Cubans were treated, and yet Cubans were also aware that we are refugees who were born in refugee camps in Lebanon…
>
> (Emphasis added)

This overlapping treatment of Palestinians as citizens who were equally identified as refugees was, according to Hamdi, one of the key foundations 'for our mutual respect'.

In turn, Ibrahim also drew upon the notion of Palestinians being identified as refugees and treated as citizens:

> Cubans were fully aware that we were Palestinians from the refugee camps in Lebanon – indeed, given the Cuban revolutionary experience, and our mutual culture [sic], there was a great appreciation for the Palestinian students and *full knowledge of their cause, and their suffering as refugees*. However, that being said, *we were treated as complete citizens*.
>
> (Emphasis added)

Precisely what these terms – citizen and refugee – might actually mean in the Cuban context was touched upon by Mohammad, who drew a comparison between the experiences of Palestinians in Cuba and the ways in which refugees are conceptualised in other states: 'We were treated as refugees, but in a different manner to the way that refugees are treated in other countries. The refugee in Cuba means that this individual should receive special treatment.' Indeed, this reference implicitly compares Cuba's approach to refugees and the prevalence of two archetypal discourses vis-à-vis refugees and asylum seekers as reproduced in the Global North: the first pertains to victimisation discourses which negate the agency of refugees by representing them as objects to be pitied (Malkki 1996; Rajaram 2002), while the second relates to intersecting criminalisation and securitisation discourses which demonise asylum seekers and refugees as threats to national security (Kampmark 2006). These discourses are both intimately gendered in nature and tied to specific geographies: innocent and apolitical 'madonna-and-child' in desperate need of assistance are perceived to be in refugee camps 'over there', while these figures become bogus asylum-seeking men who aim to exploit socio-economic benefits and threaten 'our way of life' when they apply for asylum in the Global North (Fiddian-Qasmiyeh 2009; Fiddian-Qasmiyeh and Qasmiyeh 2010).

In contrast, rather than eliciting feelings either of pity or fear, mutual respect emerged throughout the interviews as the primary mode of engagement between

Palestinians and Cubans, with Younis and Khalil alike concluding that, in effect, Palestinians were treated as equals precisely because they were 'part of the Cuban revolution': 'How were we treated in Cuba? As citizens? As refugees? As stateless people? In fact, none of these: in their eyes, we were revolutionaries.' Such a declaration is, in many ways, consistent with the notion of Cuba as a space which both trans/formed and consolidated Palestinian students' understandings of revolution and pre-existing ideological connections between Palestinian factions and the Cuban state. Furthermore, in her research in and about the Palestinian refugee camps in Lebanon, and with specific reference to the *Palestinian* revolution, Khalili indicates that 'the refugees in the camps became the emblem of the Thawra or the revolution', with camp-based Palestinian refugees becoming 'emblematic revolutionaries' (2007: 49). While Hanafi and Long assert that 'From 1969 to 1982, the PLO played a key role in promoting a collective political and national identity among the exiled Palestinians, who until then had seen themselves "merely" as refugees' (2010: 138), Cuba can in many regards also be perceived to have played a central role in influencing the development of personal, political and national identities amongst Palestinian students as 'more than' refugees.

In many ways, such accounts align with Cuba's broader ideological commitment that its revolutionary education programme should lead to the constitution of *el Hombre Nuevo* (the New Man), a self-sacrificial figure who would work tirelessly for the greater good.

Bearing in mind the paradoxical impacts of the programme as explored in the Sahrawi case study, the remainder of this chapter will now turn to the ways in which Palestinians experienced their return to their home-camps in Lebanon after their 'long absence', focusing in particular on the ways in which these graduates have – or have not – represented their educational experiences in Cuba, and whether they can be considered to have become representatives of Cuba's New Man or emblematic Palestinian revolutionaries. Indeed, while Cuban-educated Sahrawis are hyper-visible figures in the Algeria-based camps, one of the most notable findings emerging from this research is the extent to which many Palestinian graduates have erased Cuba from their public accounts of their personal history. As such, this case study reveals an alternative understanding of development and self-sufficiency to that offered in the preceding chapters: becoming independent from Cuba, rather than continuing to be prominently identified with Castro's revolutionary state as in the case of Cubaraui doctors in their Algerian-based home-camps, but also of distancing themselves from the factions which, they had declared, facilitated their access to the scholarship system itself.

Experiences of return

Palestinian interviewees argued that the vast majority of Palestinian refugees had returned to their home-camps upon graduation, declaring that they had decided to return because 'our people need us' (Nimr), and in order to 'to serve our people' (Younis and Khalil). As in the case of the interviews conducted in Cuba and in the Sahrawi camps, the specialisms offered through the scholarship programme were perceived by interviewees in Lebanon to be 'perfect' to enhance the medical self-sufficiency of the Palestinian refugee camps, meeting the Cuban aim for the individual to work for the collective (Abdullah) in order to benefit the 'local community' (Ibrahim).

A further reason underpinning graduates' return to their home-camps was because of a sense of community with both their family and their 'people' (Mustafa and Abdel-Wahid). Such responses are closely related, almost verbatim, to Cuba's official justification for the educational migration programme, with graduates appearing to embody the self-sacrificial nature of the revolutionary New Man. In spite of this stated desire, Ahmed stressed that 'although Palestinians did decide to return to the camps, Lebanese legislation vis-à-vis Palestinians and the bad economic situation in Lebanon forced some Palestinians to leave the camps'.

Indeed, Saadi, Hamdi, Khalil and Mustafa separately confirmed that some graduates had attempted to leave the Palestinian camps after their return (one interviewee, for instance, had travelled to the United Arab Emirates and then to Germany to apply– unsuccessfully – for asylum before being deported to Lebanon). Furthermore, Hamdi, Khalil and Ahmed indicated that these attempts to leave arose due to the precarious socio-economic conditions and discriminatory laws faced by Palestinians in Lebanon: limited opportunities for employment exist within the camps, and yet it is illegal for Palestinian refugees to work outside of the camps in at least 25 professions, including as doctors and engineers (Hanafi and Tiltnes 2009; also see Qasmiyeh and Fiddian-Qasmiyeh 2013).

Ironically, perhaps, structural conditions within the camps, in the host country, and in the broader international arena have ultimately ensured that the majority of Palestinians educated in Cuba have continued working within the refugee camps: being unable to work legally outside the camps has meant that refugees have indeed been the direct beneficiaries of the Cuban education programme, while the absence of legal avenues to migrate to the European Union has, as a whole, prevented Palestinian graduates from following in Cubaraui students' footsteps (at least thus far). Although Cubaraui students have, since the mid-2000s in particular, been supported by members of Spanish civil society to migrate to Spain, using the camps as transit zones to reach a European state where their Cuban medical degrees are recognised and they speak a common language (Chapter 4), no such connections exist en masse for Palestinians.[13]

Nonetheless, returning to, and remaining in, the refugee camps in Lebanon does not necessarily mean that Palestinian refugees' individual and collective needs have been met by these graduates in the way envisaged by Cuba.

On the one hand, the Palestinian refugee camps are independent, and yet lawless, spaces which are beyond Lebanese jurisdiction[14] without being administratively 'independent' or self-sufficient in the way that the Sahrawi camps are run (with international support) by the Polisario Front and the SADR. Rather than medical centres being under the direct control of the PLO or the multiple factions which vie for control in/over the camps,[15] medical, educational and other social services are provided via UNRWA and related NGOs. In this regard, although interviewees repeatedly asserted the centrality of the PLO and/ or factions in allocating scholarships to study in Cuba, the PLO and the factions have an ambivalent role within the camps themselves: the (past and ongoing) power to allocate scholarships is not paralleled by control over the principal service institutions within the camps.

On the other hand, although the Cuban education system has not enabled the development of self-sufficient camps on a collective level, Palestinian graduates have clearly benefited on an individual, and arguably familial level, with all of the graduates interviewed for this project holding professional jobs as doctors, engineers and lab technicians. Indeed, Mohammad and Abdullah respectively argued that 'Palestinians who graduated from Cuba have been treated favourably upon their return' and that 'I believe that Palestinians in the camps generally acknowledge Cuba's role and also appreciate their contributions in the field of education, which goes beyond politics and its unequivocal support at the UN'.

Equally – prior to the conflicts which have spread across the region since 2011 – Ibrahim indicated that Palestinians from Syria[16] and Jordan who were educated in Cuba had historically obtained 'important positions and have been treated well' in their refugee camp homes in those countries.[17]

Such positive accounts must be viewed not only alongside Abdullah's active membership of the Palestinian–Cuban Union (discussed in more detail below), and in light of the abovementioned invisibility of their having studied *in Cuba per se* to colleagues and neighbours alike, but also in relation to the fact that not all graduates embody the Cuban aim of providing self-sufficient health care as envisaged by Cuba. Many graduates have been employed by UNRWA as doctors and lab technicians, in particular, and yet others have transcended this centralised system by establishing their own private medical clinics within the camps.[18] The emergence of camp-based private clinics has in effect been instigated (and in many ways monopolised) by Cuban-educated Palestinians not/ no longer employed by UNRWA. These graduates have thus taken a further step towards *individual* professional and socio-economic self-sufficiency, in spite of Cuba's official policy of offering scholarships to students to maximise professional 'work that would be directed toward the national good and national development rather than the individual's upward mobility' (Breidlid 2013: 158).[19]

While we could identify these private clinics as Palestinian spaces permeated by Cuban influences, they are not hybrid spaces per se given that 'the Cuban connection' has effectively been rendered invisible by graduates who tend to discreetly erase the origin of their medical degrees. Indeed, although Cubaraui doctors are amongst the most visible professionals in the Sahrawi refugee camps, being key interlocutors with foreign visitors to the camps, the main protagonists of documentaries and films made about Sahrawi refugees (Fiddian-Qasmiyeh 2009), as well as offering medical care to camp residents who are fully aware of the location of their studies, Cuban-educated Palestinians have, in many ways, been rendered invisible on local and international levels alike.

As such, there are no international academic studies exploring the experiences of this group of Palestinians in the MENA region and only a small number of academics have recognised the presence of Palestinians studying in Cuba itself (i.e. Sirhan 1996; Abbas et al. 1997). Another more important international audience is represented by UNRWA itself, which in many ways can be identified as one of the main actors promoting the erasure of Cuba in this protracted refugee situation.

To an extent, UNRWA's recruitment process itself is responsible for this erasure, with all medical candidates having to sit recruitment exams in the English language in order to access positions in UNRWA clinics, thereby effectively pushing all doctors to sideline their language of medical training.[20] In addition to this marginalisation of the Spanish language by sitting exams in English and treating patients in Arabic, the fear of being identified by UNRWA as having been ideologically influenced by Cuba's education system appears to have led to graduates' suspicion of revealing their personal/educational history to other Palestinians and non-Palestinians alike. The validity of these concerns were borne out in the cases of Ghanaian graduates and graduates from Grenada and St. Lucia who respectively encountered difficulties in accessing employment in Ghana due to the 'negative perception of their education from a country in the Socialist bloc' (Lehr 2012: 96), and 'encountered fears and prejudices of some bureaucrats and employers [in Grenada and St. Lucia] about the presence of Marxist ideology in their training' (Hickling-Hudson 2012: 116; also see Preston 2012: 134 with reference to similar difficulties experienced by Namibian graduates upon their return to their newly established state).

Indeed, as noted in the introduction to this chapter, all of the Palestinian interviewees in Lebanon were initially suspicious of the researcher's intentions in wanting to gain insights into their experiences of having studied in Cuba. Furthermore, when interviewees eventually offered their reflections about the nature of the programme, ideological *connections* between Cuba and Palestinians were reasserted, rather than the ideological *influence* of Cuba. Studying in Cuba was thus presented as having strengthened *Palestinian* convictions through what I have referred to above as the intersecting tropes of formation, transformation and consolidation.[21]

This is not to say, however, that Cuba's legacy is entirely invisible in the camps. Instead, rather than a hyper-visible *personal* and *professional* connection with Cuba as represented by the Cubaraui students who continue to be identified by other Sahrawis as part of *la tribu de los Cubanos*, speaking in Arabañol and in Spanish amongst themselves, and in Spanish with non-Sahrawi visitors to the camps, when it has taken place, Palestinians' connection with Cuba following their return to the camps has been formalised and, in many ways, re-factionalised.

Cuban-esque union: intergenerational continuation and re-factionalisation

The key institutional Cuban-esque space in the Palestinian refugee context in Lebanon is The Union of [Palestinian] Alumni of Cuban Universities and Schools in Lebanon.[22] Established in 1990 by a group of Palestinian graduates 'In appreciation of Cuba's role, and honouring what it has done for us' (Abdullah),[23] the union aims to bring together Palestinian graduates from across the 12 official refugee camps in Lebanon, providing both a formal space and public occasions for them to meet.[24] Many of the union's members are reportedly Palestinian students who married Cuban women during their scholarships, and who live together (as Spanish-speaking families) in the refugee camps. In this regard, the union offers an official space which is visibly, and audibly, related to Cuba. The particular family composition of many of its members also highlights the extent to which the Cuban education programme has created hybrid figures, even if these figures are different from the Cubarauis who returned to the Sahrawi refugee camps upon graduation.

As noted in Chapter 3, it is precisely the establishment of Palestinian–Cuban families in the Palestinian refugee camps across the Middle East that has enabled the intergenerational nature of Cuba's education programme for Palestinian refugees, with Palestinian–Cuban youth reportedly being prioritised for the scholarship programme since the early 2000s.[25] These youth, furthermore, embody the overlapping legal and political statuses highlighted above: they are simultaneously Cuban citizens and Palestinian refugees, while, ideologically, it is assumed/desired that they should be/become/remain revolutionaries both at 'home' and 'away'.[26]

Indeed, the union provides a space to reinforce personal connections between graduates, but also to 'brighten bonds' between Palestinians and Cuba more broadly.[27] As such, the union remains an institution which primarily intends to facilitate contact between Palestinians and the Cuban state via its Embassy in Lebanon. As noted by Khalil:

> The Union had organised many forums and seminars in Lebanon, mainly to celebrate or commemorate Palestinian and Cuban events. The latest meeting was held in Baddawi Camp [in North Lebanon] to celebrate the victory of the Cuban revolution. Many Palestinian *factions* and Lebanese parties and prominent dignitaries attended this event, in addition to the Cuban Ambassador.
>
> (Emphasis added)

This official connection is imperative to ensure the very continuation of the scholarship programme for the next generation: 'We are still in contact with Cuban officials in order to secure more scholarships for more Palestinians in the camps [in Lebanon] and to ensure that this scientific collaboration survives for many generations to come.' The union thereby plays a central role both in providing a space for Palestinian–Cuban families and in supporting the intergenerational nature of this scholarship programme for the children born to these families. Nonetheless, these personal and institutional connections are very different from the centrality of Cuba and Cubarauis to the Sahrawi imagination, as inherited by the young Sahrawi children cited in Chapter 4, for instance.

Furthermore, the involvement of *factions* and not just graduates and their *families* in the union highlights the extent to which the survival of the scholarship programme often continues to be related to nepotism through factional membership.[28] As a whole, union members' connections with Cuba via its embassy were critiqued by *non-affiliated* graduates. For instance, Marwan confirmed that the union facilitated 'personal connections with the Cuban embassy, rather than a collective relationship' and Saadi further denounced that the union has 'failed to forge a relationship with Palestinian reality'. In effect, many of the graduates explicitly distanced themselves from the union, being notably tense while discussing the institution's role in the camps today. For many, the union was effectively perceived to duplicate the role of some of the Palestinian factions involved in 'facilitating' the scholarship programme – both the union and factions, in their view, have failed to leave any significant impact on Palestinian refugees' lives in the camps, holding decorative rituals for officials to meet officials. As such, the Cuban scholarship programme could be understood to have provided innovative ways for individual scholarship holders to develop professionally, personally and politically, but also for specific *factions* to grow over time and space.

Although 'the recognition of a transnational community of struggle was a central theme of the radical liberationalist discourse' embodied by Cuba and other non-aligned actors (Khalili 2007: 16), it could be argued that Palestinian factions have engaged with the discourse of a 'transnational community of struggle' in order to accrue different forms of political, material and social capital for the factions, without meaningfully promoting the needs and rights of the 'struggling community' on the local (camp) or national(ist) level. Factions such as the DFLP have arguably endorsed the Cuban scholarship programme and appropriated it as their own, using the scholarships as a means to enhance membership of their factions at critical historical junctures, as noted below.

Such critiques are broadly in line with research conducted by Hanafi and Long (2010: 143) with Palestinian youth in the Lebanese camps in the 2000s:

> factional and lesser party leaders in Lebanon have ... set up, in effect, petty fiefdoms in the camps... factional politics have lost sight of the nationalist cause and promote through clientelism and similar such practices individual self-interest over collective Palestinian interests.

In this regard, it is also important to note that although interviewees repeatedly highlighted the role of *factions* in the allocation of scholarships, a relatively recent change has taken place with regards to the emergence of Palestinian NGOs as mediating actors for the scholarship programme, rather than either the PLO or its constituent (or contesting) factions. NGOs' roles were only referred to implicitly by interviewees, and yet broader research in and about the role of Palestinian NGOs in Lebanon strongly suggests that these NGOs have materialised as credible alternatives to the PLO as key non-political mediators with a range of governmental bodies and their representatives (i.e. Suleiman 1997). NGOs' status as credible alternatives has nonetheless been accompanied by ongoing charges of nepotism – indeed, these NGOs can also be conceptualised as quasi-factions which continue to be run and managed by PLO veterans. Hence, for instance, the director of an NGO in Shatila refugee camp secured a scholarship for his son to study in Cuba through his close relationship with the then-Cuban ambassador in Beirut.[29] The fact that the NGO director was formerly a prominent figure in the PFLP demonstrates the extent to which certain NGOs have inherited both the members and mechanisms underpinning factions, including the central role of nepotism (including to access the Cuban scholarship).[30]

The critiques cited above reflect not only a disengagement from the Palestinian–Cuban Union itself, but also a distancing from the very factions which graduates argued had granted them the scholarships. Although a small number of interviewees have become union members, most of the graduates interviewed are no longer active members of their original factions. Far from processes of indoctrination or an imposition of either Cuba's or Palestinian factions' ideological and political positions, many graduates appear to have offered temporary 'loyalty' to specific factions in order to access the scholarships, as the only option available for their personal and professional development.

Strategically joining a given faction may have enabled students to be granted a scholarship in the first place, and yet from the outset many Palestinian graduates both identified and denounced the significance of nepotism in the allocation of scholarships, and the internal hierarchy of connections within factions which influenced the allocation of specific courses of study (in particular medicine). If this is the case, it could be posited that students' temporary loyalty to these factions may not only have been accepted but even encouraged by faction leaders wishing to expand their membership, even if only temporarily. It could, therefore, be argued that Cuba provided a framework for Palestinians to access tertiary education irrespective of their 'real' ideological belonging. This is not to claim that students' ideological and political beliefs were not influenced by their time in Cuba, but rather to suggest that their political consciousness, and indeed their identities and identifications as Palestinians, developed whilst in Cuba in ways which do not necessarily correspond either to the political priorities of the factions which sponsored their scholarships, or to the Cuban state and its respective institutions.

Conclusion: circumstantial humanitarianism?

This chapter has examined the ways in which Palestinian individuals have negotiated contexts of extreme deprivation and discrimination in Lebanon through their participation in this South–South educational migration programme. Rather than attempting to discern whether the Cuban programme can (or should) be conceptualised as humanitarian, ideological or developmental in nature on the basis of Cuba's motivations or the programme's ultimate outcomes on individual or collective levels, I have argued that many graduates have publicly distanced themselves both from Cuba and from the factions involved in the allocation of scholarships. They have done so whilst maximising their individual contributions to the camp-based infrastructure and thereby their own personal (and indeed economic) development as they have provided essential services to other refugees through UNRWA and private clinics. In so doing, I have posited that the Cuban education programme has facilitated an alternative understanding of humanitarianism, development and self-sufficiency. Unlike Cubarauis – whose prominent identification with Cuba is borne in their hybrid label[31] – Palestinian graduates have, in many ways, become independent both from Cuba and from factional intermediaries.

Indeed, working 'for the community' by providing medical and other professional services in the camps, does not mean that Palestinian graduates have become the quintessentially self-sacrificial New Man, having disengaged, as many have, from Cuba's legacy on multiple levels. If the erasure of Cuba's legacy can be linked to graduates' fears that they might be perceived by external actors (and especially by UNRWA) to have been brainwashed whilst studying in Cuba, the ongoing influence of Cuba's education programme is, in many ways, also the result of structural conditions, in this case local, national and international conditions which have (thus far) prevented Palestinian graduates from leaving the camps to work in Europe (as their Cubaraui counterparts have) or to work in Lebanese hospitals. Consequently, Palestinian refugees continue to benefit from graduates' professional training in Cuba not only because they are committed to supporting their communities, but also because they have limited alternatives. If the education programme has facilitated a high degree of Palestinian self-sufficiency in terms of medical professionals treating Palestinian patients in the camps, this outcome can, in many ways, be considered to represent a form of *circumstantial* humanitarianism.

Notes

1 This is largely due to the hyper-visibility of Cubaraui medical personnel and the importance of Spanish in the Sahrawi refugee camps.
2 As noted in Chapter 3, there were no UNRWA-run secondary schools in Lebanon throughout the 1970s and 1980s, with secondary places only being available via PLO managed/sponsored schools. By 2014, UNRWA was running 69 primary and secondary level schools in Lebanon for approximately 32,000 Palestinian refugee children (out of a total number of 455,000 Palestinian refugees registered with UNRWA in that country). Two UNRWA administered vocational training centres have a capacity for a maximum of 1,100 students.
3 The latter are run, administered and controlled by the Polisario Front and its SADR, in spite of being geographically isolated and entirely dependent in material terms upon externally provided assistance (see Chapter 4).
4 I am indebted to Mohammed (Abu Iyad) for helping me identify and interview Cuban-educated Palestinians in Lebanon. These processes were particularly complex given that this was clearly a sensitive topic for many interviewees in the Palestinian camps (unlike the relative ease of conducting research with Cubarauis, who are hyper-visible in the Sahrawi camps). Mohammed negotiated these sensitivities and fears with great care and professionalism, and provided invaluable insights at all stages of the research for this chapter, ranging from sharing feedback on the phrasing of the proposed interview questions, to explaining the nuances of key terms emerging throughout the interviews.

5 In contrast, Lehr notes that the 'recruitment program' for Cuban scholarships in Ghana is a competitive application process, including exams and aptitude tests, stressing that 'the Cubans provided technical advice in the early stages of the program on how to structure the recruitment process in order to achieve this goal of providing equal opportunities to students across the country' (2012: 90–93).

6 The implications of these bonds between Cuba and Palestinian factions are multiple, and yet Khalil, amongst others, noted that not all Palestinian students in fact shared the political and ideological convictions upheld by these factions. This point is discussed in greater detail below.

7 Although Cuba's education programme was established in the 1960s, Palestinian refugees' participation gained particular strength when a range of Palestinian Marxist factions were established in full force in the mid-1970s. This is reflected in the increasing number of students matriculating in Cuban universities between the mid- and late 1970s. The periods of study of the graduates cited in this chapter is of particular interest given that none of the interviewees arrived in Cuba in the 1980s, with eight having arrived between 1977 and 1979, and four in 1990–1991. While further analysis is required to examine whether there was indeed a reduction in the numbers of Palestinians leaving Lebanon to study in Cuba in the 1980s, an interruption in the programme during that decade could be understood as a response to the major events which devastated Palestinian lives in Lebanon at that time – such events include the overarching Lebanese Civil War (1975–1990), but more specifically the Israeli invasion of Lebanon (1982–1983) and the Camps War (1985–1989, also known as the War of the Camps). Further research would also be required to establish whether the number of scholarships offered to Palestinians across the region shifted in response to major events taking place in each of the major host states (Lebanon, Syria and Jordan) and in the Occupied Territories themselves – that is to say, whether the reduction in Palestinians able/willing to leave Lebanon in the 1980s to study in Cuba might have led to an increase in the number of scholarships available for Palestinians from Syria or Jordan in that decade.

8 Nonetheless, not *all* Palestinian factions benefited from the scholarship programme, since it was primarily those factions *supporting* the PLO, rather than those *opposing* it, which were allocated scholarships by the PLO to distribute to their respective members. Although a small number of factions not associated with the PLO were able to offer their members access to Cuban scholarships, further research is required to establish how Hamas (established in 1987) and other non-secular or overtly Islamic groups might have conceptualised the Cuban scholarship system for Palestinians.

9 As noted above, it is not in fact the case that all Palestinian factions were/are part of the PLO.

10 Fifty-five-year-old engineer.

11 This is not to say that Cuba has only 'shared' with internationalist and non-aligned partners, as exemplified by its offer to send medical brigades to the United States of America in the aftermath of Hurricane Katrina. The US government's rejection of this offer, arguably as much as Cuba's offer itself, can, of course, be seen to be inherently ideological in nature.

12 We could conceptualise this as a form of 'marginal bonding' through which the geopolitically marginalised Cuban state has created structures to bond with other margins, including multiply marginalised populations such as the Palestinians and Sahrawis (see Chapter 3).

13 Indeed, one interviewee – Marwan – left Cuba before completing his degree since it became apparent that studying there would not facilitate onward migration to either European or North American countries. Equally, Hickling-Hudson notes that in the context of the Anglophone Caribbean 'Cuban degrees are seen as being associated with Marxist perspectives, and North American degrees and diplomas are viewed as having more status and "saleability"' (2012: 123). While Hickling-Hudson's

interviewees suggest that 'Cuban trained graduates were less likely to be part of this "brain drain" of qualified people, because the degree prepared them both technically and attitudinally for contributing to the region's development' (ibid.), this outcome is related to a broader set of structural factors, including the more limited marketability of Cuban degrees (cf. Sahrawi doctors' emigration from the refugee camps, Chapter 4).

14 Many camps are also beyond the reach of the Lebanese army, although at different historical junctures specific camps have been subjected to army attacks and even destruction, as in the case of the destruction of Nahr el-Bared Camp in 2007.

15 See Hanafi and Long's account of the 'rampant factionalism' in the Palestinian camps in Lebanon (2010, esp. 140).

16 The impact of the conflict in Syria (2011–) on the future of the Cuban–Palestinian scholarship programme remains to be explored; the impact of the Libyan civil war on Palestinians' access to tertiary education in Libya is examined in Chapter 6.

17 In contrast, Marwan offered a different conclusion regarding Cuba's position within the Palestinian imagination, both when compared with other Palestinian graduates, but also Sahrawi graduates' accounts: 'I don't think that Cuba's medical advancement and expertise in a spectrum of medical fields are known in Lebanon. They [members of the Palestinian community] think of Cuba only as a Communist place, and overlook their expertise in medicine.'

18 Regarding the development of micro-economies in the Palestinian camps in Lebanon see Qasmiyeh and Fiddian-Qasmiyeh (2013).

19 Here, Breidlid is referring to Cuba's education system for Cuban citizens.

20 Y.M. Qasmiyeh, personal communication, January 2014.

21 It could be suggested that centralising the roles played by Palestinian actors during this historical stage (in particular in the 1970s) could be related to graduates' nostalgia for a period when Palestinians were recognised by international(ist) actors as active refugees who had the right to fight for their cause.

22 *RabiTat al-Hirijiin min Al-Jamiaat wa al Maahid al Cubia fi Lubnan.*

23 While Martínez-Pérez argues that 'the affection and gratitude of these [Cuban-educated] professionals towards Cuba is shown by the establishment of Cuban friendship and solidarity groups in their own countries' (2012: 82), other reasons for engaging in such groups are explored below.

24 Given Palestinian graduates' geographical spread not only across Lebanon but also across the Middle East as a whole (having also 'returned' to Jordan, Syria, Gaza and the West Bank), such an institution is arguably a core means of maintaining social networks and contacts across an otherwise widely dispersed group. Such a centralised meeting space is less necessary in the Sahrawi context given that the approximately 4,000 Sahrawi graduates are situated across four main camps within the broader Sahrawi refugee camp complex, and are therefore typically able to maintain contact much more informally. Given the large number of Sahrawi graduates who spent such a significant part of their childhoods and adolescences in Cuba, a major Internet-based social group does exist, providing an alternative forum online to maintain social and professional connections.

25 In many other instances, however, the children of Palestinian–Cuban unions have remained in Cuba with their Cuban parent (almost invariably, the mother).

26 However, precisely how Palestinian–Cuban graduates are categorised by the Cuban state upon their arrival in Cuba remains ambiguous (Chapter 3).

27 It could be argued that such encounters also provide space to nurture nostalgia on behalf of the PLO.

28 Or, as noted below, through the more recently established 'NGOs' in the camps.

29 Field notes, December 2013.

30 Through nepotism, factions and NGOs alike have developed the means for the politically powerful to allocate scholarships to their relatives, who have returned to

the camps as medical professionals who not only control the body (via medicine) but also the body politic (by inheriting positions of power in 'their' factions).

31 In many ways, ambivalence towards Cuba as an education provider is consistent with other research regarding both Cuban and non-Cuban students' experiences of studying in revolutionary institutions (i.e. Berg 2014). The strong identification which many Sahrawi students developed following their arrival on the Island of Youth as 11- and 12-year olds leads us to ask whether children's identification with a school and classmates may be stronger than the impact of tertiary level education on young adults arriving in Cuba.

References

Abbas, M., Shaaban, H., Sirhan, B. and Hassan, A. (1997) 'The Socio-economic Conditions of Palestinians in Lebanon', *Journal of Refugee Studies*, 10(3): 378–396.

Alba, R. (2005) 'Bright vs. blurred boundaries', *Ethnic and Racial Studies*, 28(1): 20–49.

Berg, M. (2014) '"La Lenin is my Passport": Schooling, Mobility and Belonging in Socialist Cuba and its Diaspora', *Identities*, doi: 10.1080/1070289X.2014.939189.

Bhabha, H.K. (2006) *The Location of Culture*. 3rd ed. London: Routledge.

Brazier, C. (1997) 'Special Edition: War and Peace in Western Sahara', *The New Internationalist*, 297.

Breidlid, A. (2013) *Education, Indigenous Knowledge, and Development in the Global South: Contesting Knowledges for a Sustainable Future*. New York: Routledge.

Chimni, B.S. (2000) Globalisation, Humanitarianism and the Erosion of Refugee Protection, Refugee Studies Centre Working Paper No. 3. Oxford: Refugee Studies Centre.

Dominguez, J.I. (1989) *To Make a World Safe for Revolution: Cuba's Foreign Policy*. Cambridge, MA: Harvard University Press.

Ferris, E. (2011) *The Politics of Protection: The Limits of Humanitarian Action*. Washington, DC: Brookings Institution Press.

Fiddian-Qasmiyeh, E. (2014) *The Ideal Refugees: Gender, Islam and the Sahrawi Politics of Survival*. Syracuse, NY: Syracuse University Press.

Fiddian-Qasmiyeh, E. (2013a) 'The Inter-generational Politics of "Travelling Memories": Sahrawi Refugee Youth Remembering Home-land and Home-camp', *Journal of Intercultural Studies*, 34(6): 631–649.

Fiddian-Qasmiyeh, E. (2013b) 'Transnational Childhood and Adolescence: Mobilising Sahrawi Identity and Politics across Time and Space', *Journal of Ethnic and Racial Studies*, 36(5): 875–895.

Fiddian-Qasmiyeh, E. (2010) 'Education, Migration and Internationalism: Situating Muslim Middle Eastern and North African Students in Cuba', *The Journal of North African Studies*, 15(2): 137–155.

Fiddian-Qasmiyeh, E. (2009) 'Representing Sahrawi Refugees' "Educational Displacement" to Cuba: Self-sufficient Agents and/or Manipulated Victims in Conflict?' *Journal of Refugee Studies*, 22(3): 323–350.

Fiddian-Qasmiyeh, E. and Qasmiyeh, Y.M (2010) 'Asylum-seekers and Refugees from the Middle East and North Africa: Negotiating Politics, Religion and Identity in the UK', *Journal of Refugee Studies*, 23(3): 294–314.

Hanafi, S. and Long, T. (2010) 'Governance, Governmentalities, and the State of Exception in the Palestinian Refugee Camps of Lebanon', *Journal of Refugee Studies*, 23(2): 134–159

Hanafi, S. and Tiltnes, A. (2009) 'The Employability of Palestinian Professionals in Lebanon', *Knowledge, Work and Society*, 6(1): 56–78.

Hickling-Hudson, A.R. (2012) 'Studying in Cuba, Returning Home to Work: Experiences of Graduates from the English-speaking Caribbean', in A. Hickling-Hudson, J. Corona González and R. Preston (eds) *The Capacity to Share: A Study of Cuba's International Cooperation in Educational Development*. New York: Palgrave Macmillan, 107–126.

Hickling-Hudson A.R., Corona González, J. and Preston, R. (2012) 'Introduction: Cuba's Capacity to Share', in A.R. Hickling-Hudson, J. Corona González and R. Preston (eds) *The Capacity to Share: A Study of Cuba's International Cooperation in Educational Development*. New York: Palgrave Macmillan, 1–12.

Kampmark, B. (2006) '"Spying for Hitler" and "Working for Bin Laden": Comparative Australian Discourses on Refugees', *Journal of Refugee Studies*, 19 (1): 1–21.

Khalili, L. (2007) *Heroes and Martyrs of Palestine: The Politics of National Commemoration*. Cambridge: Cambridge University Press.

Lehr, S. (2012) 'The Children of the Isle of Youth: How Ghanaian Students Learned to Cope with "Anything in Life"', in A. Hickling-Hudson, J. Corona González and R. Preston (eds) *The Capacity to Share: A Study of Cuba's International Cooperation in Educational Development*. New York: Palgrave Macmillan, 83–105.

Malkki, L.H. (1996) 'Speechless Emissaries: Refugees, Humanitarianism, and Dehistoricization', *Cultural Anthropology*, 11(3): 377–404.

Martínez-Pérez, F. (2012) 'Cuban Higher Education Scholarships for International Students: An Overview', in A. Hickling-Hudson, J. Corona González and R. Preston (eds) *The Capacity to Share: A Study of Cuba's International Cooperation in Educational Development*. New York: Palgrave Macmillan, 73–82.

Pacitto, J. and Fiddian-Qasmiyeh, E. (2013) 'Writing the "Other" into Humanitarian Discourse: Framing Theory and Practice in South-South Humanitarian Responses to Forced Displacement', *UNHCR New Issues in Refugee Research*, Research Paper No. 257, July.

Preston, R. (2012) 'Cuban Support for Namibian Education and Training', in A. Hickling-Hudson, J. Corona González and R. Preston (eds) *The Capacity to Share: A Study of Cuba's International Cooperation in Educational Development*. New York: Palgrave Macmillan, 127–140.

Qasmiyeh, Y.M. and Fiddian-Qasmiyeh, E. (2013) 'Refugee Camps and Cities in Conversation', in J. Garnett and Harris, A. (eds) *Migration and Religious Identity in the Modern Metropolis*. Farnham: Ashgate, 131–143.

Rajaram, P.K. (2002) 'Humanitarianism and Representations of the Refugee', *Journal of Refugee Studies*, 15(3): 247–264.

Sahrawi Arab Democratic Republic (2003) *Constitution of the Sahrawi Arab Democratic Republic*. Rabouni: Sahrawi Arab Democratic Republic.

Sayigh, R. (2000) 'Greater Insecurity for Refugees in Lebanon', Middle East Research and Information Project, 1 March.

Sirhan, B. (1996) 'Education and the Palestinians in Lebanon'. Paper presented at the Palestinians in Lebanon Conference organised by the Centre for Lebanese Studies and The Refugee Studies Programme, Queen Elizabeth House, 27–30 September. Available at http://www.lpdc.gov.lb/getattachment/6fd90905-1379-45e1-9a40-8db11c095501/Education-and-the-Palestinians-in-Lebanon.aspx, last accessed 27/05/2014.

Suleiman, J. (1997) 'Palestinians in Lebanon and the Role of Non-governmental Organizations', *Journal of Refugee Studies*, 10(3): 397–410.

6 Libyan *hostipitality* through Sahrawi and Palestinian eyes

Introduction

Following the *coup d'état* led by Gaddafi in 1969, education in Libya became 'practically free'[1] for all students in the country, irrespective of their country, or refugee camp, of origin. Indeed, Libya, like Cuba, offered Sahrawi and Palestinian refugees – along with thousands of other citizens and refugees from Sudan, Egypt, Mauritania, Syria, Morocco, Tunisia and Yemen – the opportunity to study free of charge at primary, secondary and tertiary level institutions from the 1970s until the 2011 uprising, the year when Gaddafi was killed and over 900 Sahrawi and tens of thousands of Palestinians were displaced by the conflict.

Although Cuba offered educational opportunities to Sahrawi and Palestinian refugees via similar – although not identical – scholarship initiatives, this chapter examines the nature and implications of Libya's bifurcated approach to supporting Sahrawis on the one hand and Palestinians on the other. It starts by briefly tracing the history of Libya's structured support for Sahrawis, including through reference to Sahrawi graduates' experiences of having been allocated scholarships as young children through a bilateral agreement between the Polisario Front and the Libyan state. Given the extent to which this agreement, and Sahrawi experiences of studying in Libya, are in many ways reminiscent of the Cuban framework, and with the echo of Sahrawi and Palestinian experiences and retrospective perceptions of the Cuban scholarship system in mind, the remainder of this chapter primarily explores how, why and with what effect Libya supported Palestinians' access to its educational establishments through a range of overlapping mechanisms. These included the provision of a small number of scholarships – primarily for individual Palestinians affiliated with particular factions to attend military colleges – but more broadly the implementation of policies which facilitated the South–South migration of tens of thousands of Palestinians to Libya both as refugee-students but also as refugee-migrant workers.[2]

Exempting Palestinians from visa and other bureaucratic requirements to enter and remain in Libya,[3] and providing Palestinians with access to the Libyan labour market and national education system alike were particularly notable policies in light of the broader regional insecurity faced by Palestinians, including as a result of the discrimination and xenophobia, occupation, civil wars and mass expulsions which affected Palestinians across North Africa, the Middle East and the Gulf. However, far from idealising Libya's approaches towards Palestinians, this chapter draws on Derrida's conceptualisation of *hostipitality* (2000a, 2000b) to explore how and why Libya itself replicated these and other forms of discrimination and expulsion at different points of time.

The substantive analysis of the Palestinian–Libyan case study thus starts by introducing the diverse motivations and structures which led Palestinians to migrate to Libya, especially in light of the general insecurity faced by Palestinians in Lebanon – as introduced in the previous chapter. Inter alia, it notes the extent to which Palestinians' presence in Libya and their access to the education system was simultaneously much more individualised (in terms of travelling as individuals to Libya, rather than as part of a cohort) but also more communal in nature in light of the long history of Palestinian migration to Libya and the well-established Palestinian community based in the North African country.

Reflecting the multifaceted routes followed by Palestinians to reach Libya, the Palestinians interviewed in Lebanon for this chapter[4] included one individual who had travelled specifically to complete his university degree in Libya, one who had travelled to pursue his studies with the expectation of also working as a teacher in Libyan institutions, three Palestinians (with degrees in music from an Egyptian university, and in physics and history from Lebanese universities) who had travelled to Libya specifically to work as teachers, and four Palestinians who were born in Libya to Palestinian refugee-migrants. This latter group – including three women – had completed their primary, secondary and (in some instances) their tertiary studies in Libya before returning to the Palestinian camps in Lebanon for a variety of personal and political reasons examined in greater detail below. Notably, none of the Libyan-educated interviewees identified in the Palestinian refugee camps in Lebanon had been in receipt of Libyan scholarships per se, even when they had travelled to Libya specifically to pursue their studies.[5]

Drawing on these Palestinian interviewees' experiences of studying and teaching in Libya, the chapter then critically reflects on the nature, content and quality of the Libyan education system, and concurrently examines the shifting policies which variously constituted Palestinians as part of the Libyan Self or as the quintessential Other. As the culmination of the latter, in spite of the differences which characterise Sahrawi and Palestinian experiences of accessing and studying in Libyan educational institutions as a whole, the third part of the chapter focuses on Sahrawis' and Palestinians' shared experiences of having been subjected to mass expulsions from Libya on Gaddafi's orders in the 1980s and 1990s. It consequently concludes with an analysis of the displacement of both of these refugee-student/ refugee-migrant groups as a result of the 2011 Libyan uprising. Outlining the ambivalence of South–South programmes designed to support MENA refugees, and the tensions and violence which have led to expulsion at different geopolitical junctures, thereby demonstrates the need to engage critically with the diverse opportunities and challenges which may emerge in South–South development/ humanitarian initiatives which can, in turn, create and perpetuate, rather than reduce or eliminate, diverse forms of vulnerability and dependence.

Pan-Arabism, 'self-service' and hostipitality

Throughout this chapter I analyse Libya's mode of South–South cooperation through the lenses of 'self-service' on the one hand, and hostipitality (following Derrida 2000a and 2000b) on the other, concepts which are introduced in the following pages, before turning to the Sahrawi and Palestinian case studies in turn.

Palestinian 'self-service'

In contrast with the formal scholarships institutionalised by Libya on behalf of Sahrawi refugees, this chapter argues that Palestinians' migration to form part of Libya's transnational eduscape can be best conceptualised as a process of 'self-service'. I use this term to capture the extent to which Palestinians were encouraged to 'help themselves' by migrating to Libya, but also to centralise the practical and political benefits which Libya itself accrued by virtue of Palestinians' presence in North Africa. A key question guiding the analysis presented in the following pages is therefore the extent to which Libya's support for refugees' education can be conceptualised as a mode of South–South cooperation designed to promote the self-sufficiency of refugees, and/or is more readily identifiable as part of Gaddafi's Pan-Arabist ideology and regional aims.

With reference to the former, I posit that educational migration to Libya has not enhanced the professional and/or political self-sufficiency of the Sahrawi or Palestinian home-camps to the same degree as the Cuban scholarship system. Nonetheless, the 'self-service' system promoted in particular for Palestinians, enabled refugee-migrants to engage in paid employment and, therefore, not only to be self-sufficient, but even prosperous, within Libya, and to support the socio-economic well-being of their families in the refugee camps in Lebanon and elsewhere by sending remittances from Libya. While providing these opportunities for employment and education in the Libyan arena, I argue that the self-sufficiency of those Palestinians who taught and studied in Libya has not 'travelled' with Palestinians upon their return to their home-camps.[6]

Hence, although nine out of the twelve Cuban-educated Palestinians cited in Chapter 5 were employed in Lebanon by UNRWA – Palestinians' main employer in the camps[7] – or NGOs as doctors, technicians and engineers, or had established private clinics or personal businesses within the camps, only four of the Palestinians interviewed for this chapter were employed and/or had been reabsorbed as teachers by UNRWA in Lebanon, while two were working as private tutors since they had been unable to secure a position at UNRWA schools. In turn, one interviewee was working as an accountant and NGO driver, another in a beauty salon, and a third was running a small sweet kiosk in the grounds of an UNRWA school.

The relatively poor employment outcomes experienced by these Palestinians following their return to the camps in Lebanon are all the more noticeable given that four of these interviewees had in factworked as teachers in Libyan schools during their time in North Africa: while two of these former teachers are currently employed in UNRWA schools, one has only been able to find work as a private tutor and the other is running the abovementioned sweet kiosk. This reality suggests the extent to which an inverse form of self-sufficiency has been promoted through this programme: Palestinian teachers enhanced Libya's educational self-sufficiency, but they were ultimately unable to transport this self-sufficiency with them upon their return to the Palestinian refugee camps in Lebanon.

I, therefore, argue that Libya's model of South–South assistance for Sahrawi and Palestinian refugees can be conceptualised as a form of 'unintentional' humanitarianism. This concept draws on the term used by Saad – a 62-year-old man who worked as a history teacher in Libya between 1978 and 1984, and currently runs a sweet kiosk in an UNRWA school in Baddawi camp – in his interview:

> Work and education were available to Palestinians in Libya, and I would not say that these were seen as scholarships… I think that Libya offered a form of unintentional help to Palestinians. Gaddafi offered support because he saw himself as a national Arab leader.

This notion aims to reflect that selected benefits arose for Palestinians and the Libyan government alike, *in spite of* an absence of a structured humanitarian/ scholarship programme, a weak national education system, and an absence of policies such as those designed by Cuba to maximise refugees' professional and political contributions to their home-camps upon return. In effect, while even the most critical interviewees highlighted the positive features of their experiences of studying in Libya, the provision of a high quality education or specialist training to support refugees' socio-economic and political self-sufficiency in their home-camps was arguably not at the core of Libya's support for Sahrawis and Palestinians. The benefits *for* refugees travelling to study and/or teach in Libya, of which there were reportedly many, thus arguably arose 'accidentally' rather than by design. In contrast, it can be argued that the benefits *of* refugees migrating to Libya, as accrued by Gaddafi, were more intentionally framed in line with Gaddafi's (fluctuating) ideological position and political aims.[8]

As a constituent part of the broader model(s) of South–South cooperation examined in Chapter 2, Gaddafi's worldview was in many ways similar to Castro's ideological commitment to anti-colonial and liberation struggles. As discussed through the case study of Cuba in Chapter 3, the emergence of internationalism in Latin America and the Caribbean was intimately related to the increasing commitment of anti-colonial political (and military) leaders to Marxism and socialism in the region, as a means of achieving the development of egalitarian and fair societies. Structured by these ideological frameworks, education and educational migration were viewed as means for beneficiaries to escape poverty and underdevelopment, enhancing their national and collective self-sufficiency, and, therefore, widening the gap between formerly colonised peoples and colonial powers (Fiddian-Qasmiyeh 2010a; Hickling-Hudson et al. 2012).

However, in contrast to the internationalist approach represented by Cuba's education programme – which created and strengthened bonds of solidarity and cooperation between formerly colonised, exploited and occupied peoples from around the world, on inter- and trans-regional levels – Pan-Arabism has an intrinsically regional approach and prioritised the (socio-political, religious and linguistic) sovereignty and independence of Arab peoples and nations (see Khalidi et al. 1991; Choueiri 2000). By denying colonial (and neocolonial) powers the right to intervene in regional affairs, and demanding the independence of colonised and occupied territories and peoples – including, in particular, Palestine and Palestinians – Pan-Arabist approaches have simultaneously been founded upon Arab nationalism, Arab socialism, and the aim to politically unify these sovereign Arab states through the development of an overarching 'Arab Ummah' (Choueiri 2000).

In support of these processes, education was perceived to be a means to enhance the younger generation's awareness of and commitment to Arab nationalism, including to Arabic culture, language, and religion.[9] Access to such an education was available to 'foreign' Arab nationals, and indeed Arab refugees such as the Palestinians and Sahrawis, given that Pan-Arabism meant that they were 'broadly perceived as Arab brethren to whom the same type of rights as those accorded to nationals should be granted' (Chatelard et al. 2009: 5).

After Nasser's death in 1970, Gaddafi presented himself as the inheritor of, and the Protector of Pan-Arabism, and aimed to situate Libya at the core of the Arab world, and, from the 1990s onwards when he merged his prioritisation of Arab Unity with a commitment to 'Africa', at the core of the African continent. This was itself influenced by Gaddafi's personal/political aim – especially in the mid -to late 1980s – to position himself as the region's main revolutionary; Gaddafi effectively presented himself as The Revolutionary who was supporting Other Revolutionaries, including through the development of intra-regional initiatives to support Palestinian and Sahrawi liberation movements.

It could be posited that the success of Gaddafi's model was itself embodied through Libya's intrinsically international education system, characterised not only by the presence of diverse non-Libyan Arab students who accompanied Sahrawi and Palestinian refugees in Libya from the 1970s onwards, but also through the non-Libyan Arab teachers – Palestinians, Egyptians, Sudanese and Shi'a Iraqis –who taught Libyan and non-Libyan citizens alongside MENA refugees such as Sahrawis and Palestinians.

In spite of these students and teachers embodying the 'unity' of the Pan-Arabist eduscape, this chapter argues that Gaddafi's ideology and policies simultaneously offered key opportunities to individuals, families and communities and yet also undermined the physical and political security of such recipients. In particular, Sahrawis and Palestinians experienced oscillating forms of 'reward and punishment' which demonstrate the conditional nature of the support offered by Gaddafi to these refugee groups. Most acutely, members of both groups were physically expelled from Libya in the 1980s and 1990s when Gaddafi's relationships with the Polisario/SADR and with the PLO were fraught, and yet such expulsions were, ostensibly, ordered by Gaddafi in the name of Maghrebian Unity in case of the former, and in the name of the Palestinian national cause in the case of the latter.

Palestinians and Sahrawis were thus welcome, from the 1970s onwards, to travel to Libya without legal obstacles and even, in the case of thousands of Sahrawis and several hundred Palestinians, with full scholarships, and yet they were repeatedly expelled from Libya and (dis)placed on the margins of the North African state. Far from creating a 'central margin' via education, Libya's approach to Sahrawi refugees, but especially Palestinians, can thus be conceptualised as a policy of hostipitality towards these refugees.

This coinage highlights that 'hospitality' – in this context, the welcoming attitudes, policies and practices which are presumed to exist towards Arab brothers and sisters – is always 'parasitized by its opposite, "hostility", the undesirable guest which it harbours as the self-contradiction within its own body' (Derrida 2000a: 3).

Such self-contradictions are 'violently imposed on the very concept of hospitality' through the 'law of hospitality' itself, since hospitality is 'necessarily'

> a right, a duty, an obligation, the *greeting* of the foreign other as a friend but on the condition that the host, the Wirt, the one who received, lodges or gives asylum remains the patron, the master of the household…
>
> (Ibid.: 4)

A law of hospitality thus depends upon the host's ability to

> [maintain] his own authority in his own home, that he looks after himself and sees to and considers all that concerns him and thereby affirms the law of hospitality as the law of the household, *oikonomia*, the law of his household … the law of identity which de-limits the very place of proffered hospitality and maintains authority over it, maintains the truth of authority … thus limiting the gift proffered and making of this limitation, namely, the being-oneself in one's own home, the condition of the gift and of hospitality.
>
> (Derrida 2000a: 4)[10]

Although the host 'imagines itself narcissistically as being hospitable, (Germann Molz and Gibson 2007: 9), Derrida argues not only that do we *not know what hospitality is* – it is ultimately unknowable (it 'is not a concept which lends itself to objective knowledge') and also unachievable – but that hospitality itself inherently bears its own opposition, the ever present possibility of hostility towards the Other who has, at one time, been welcomed at the threshold; yet, 'Perhaps no one welcomed is ever completely welcome' (Derrida 2000a: 6).

In effect, Sahrawis and Palestinians have never 'known' what it is to 'be' 'completely welcome[d]': they were invited to cross the Libyan threshold through official declarations and policies of 'hospitality' – including the scholarships for Sahrawis introduced in the next section – and yet the 'gifts' offered by Gaddafi

– economic and educational, but also existential in the sense of being offered the gift of the right to 'be' Sahrawis and Palestinians – were not only controlled but revoked, followed by tens of thousands of Sahrawis and Palestinians being physically expelled when they did not directly endorse Gaddafi's views. This overarching hostipitality[11] in turn highlights the second dimension of what I have referred to above as a form of unintentional humanitarianism – Libya's support for/to Sahrawi and Palestinian refugees was accidental rather than by design, but it was equally permeated with injury, disaster and renewed processes of displacement and dispossession.

With this framework in mind, the remainder of the chapter examines the nature and implications of Muammar Gaddafi's hostipitality towards Sahrawi and Palestinian refugees from the 1970s until his death in 2011.

The Libya–Polisario nexus: a history of structured support, and occasional expulsion

In line with his support for anti-colonial movements throughout the 1960s, 1970s and 1980s (Hulieras 2001), Gaddafi expressed his support for the liberation of the Spanish Sahara even before the birth of the Polisario Front. El-Ouali, the Polisario Front's Secretary-General from 1973 until his death in 1976, had visited Libya (in addition to Algeria and Mauritania) in 1972 and 1973 to establish the North African state's support for the embryonic anti-colonial movement, with Libya calling for the liberation of the 'Arab Sahara' in 1973 (Miské 1978; Barbier 1982). Following the establishment of the Polisario Front, Gaddafi repeatedly announced that if Spain did not withdraw from the territory, Libya would provide military support to the Sahrawi, would open an office for the Polisario Front in Tripoli, and would establish a radio station for the Polisario to engage directly with the Arab world (Hernández Moreno 1988). Paralleling the provision of humanitarian and military supplies to the camps,[12] with Libya's support, the Polisario's youth wing was admitted to the *Congres des Jeunesses Euro-Arabes* and the *Movement Panafricain de la Jeunesse* in 1974 (Miské 1978; Barbier 1982). After the birth of the SADR, Libyan, Algerian and Sahrawi delegations also worked together between April 1976 and 1978 to ensure that the camp-based NUSW would be accepted as a full member of the Organization of Arab Women – it succeeded in 1978 (Yara 2003: 51; Gimeno-Martín and Laman 2005: 125).

Despite Libya's political support for the Polisario Front, and its clear positioning of this support via Pan-Arabist and Pan-Africanist frameworks, it was only four years after the establishment of the SADR, in 1980, that Libya formally recognised and established full diplomatic relations with the Sahrawi state-in-exile. Gaddafi then played a key role in lobbying for the admittance of the Polisario/SADR to the Organization of African Unity (OAU), a process which led to Morocco eventually suspending its membership of the regional organisation in 1982 and officially withdrawing from the OAU in 1984 after that organisation recognised the SADR (Lynn Price 1981; Damis 1983).[13] During this period, the Polisario/SADR 'frequently endorsed the Arab "unionist" goals propounded by Qadhafi [sic] and before him by Nasser and the Baathists' (Hodges 1984: 86). Citing the 1982 General Programme of National Action adopted by the Polisario's Fifth Congress, the Polisario's stated aims in 1982 included 'strengthen[ing] the tripartite, progressive front of the Saharawi, Algerian and Libyan revolutions, as a basic step towards the concretisation of the revolutionary alliance of the peoples of the Maghreb' (ibid.).

However, it was precisely Libya's determination to develop a Maghrebian alliance which led to the end of Gaddafi's material and diplomatic support for the Polisario in 1983 (Pazzanita and Hodges 1994), with the Libyan leader stating on 16 June of that year that 'Libya has finished carrying out its duty with respect to Western Sahara. There is no longer any dispute between Morocco and Libya about this region' (cited in ibid.). While Libya cut diplomatic ties with SADR due to its rapprochement with Morocco in 1983, Africa Confidential (1984) noted that as of May 1984, 'Polisario's office in Tripoli has not been closed', and an estimated '3,000 Polisario military and civilian personnel were still receiving training there' (also see Velloso de Santisteban 1993). In August 1984, the Moroccan–Libyan treaty of 'Arab-African Unity' was signed (Mace 1985), leading to a short period of regional unification which was interrupted when Libya protested at King Hassan of Morocco's talks with the Israeli Prime Minister in July 1986, and Hassan in turn abrogated the 1984 treaty of Union (Mace 1985; Pazzanita and Hodges 1994). While the Polisario had eventually re-established relations with Gaddafi by the early 1990s, this incident was a significant turning point in the history of Sahrawi relations with Libya, leading, amongst other things, to a hiatus in the scholarship programme for Sahrawi children and adolescents.

Re-membering the Sahrawi–Libyan education programme

From 1975 onwards, Sahrawi children as young as six left their Algerian-based refugee camps to study in Libya, with Libya having historically been the second largest educational host for this refugee population.[14] If 16 of the Sahrawi children whom Crivello and I interviewed in Madrid had relatives who had studied in Cuba (see Chapter 4), thirteen of these children referred to relatives (including parents, aunts and siblings) who had studied in Libya since the camps' establishment (Crivello and Fiddian-Qasmiyeh 2010).[15] Six of these children expressed an intention to study in Libya themselves in the future, reflecting a similar position as that held by Cuba in Sahrawi children's imaginary landscapes.[16]

Recounting her experiences of studying in Libya in the late 1970s and early 1980s, a 32-year-old Sahrawi woman explained:

> When I arrived there [in 1978 at the age of eight], the Libyans were very nice to us, they gave us everything that we need, food, clothing and materials that we needed to study. The children that went to Libya were very young, some six or seven years old, the age ranged between six and nine years old. In any case, the Libyans welcomed us warmly. The Libyans provided us with

everything that we needed and tried to compensate for the separation from our families.

(cited in Chatty, Fiddian-Qasmiyeh and Crivello 2010: 72)

Precisely why 'the Libyans' would try to 'compensate for the separation from our families', was elaborated upon by a 34-year-old woman who also completed her primary level studies in Libya from the age of seven:

I left for Libya to study and I used to cry all day long, looking for my mother. There, they gave me toys to distract me ... with time I became accustomed to my mother's absence... At that time we visited the camps and our families every two years during the summer holidays. Each time we left the camps to [return to] Libya we cried and remembered the camps and our families.

(cited in Fiddian-Qasmiyeh 2013a: 640)

Despite the pain of separation, she indicates that 'as the years passed, we got used to this, and now I do not see anyone crying, because she [sic] left the camps'.

In addition to the emotional loss experienced by virtue of having travelled to Libya as young children, a second major challenge arose as these boys and girls travelled to different countries to complete their studies; hence, after leaving her primary studies in Libya in 1984 (for reasons explained below), the above-cited young woman did not return to the Sahrawi camps, but rather pursued her secondary level studies in northern Algeria. Eventually, upon her return to her home-camp, the pain of having been separated from her family from such a young age, and the socio-linguistic and educational challenges faced in Algeria, were compounded, rather than mitigated:

[when I returned] I began living in a society that was different from the societies I had lived in previously, and therefore our lives were very difficult in the beginning. We were ridiculed a hundred times a day, they did not let us speak the Libyan dialect. If we behaved differently they used to laugh at us and made jokes. However, while studying in Algeria, it was easier to get accustomed again to the Sahrawi ways, because we returned to the camps every summer and we met many Sahrawi students who helped us to adapt to our traditions.

(cited in Chatty, Crivello and Fiddian-Qasmiyeh 2010: 69)

Libya and Algeria have often been conceptualised by Sahrawi children, youth and their families as being 'closer' than Cuba in a religious, cultural and dialectal sense, and yet graduates from Libya regularly referred to a wide range of difficulties upon their return to the camps, ranging from alienation from family members, to marginalisation and different forms of discrimination on the basis of linguistic differences and a lack of familiarity with the camps' socio-cultural and religious norms.[17]

Importantly, Cuban-educated Sahrawis' experiences of alienation, discrimination and marginalisation have typically been paralleled by high degrees of professional visibility and political audibility in the Sahrawi refugee camps (Chapter 4), and yet I would argue that Libyan-educated Sahrawis have in many ways remained on the margins in the camps following their return. A number of high profile Sahrawi/Polisario figures have, of course, studied in Libya, such as Fatma Mehdi, who was elected to be the Secretary General of the NUSW in 2002 (Fiddian-Qasmiyeh 2014a); nonetheless my interviews with a Libyan-educated male shopkeeper in the 27 February Refugee Camp were more representative of the accounts offered throughout my research in the Sahrawi camps: he reflected that he had found our conversations important since people 'like him' – who had been educated in Libya and spoke only Arabic – were rarely interviewed or listened to by Northern visitors to the camps.

This brief example draws attention to the fact that attending school in Libya enabled/required Sahrawi children and youth to study in Modern Standard Arabic (*Fus-ha*), in addition to learning the Libyan dialect, with a view to either continuing their studies in Libya, or to undergo onwards *educational* migration within the region (i.e. to study in Algeria or Syria). Unless these students subsequently travelled to Cuba (as had been the case for two of my interviewees in Cuba), these students could speak and understand multiple dialects and yet were effectively mono-lingual upon their return to the camps, and therefore had fewer opportunities to engage directly with European and North American *solidarios*, NGOs or researchers than their bilingual or trilingual counterparts. In turn, they had more limited opportunities to access professional employment with NGOs in the camps, to share their experiences with non-Sahrawi visitors, or to pursue onward migration as Cubaraui graduates have increasingly done to work across Spain.[18]

Views from (and of) the margins

Libyan-educated refugees have also remained marginal in at least two other regards. First, Sahrawi students' presence in Libya was not acknowledged by any of the Palestinians interviewed in Lebanon, in spite of Sahrawi graduates not only being aware of the presence of Palestinians in Libya but having themselves been taught by Palestinian teachers whilst completing their primary, secondary and tertiary level studies there.[19]

Second, Sahrawi *and* Palestinian refugees alike experienced multiple forms of marginalisation upon their return to their home-camps, reflecting implicit, and at times explicit, perceptions of a hierarchy of educational value and worth. Not only were Palestinian interviewees unable to secure employment opportunities in their areas of expertise following their return from Libya, but two Palestinians who had been forced to withdraw from their university degrees in chemistry in Libya for personal and political reasons (including as a result of mass expulsions) were unable to complete the equivalent degrees in Lebanon – both of these Libya-born students (Lina, a 40-year-old woman currently employed as an UNRWA Arabic language teacher, and Anas, a 36-year-old man working as an accountant and driver in Tripoli, Lebanon) had to start their degrees from the very beginning, and both shifted to study Arabic language and literature, rather than continuing with chemistry. While Palestinians who studied in Cuba were ultimately absorbed by UNRWA, those who were educated in Libya had to repeat or restart their studies, as if the value of a Libyan education were not recognised in Lebanon.

A third experience was also shared by Sahrawis and Palestinians in Libya – that of being physically displaced by, and from, the Libyan state (the experiences of the latter group are addressed in greater detail below): Sahrawi children who were based in Libya in the 1980s were directly affected by the diplomatic shifts that took place as a result of the Libya's rapprochement with Morocco, leading not only to a rupture in Gaddafi's political ties with the Polisario Front, but also to a temporary cessation of the educational programme and the expulsion of all Sahrawi students from the North African state:

> Since Libya re-established its diplomatic ties with Morocco in 1984, all Sahrawi students were expelled until the beginning of the 90s, when they returned again, but this time we were not treated like before… in recent years, young students in Libya have faced a degree of marginalisation and discrimination due to the good relations between this country [Libya] and Morocco
> (in Gimeno-Martín and Laman 2005: 31, my translation from Spanish)

Importantly, when the scholarship programme was eventually reinitiated in the late 1980s (when Libya protested at King Hassan's talks with the Israeli Prime Minister in July 1986), it was designed solely for secondary and tertiary level students. As such, although Libya had primarily been a location for young Sahrawi children to receive a primary education before moving on to complete their secondary and tertiary studies elsewhere in the region and further afield, when the programme restarted in the 1990s, no primary-level children were among the hundreds of (and at times over a thousand) Sahrawi youth who received a Libyan scholarship every year between the 1990s and early 2011. In light of the pain of separation, the difficulties of/upon return, and the violence experienced by those Sahrawi who were studying in Libya at the outbreak of the uprising in 2011, it is not entirely evident that this shift was necessarily a negative one overall.

It could be argued that the historical shifts which led Gaddafi to end the primary level scholarship programme in the mid-1980s had a significant impact on the educational trajectories of all Sahrawi children, since the satisfactory completion of a primary level education is a prerequisite to accessing secondary and tertiary level institutions; it could furthermore be argued that this could have had an even greater impact on Sahrawi girls than on boys. This is arguably the case because completing primary level education outside the Sahrawi camps has historically not only supplemented the limited educational infrastructure in the camps, but has also been as a way of redressing gender disparities in camp-based school attendance, lower female enrolment rates in the camps, and the early withdrawal of girls from camp schools, especially from the upper primary level onwards (WFP 2004: 6–7; Fiddian-Qasmiyeh 2011, 2014a).

However, even after the shift away from primary level schooling, a high proportion of Sahrawi girls and young women continued to participate in the Libyan scholarship programme throughout the 2000s: for instance, 350 female students – out of a total 700 Sahrawi students – were reportedly studying in Libya by the early 2000s (SPS 2001), and it is calculated that teenage girls and young women in their early twenties accounted for the majority of over 900 Sahrawi refugee-students who were waiting to be evacuated from the Libyan uprising at the end of February 2011 (see Fiddian-Qasmiyeh 2012). The high rate of female participation throughout this period is itself particularly pertinent when compared with the gender ratio of Cuban-educated Sahrawi students, but also because it highlights the longer-term gendered implications of the end of the Libya scholarship programme following the 2011 uprising: girls and young women can no longer study at primary, secondary or tertiary levels either in Cuba (see Chapters 3 and 4) or in Libya, leaving them with only one opportunity to study on a collective level outside the camps – in schools and universities dispersed across the Algerian territory.[20]

Algeria has always been the country offering an education to the largest number of male and female Sahrawi students alike, both because Algeria has 'hosted' the Sahrawi since the mid-1970s, but also because of the abovementioned conceptualisation of certain national and regional spaces as being 'closer' to the Sahrawi – this proximity has been perceived to exist not only in religious, cultural and dialectal terms, as indicated above, but also in gendered terms. That a large number of Sahrawi girls have historically studied in Libya – with many of my camp-based interviewees reporting that girls were in fact the *majority* of Sahrawi students in that country – and in Algeria, while girls and young women effectively stopped travelling to study in Cuba from the late 1980s onwards, reflects the extent to which Algeria and Libya have effectively been perceived to be 'fraternal', and even 'core', spaces while Cuba has been viewed as 'foreign', and 'peripheral'.

As such, Sahrawi girls and women not only remained – figuratively speaking – 'within their families' sight' when studying in Algeria and Libya, but were also seen to be embraced by a common socio-cultural sphere. These markers and identifiers were not only perceived to be 'similar' to Sahrawi norms and views, but were at times even perceived to be 'better' than those in students' home-camps. This conclusion was also shared by a number of Palestinian interviewees in Lebanon, including 36-year-old Anas – who referred to Libyans as 'very devout Muslims' – and Lina, who was born in Libya and now works as an Arabic teacher in UNRWA schools in Lebanon: 'In Libya my family and I used to live in an environment characterised by profound family values and ideal social relations but when we returned to the camp in Lebanon we felt that these dynamics have lost their value.'

Whilst experiencing a form of alienation upon her 'return' to the Palestinian camps in Lebanon, Lina's account of the strength of family values in Libya is in direct contrast, on the one hand, with MENA interviewees' fears of 'losing your Arabness' and needing special tools to 'defend yourself' from Cuban society (cited in Chapter 3), and, on the other hand, with the experiences of family fragmentation which arose as a result of young Sahrawi boys' and girls' participation in the Libyan scholarship system.

Palestinian 'self-service' in Libya: individual and family migration

If Sahrawi refugees taking up Libyan scholarships were separated from their families and broader community from as young as the age of six until the 1980s and as older children and adolescents from the 1990s until 2011, Palestinians migrated to Libya individually as (young) adults, or as families who, in turn, became part of the extensive and well-established Palestinian community in Libya.[21]

When addressing the motivating factors behind their migratory trajectories, the combination of being able to access work and education in Libya, rather than benefiting from (or requiring) an institutionalised form of support such as an official scholarship system, emerged throughout all of the interviews in Lebanon; this was the case whether interviewees had migrated individually to Libya in the 1970s and 1980s, or had been born in Libya to parents who had left the refugee camps in Lebanon in search of a 'better life' in the late 1970s and 1980s.

Hakim – a 60-year-old man who taught at Libyan institutes and completed a postgraduate degree in music there between 1979 and 1984, and who was working as a private tutor in Baddawi Camp when interviewed in 2014 – indicated that he had decided to leave Lebanon for Libya because 'it was the only available option' as a result of the restrictions faced by Palestinians attempting to travel to work in the Gulf. He stated:

> I graduated from Egypt holding a degree in musicology, but when I looked for a job in Lebanon, I couldn't find anything. I also considered travelling to the Gulf, but my attempts were not fruitful. Libya was the only opportunity available then.

He and three other interviewees explained that they had travelled to Libya in the late 1970s and early 1980s with the expectation of working as teachers there: 'In every Libyan city there was a Palestinian Teachers' Union – that tells you a lot about the huge numbers of Palestinian teachers who were working across Libya in different cities during that time' (Saad, Baddawi Camp).

While the restrictions on Palestinians' employment in Lebanon outlined in the preceding chapter clearly influenced many Palestinians' decision to leave their home-camps to find jobs elsewhere in the region, depicting Libya as a destination chosen by Palestinians from Lebanon solely for economic/employment reasons is misleading for many reasons.

The difficulties faced by Palestinians attempting to work and live in other Arab states, including in particular the oil-rich Gulf states, at this time were perhaps most clearly embodied by Kasem, a 42-year-old man originally from Baddawi Camp in Lebanon but whose parents had migrated to work in the Gulf in the 1970s and who indicated that he had travelled to pursue his studies in Libya because he was one of the hundreds of thousands of Palestinians who was 'expelled from Kuwait [as a result of the Gulf War] and I wasn't able to travel to any other countries in the Gulf'. The expulsion of Palestinians from Kuwait is part of the long history of mass expulsions of Palestinians from host countries across the region, including from Jordan in 1970, from Iraq in 2003, and from Libya in 1971, 1995, 2007 and, most recently, in 2011, as discussed below (also see Lesch 1991; Shiblak 1996; Fiddian-Qasmiyeh 2012). Such experiences of individualised and mass violence and displacement were justified on diverse grounds, including the perception that Palestinians were a threat to the host state's political or sectarian balance (Mason 2011: 357, also 2008; Brand 1988), and due to Palestinians' imputed political affiliation with nationalist leaders precisely because these leaders – such as Saddam Hussein (Mason 2011: 366), but also Gaddafi – had tolerated or encouraged their presence. This reminds us that, throughout the region, both official and popular forms of hostipitality towards Palestinians have prevailed in spite of declarations of support for Pan-Arabism in general and the Palestinian cause and people in particular (also see Badwan 2011).

Indeed, the Palestinians who migrated to work in Libya in the 1960s, 1970s and 1980s, and whose Libyan-educated children were interviewed as part of this research, had made this decision both as an employment strategy, but also in light of the socio-economic, political and physical insecurity faced by Palestinians in Lebanon at the time. With reference to the former, Lina's father had reportedly 'travelled to Libya hoping to find a job in the field of teaching in 1968' – a year before the Libyan *coup d'état* led by Gaddafi – and yet by the mid-1970s, Anas explained that his family had travelled to Libya for a number of intersecting reasons:

> I was born in Libya in 1978, after my father had travelled there in 1976, during the Lebanese civil war [which started in 1975]. He travelled there to escape the difficult security situation in Lebanon, and went to Libya because it was the only Arab country which allowed Palestinians access with relatively easy bureaucratic procedures. For instance, Palestinians were able to enter Libya without a visa, and job opportunities were available to Palestinians [while they were not available in Lebanon].

He summarised his father's decision as follows: 'My father chose Libya because it was the only country available then, especially after the Lebanese civil war, but also because Palestinians were welcomed in Libya and we felt embraced by Gaddafi.'

The relative ease with which Palestinians were able to access Libya, and the sense of being 'embraced by Gaddafi' were repeatedly highlighted throughout the interviews, with Hakim noting the extent to which Gaddafi supported the Palestinians for 'humanitarian reasons' as part of what Saif – a 60-year-old man who had spent the 1980s teaching in Libya – referred to as a broader form of

'Libyan solidarity for Palestinians'. Nonetheless, as explored in more detail below, Hakim situated this humanitarian dimension within Gaddafi's broader tendency to 'manipulate Palestinians', as reflected in his 'fluctuating temperament' (a term used by Saad) and the implementation of divergent policies towards Palestinians at different geopolitical stages.

Support and dependence: Palestinians and Gaddafi

The multi-directional, if fluctuating, nature of the relationship between Palestinians and Gaddafi was highlighted by Ameen, a physics specialist who taught in Libya for five years in the late 1980s and early 1990s before returning to work in an UNRWA school in Lebanon. He argued that

> I think that Libya's support for Palestinians emerged in the 1950s, but it was after the Fatih Revolution led by Gaddafi *that Libya started to rely on Palestinian teachers and specialists*. This was mainly because he had a very strong relationship with some of the Palestinian factions during that time. He was also trying to present himself as The Arab Leader, and was using Libya's extensive natural resources to maintain these programmes.
>
> (Emphasis added)

Ameen thus argues that Gaddafi's support for Palestinians was paralleled by his dependence upon Palestinians in educational terms, but it could be posited that this dependence also had political, and indeed military, dimensions – through supporting Palestinians, Gaddafi's position as The Arab Leader could be reasserted both externally, and internally. The presence of Palestinians, and, indeed, other refugee groups, in Libya therefore simultaneously enabled Gaddafi to strengthen his external claims to be the Protector of Arab Unity but also helped him maintain and strengthen an otherwise weak national education system, thereby officially fulfilling his duty towards his own citizens.

In effect, throughout this period Samira recalled that

> School teachers were mainly Libyan and Egyptian whereas at university the majority of the lecturers were exiled Shi'a Iraqis [from the Saddam Hussein era] who were adopted politically by Qaddafi. As a sign of support, Qaddafi built their dormitories near the universities.

In addition to supporting Iraqi lecturers in this way, Lina indicated that 'some Iraqis, in particular lecturers during that time, who feared persecution in their home country, were given political asylum and the opportunity in live in Libya permanently'. By relying on exiled and refugee groups such as Shi'a Iraqis and Palestinians (in particular those from the Popular Front General Command and Fatah al-Intifada[22]) as teachers, and offering scholarships to groups such as the Sahrawi and Palestinians from specific factions, Gaddafi could simultaneously uphold himself as a hospitable Pan-Arabist leader committed to the liberation and claims for self-determination of Arab peoples across the region, whilst refusing to allow such opportunities for groups such as the Amazigh or Tuareg within Libya itself. Presenting himself, externally, as a supportive, anti-colonial leader thereby enabled him to continue implementing oppressive and discriminatory policies internally, reflecting the accolades which he received externally (including the Grand Cross of the Order of Good Hope which he received from South Africa in 2007) and the denunciations of human rights violations internally (i.e. Amnesty International 2010).

Military scholarships

The role of education in Libya as part of a broader context of Palestinian–Libyan collaboration comes to the fore when we consider the extent to which schooling and university studies were primarily undertaken by Palestinians via a strategy of self-service, but formal scholarships were offered for certain Palestinians to attend *military* colleges in Libya.

The discrepancies between the different models of support for non-Libyan students were highlighted by Kasem, who noted that not all scholarships were equal:

> To a large extent, the scholarships which Palestinians were offered to study in Libya were symbolic, especially when compared with the scholarships which were offered by the Libyan government to other Arab students who also received some financial help. Some Yemeni and Syrian students, for instance, were offered pocket money and a daily allowance, in addition to a scholarship to cover the small tuition fees.

While arguing that Palestinians were not offered scholarships to complete *university* degrees, Anas, Kasem and Saif all stressed that when Palestinians *were* offered scholarships, these were specifically granted to support Palestinians' access to *military college*:

> Non-Arab students chose to study in Libya because of the difficult socioeconomic situations in their home countries and because education was available free of charge and without obstacles. Although studying at university was free of charge, a scholarship scheme existed to give Palestinian students access to military education.

> (Anas)

With reference to this military training, Kasem argued that

> Before I travelled to Libya, I was aware that there had been a strong military collaboration between Libya and some Palestinian factions in the late 1980s, and I knew that some Palestinians were studying and teaching on such programmes [i.e. members of the Popular Front, General Command, and Fatah al-Intifada].

I think that the main reason behind Gaddafi's scholarships for Palestinians was that he was trying to promote his notion of the People's Republic.

As was the case in Palestinian accounts of the Cuban scholarship system, a discrepancy also emerged regarding the system through which scholarships were selected. For instance, Samira, an UNRWA teacher who was born in Libya in 1973 and who completed her primary and secondary schooling, in addition to three years of her chemistry degree, in Libya, explained that

> Education in Libya was available to everybody indiscriminately, but during our time living there, Libya used to receive Palestinian students from Gaza and the West Bank who *were also funded by the PLO*. I believe that these scholarships used to cover the students' daily expenses and their travels.
> (Emphasis added)

In turn, Kasem believed that 'Palestinian factions, rather than the Libyan government, allocated scholarships for Palestinian youth to study in Libya'. Indeed, although Saif posited that the Libyan government was the overarching administrator of the scholarships which were offered to non-Palestinian Arab students, he remained convinced that

> Scholarships were secured through collaboration between the Libyan regime and some Palestinian factions which were politically close [to the Libyans]. Certainly, students' political affiliation played a significant role in the allocation of these scholarships and also in the way that certain specialisations were distributed and shared amongst candidates.

Education: quality and content

The Cuban education system is internationally recognised, and even 'ranked as one of the best, if not the best in the global South' (Breidlid 2013: 141), with Sahrawi and Palestinian students and graduates referring to it as a well-structured education programme which aimed to provide Sahrawis and Palestinians with a professional training which would maximise their professional, and national, self-sufficiency upon their return to their places of origin. Conversely, although even the most critical of interviewees highlighted the advantages and opportunities accrued by virtue of teaching and/or studying in Libya, four interviewees in particular referred to the inherent weaknesses of Libya's education system, for Libyans and non-Libyans alike. Drawing a direct comparison between the Cuban and Libyan education systems, Hakim denounced that

> The education programmes in Libya weren't of a good standard, especially when compared to countries such as Cuba which had very minimal economic capabilities. Libya did not have the educational infrastructure and experience necessary, and these programmes were mismanaged as a result.

Saif equally argued that 'The programmes were chaotic and lacked sense of direction. They lacked relevant specialisations', explaining further that the 'teaching there lacked good cadres and effective administration'.

These Palestinian teachers' perspectives were echoed by Lara, who was born in Libya in 1981 and completed her primary and secondary schooling in Libya before starting her foundation year at university there:

> Studying in Libya was not good at all. It lacked qualified cadres with relevant experience. I would say that teachers in Libya were merely employees and not individuals who carried a human message. Actually, the majority of the teachers in Libya were not Libyan, which shows that this domain was totally neglected by the Libyans themselves.

Despite these and other criticisms of the Libyan education system, including Lara's implicit critique of the non-Libyan teachers who taught there, as a whole interviewees praised both the education system and the non-Libyan teachers and university professors who sustained the system. At tertiary level institutions, Iraqi university professors in particular were celebrated as quintessential Arab brothers who transcended the Libyan curriculum, drew on their own academic materials and effectively started an educational revolution from within the Libyan system.

Supplementing the Libyan curriculum in this way was, it was argued, particularly welcome given the extent to which the official curriculum was ideologically, rather than pedagogically, oriented: although Lara argued that education in Libya 'carried a humanitarian outlook', Kasem held that far from promoting the development of a professional specialisation, 'The education programme was largely based on a Pan-Arabist model, and the basic principle of the education system was to promote the idea of Arab unity, of transforming the Arab peoples into one country.'

Interviewees such as Hakim thus recalled that 'classes in Libyan schools were mainly pan-Arabist – reading the Green Book was more important than pursuing a specialisation itself', with Samira indicating that 'at secondary school we studied a module called "Cultural Awareness" and also the *Green Book*, which focused on Gaddafi's ideas on Arab nationalism'. Far from the internationalist framework espoused in Cuba's education system, students in Libya were thus exposed to a firmly regional approach – Lina recalled that 'History and Geography both revolved around the Arab region, mainly focusing on the paradigm of Arab Unity.'

The explicit ideological component of the Libyan education system did not lead to the indoctrination of Palestinian students, with interviewees paralleling the experiences and accounts of Cuban-educated Palestinians both through the clear critical distance which the interviewees reflected in their accounts of the respective education system, but also given the multi-directional relationship between the ideological underpinnings of the Palestinians on the one hand and of the education providers on the other. The latter was explained most clearly by Ameen: 'Libya's liberation ideology benefited greatly from the Palestinian liberation project.'

Palestinian–Libyan relations: a 'special' relationship?

The relationship between Gaddafi and the Palestinian liberation project, however, was intrinsically fraught, fluctuating as Gaddafi's relationship with the Sahrawi leadership had done in the 1980s when Libya prioritised the broad ideological aim of establishing a Maghrebian alliance over the individual or collective rights of the Sahrawi students who were expelled in 1984 or of the Polisario/SADR which was disowned in order to strengthen Gaddafi's negotiating position with Morocco.

This prioritisation of a particular interpretation of ideological imperatives was recognised by interviewees as being both highly political, but also intrinsically personal, both in terms of Gaddafi's motivations, and in terms of the ultimate outcomes for the Palestinians affected.

With reference to Gaddafi's role(s) in allowing or encouraging Palestinians to work and study in Libya, Ameen argued that 'sadly, these programmes didn't evolve due to a variety of *political* reasons, including disagreements between Gaddafi and Arafat' and Saif equally noted that 'these programmes did not evolve due to the *personal* clashes between Gaddafi and Yasser Arafat' (emphasis added). Whether denominated a political or personal disagreement,[23] numerous examples demonstrate the extent to which Gaddafi's relationship with Palestinians in Libya was dependent upon a combination of national (internal) and regional (external) tensions.

On the one hand, Palestinians were offered many opportunities in Libya, with interviewees including Hakim, Lina and Saad remarking that they were welcomed and treated like brothers (sic) or even, in Ameen's view, as Libyan citizens; effectively, they had become part of the Libyan Self. A number of relevant policies were identified in this regard, with Anas indicating that

> We [Palestinians] were treated as if we were Libyans. For instance, when a new decree or law was issued, like when the state introduced certain fees for Arab visiting students, that law was always followed by another decree which would automatically exclude Palestinians from this legislation.

A concrete example of this approach was referred to by Samira, who explained:

> When I studied there, education in Libya was free of charge – even the textbooks were free each year. I recall once that in the early 1990s the Libyan government decided to impose tuition fees on non-Libyan students, but shortly after the issuing of this ruling the Libyan government issued another law which immediately excluded Palestinians from having to pay this fee.

Within the broader context of an open Pan-Arabist education system, Palestinians were thus made the exception,[24] positioning them as quasi-Libyan citizens, rather than as non-Libyan Arab visiting students. Samira argued that 'Gaddafi treated Palestinians as Libyans and we were favoured at times because we are both refugees and Arab', and Kasem equally specified that 'on the basis of their refugee status, on an official level Palestinians enjoyed some special privileges which facilitated their daily lives in Libya'.

On the other hand, this special status was ultimately dependent upon Gaddafi's official statements, which oscillated in line with internal and external events. Far from Palestinians systematically being treated 'as Libyans' and being exempted from legislation which differentiated between Libyan and non-Libyan students, Anas explained that:

> University subjects were allocated according to the student's average mark, and during that time, Palestinians and other non-Libyan Arabs studying in Libya had to obtain a 10% higher mark than Libyan students to secure their preferred subject. If Libyan students were able to study Engineering with 85 per cent, Palestinians and other visiting students needed to get 95 per cent.

This uneven mechanism for the allocation of subjects was complemented by other measures described by Lina: 'During my time at university Gaddafi issued a law banning Arabs, including Palestinians, from joining university in first term. This procedure was employed in order to differentiate between Libyans and the rest of Arabs in Libya.'

In addition to institutionalising this educational edge for Libyans, at other times Gaddafi reportedly excluded Palestinians from undertaking specific courses in order to strengthen his position *vis-à-vis* Libyan citizens: 'In some years Gaddafi banned Palestinians from doing medicine or engineering because he perceived us as being high-achievers and believed that [our results] would affect the opportunities of Libyan citizens who wished to study the same subjects...'

Such an approach corresponds closely to what Derrida refers to as the law of hospitality's prerequisite that the host 'looks after himself and sees to and considers all that concerns him and thereby affirms the law of hospitality as the law of the household' (2000a: 4). In this regard, Samira explained,

> Gaddafi was a very inconsistent leader... In the end, he decided to ban Palestinians from studying medicine because they had always achieved the highest grades and also due to the large sums of money the Libyan regime used to spend on medical students.

The exclusion of Palestinians specifically from medicine and engineering is particularly significant given that these are precisely the degrees which Cuba prioritised for Palestinians and Sahrawis for over three decades.

In addition to these bureaucratic measures revealing that Gaddafi's 'hospitality' and 'generosity' could always be withdrawn, the potential for broader discrimination and physical violence on both an official and on a communal level were also present. Lina argued that on an official level during most of her time living in Libya 'we were treated as brothers [sic] who were living amongst their own people' and yet in the late 1980s

Gaddafi institutionalised two different colour codes for [car] registration plates: the green one was for Libyans and the yellow and green one was for the rest of the population. Because of these colours, some Palestinians were identified as foreigners and as a result they were beaten by locals. For some Libyans, Palestinians were stealing Libyan resources.

More acutely, as reflected by Saad,

Palestinians' opportunities to work and study in Libya relied heavily on Gaddafi's temperament. At times there were too many opportunities for us but at other times these same opportunities were blocked. I would like to share an incident with you that involved five Palestinian teachers who were caught and hanged by the Revolutionary Committees for teaching the principles of Islam to students in the city of Adjabia on the morning of the Eid in 1982. That incident was mainly prompted by a well-known saying by Gaddafi which read: *Man TaHazzaba Khaana* – 'He who joins a party is deemed to be a traitor'.

Such policies, inter alia, were designed to control Palestinians and other populations within Libya, but their influence also extended beyond North Africa both to Palestinians' home-camps and also across the broader Palestinian refugee diaspora, as evidenced in the 1980s when Saad indicated that 'Palestinians were banned from transferring money to their families in the refugee camps in Lebanon'.

In addition to controlling remittances, tensions between Gaddafi and the PLO repeatedly led to accentuated processes of exclusion and discrimination towards Palestinian individuals, families and communities, as the culmination of the processes of hostipitality outlined above, effectively sacrificing the Palestinian individual, family and broader community in order to 'protect' Gaddafi's vision of/for the Palestinian nation on the one hand and his Pan-Arabist dream on the other. The increasing insecurity experienced by Palestinians, and the resurgent threats of expulsion experienced by Palestinians, and indeed by Sahrawi refugees as discussed above, thus represent the *hostipitable* dynamics inherent within Gaddafi's approach to these groups, and yet are also consistent with Gaddafi's ideology and view of himself at the Protector of the Palestinians, of the Sahrawi and of Arab Unity.

Protection through expulsion?

And as I care about the Palestinian cause, and in order to achieve the best interest of Palestinians, I will expel the thirty thousand Palestinians who currently live in my land, and *try to secure their return to Gaza and Jericho.* If Israel would not let them in, while Egypt does not allow them to pass through its territories, then I shall set a great camp for them on the Egyptian-Libyan borders.

(Gaddafi, quoted by Sarhan in Al-Majdal 2010: 46, emphasis added)

As a means of protesting the PLO's signing of the Oslo Accords, in September 1995 Gaddafi threatened to expel all of the estimated 30,000 Palestinians who were based in Libya. Irrespective of Palestinians' factional or organisational affiliation (or none), Gaddafi ultimately considered the PLO to be 'the' representative of all Palestinians in Libya, leading him to collectively punish Palestinians through the threat of expulsion, and subsequent implementation of this threat, in 1995.

Three of the interviewees who participated in this research had personally experienced expulsions in the region: Kasem was expelled from Kuwait during the Gulf War, while Hakim and Anas were both expelled from Libya by Gaddafi in 1995, with Hakim returning to Lebanon, while Anas remained stranded on the Libya/Egypt border for a year:

> It was not my choice to leave Libya. Gaddafi expelled the Palestinians after his disagreement with Yasser Arafat – in spite of the majority of Palestinians in Libya opposing Yasser Arafat and his policies, Gaddafi considered that Yasser Arafat embodied all Palestinians. If Arafat made a mistake, all of us would suffer as a result.

It is estimated that 13,000 Palestinians were deported over the course of the following eight months, with 17,000 reportedly remaining in the country by May 1996 (Al-Majdal 2010: 47; on the processes of deportation, and the challenges of gaining access to other MENA countries at the time, see Fiddian-Qasmiyeh 2012).

In line with Gaddafi's highly paradoxical conceptualisation of 'protection',[25] Palestinians' expulsion from Libya in 1995 was presented in his 1995 speech (cited above) as a means of securing 'their return to Gaza and Jericho'. In effect, the name of the 'great camp' which Gaddafi established in September 1995 on the Salloum border between Libya and Egypt clearly centralised the Palestinian right of return, as enshrined in UN Resolutions 194 and 3236: *Mukhayyam Al-Awda* (the Return Camp).

It can be argued that Gaddafi's strategy in 1995–1996 was ostensibly to draw attention to Palestinians' *inability* to return to Gaza and Jericho, utilising the mass concentration of highly visible Palestinians at the border to challenge the political status quo: in September 1995, 32 Palestinians were stranded in the 'Egyptian-Libyan no-man's land', by October 1995 approximately 900 Palestinians were stuck at the border, and over 200 remained by January 1996, unable to leave Libya and enter Egyptian territory (Goddard 2009: 502; Al-Majdal 2010: 47).

Indeed, unlike the 2011 Libyan uprising, which witnessed thousands of Palestinians actively attempting to leave Libya in order to escape the violence engulfing the country (Fiddian-Qasmiyeh 2012), in 1995–1996 a large proportion of Palestinians were forcibly collected, transported and deported by Gaddafi's forces; by the end of September 1995 alone, 1,500 Palestinians had been transported to the Tubrok Camp in the north-east of Libya, in preparation of deportation by land (via the Salloum border) or sea (Al-Majdal 2010: 47).

Thirty-six-year-old Palestinian, Anas, recounted his personal experiences of expulsion to the Libyan margins:

> Sadly, I had to desert my studies in Chemical Engineering as Gaddafi's regime forced me to leave my family in 1995 and to reside on the border for an entire year. This happened after I had finished my second year at university, and it was prompted because of Gaddafi's stance on the Oslo Accords. When I was allowed to return to Libya, the University refused to allow me to continue my studies; I was denied my right to return. My dreams were shattered... On a social level, forcing an individual to leave all of his family and to live on his own in the desert for an entire year, was a very difficult experience which imposed suffering not just on me individually but on my entire family.

Following the 1995–1996 mass expulsions, an unknown number of Palestinians, including Anas, eventually returned to Libya, but found themselves in a highly tentative and uncertain situation; thousands reportedly stayed in an irregular status, fearful of renewing their work permits and engaging with the Libyan authorities.[26]

Such fears are grounded in an acute awareness of the vulnerability of Palestinians in the country (and, indeed, broader region), as the 1995–1996 episode was neither the first, nor the last, instance of Palestinians' expulsion from Libya: hundreds of Palestinian migrant workers were expelled in March 1971 (Otman and Karlberg 2007: 36) and, in March 2007, Gaddafi had once again threatened to deport all Palestinians to Gaza 'in retaliation for the latest Arab peace initiative' (Nahmias 2007). This vulnerability was accentuated even further in the context of the 2011 Libyan uprising, to which the chapter now turns.

Palestinians and Sahrawis in the 2011 Libyan uprising

Following the North African popular uprisings (known as the *Arab Spring*) which started in Tunisia in December 2010, by February 2011, anti-government protests in Libya had rapidly escalated to a major conflict characterised by widespread attacks between pro- and anti-Gaddafi forces, a NATO-coordinated bombardment of the country, and mass internal and international displacement. Between February 2011 and late August/early September, UNHCR reported that over 990,000 people – including Libyans, third country nationals and MENA refugees – had crossed from Libya to Tunisia, and 468,000 had fled to Egypt via the Salloum border crossing; it was estimated that over 200,000 people had been internally displaced within Libya itself (UNHCR EXCOM 2011). Amongst others, this acute crisis affected approximately 900 Sahrawi refugees participating in the official scholarship programme, 104 Palestinian students who were reportedly attending university and military academies in Libya as scholarship holders, and an estimated 50,000–70,000 Palestinians who were working and studying in Libya at the time.

Sahrawis

Although Sahrawi refugees' experiences in Libya were generally invisible in English-language sources, the Spanish media, including Spain's national newspaper *El País*, placed Sahrawis in Libya at the forefront of its reports,[27] drawing upon Sahrawi students' testimonials alongside those of Libyan citizens and third country migrant workers to outline conditions in the country. For instance, the experiences of two Sahrawi young women aged 17 and 19 who had studied in Libya since they were 12 were relayed to/by *El País* through two main news articles (*El País* 2011; Muñoz 2011) specifying that:

> All of the Libyan personnel in the Centre [the Sahrawi boarding school in Benghazi] abandoned the institution when the conflict started between the security forces and the demonstrators. Not even the cooks remained. They left the girls, without food, until the people on the street started to feed them out of charity.
>
> (Muñoz 2011, author's translation)

On 7 March 2011 the Sahrawi Press Service (SPS) reported that two days earlier, 'some 916 Sahrawi students who pursued their secondary and university education and vocational training in Libya' had returned safely from Libya to the Sahrawi refugee camps (El-Hafed 2011). SPS (2011) was informed by the Sahrawi Minister of Education, Mariem Salek Hmada, that

> All the Sahrawi students in Libya, including girls, arrived safe and healthy [sic] in the Sahrawi refugee camps... The students have been repatriated[28] under good conditions and without incident.
>
> (Ibid.)

Shortly after the outbreak of violence in 2011, the Polisario representative to Madrid is reported to have stated that: 'the Sahrawi adolescents who are studying in Libya are "safe"', reiterating that 'the Sahrawi authorities have not considered an evacuation plan "yet"'.[29] These statements were made as a 'response' to the 'concerns demonstrated by various Spanish families who, years ago, hosted some of these young Sahrawis when they were children'.[30] In this instance, Spanish civil society, therefore, felt a responsibility not only to trace the situation of Spanish citizens affected by the conflict in Libya, but also that of one particular refugee group with whom they have a long-standing connection, including through the migration of Sahrawi children to Spain via a Holidays in Peace programme (on the latter, see Crivello and Fiddian-Qasmiyeh 2010). Despite their initial dismissal of an evacuation plan, Polisario ultimately secured the evacuation of these children and adolescents.[31]

Upon the children's departure, UNHCR reported that they have been 'informed' of the evacuation of 753 Sahrawi from Benghazi on an Algerian boat.[32] This in turn leads us to ask why UNHCR was 'informed' rather than more proactively involved in (if not *responsible for*) their evacuation. Furthermore, it is unclear to what extent UNHCR was in fact aware of the presence, whereabouts, total number and protection needs of these refugee children in Libya, or whether it considered itself to be responsible for the protection of these refugees (as they have been in the past in the case of Cuban-based Sahrawi students). While Algeria's intervention to evacuate the Sahrawi children and youth from Libya could be interpreted as a 'normal' part of its responsibilities as the Sahrawi's asylum state, it is notable that Algeria has in the past explicitly refused to accept that it is legally responsible for the human rights of Sahrawi refugees, *as* the Sahrawi's 'host state' and *de jure* authority over the camps. Rather, Algeria 'holds that it bears no responsibility with regard to the human rights situation of the Sahrawi people', since it recognises the SADR's jurisdiction and, in effect sovereignty, over the camps (OHCHR 2006: 13; Fiddian-Qasmiyeh 2014b).

Palestinians

Although the presence of Sahrawi refugees in Libya remained largely unnoticed by the international community (with the exception of Spanish audiences) until their evacuation in March 2011, the UN, United States Department of State and OCHA regularly documented the numbers of Palestinians attempting to cross the Libyan–Egyptian border, those prevented from doing so, and those evacuated to a number of locations(see Fiddian-Qasmiyeh 2012). UNHCR regularly included such details under the 'protection' heading of its reports: for instance, by 18 May, 'some 655 Palestinians' had been supported by UNHCR (UNHCR 2011a), and by 3 June 'UNHCR ha[d] also helped 765 Palestinians stranded in a no man's land to travel to Gaza, through the Rafah border crossing, in Egypt' (UNHCR 2011b). As in 1995, the Salloum border witnessed mass population movements, and major restrictions on Palestinians' attempts to cross the Libyan–Egyptian border to seek safety.

With reference to the evacuation of Palestinian students from Libya, the Palestinian ambassador in Tripoli (Atif Mustafa Auda) informed the media that by 6 March 2011 all 104 Palestinian refugee students who were attending university and military academies in Libya at the time had been evacuated from the country (*Ma'an* 2011b). While the Palestinian ambassador is cited as declaring that the evacuation of the Palestinian students had been ordered by Palestinian President Mahmoud Abbas, the students themselves contested this account in the media, claiming that the Palestinian Authority failed to evacuate the students, with Jordan having reportedly offered to transport them alongside their own citizens, even if they did not hold Jordanian travel documents (*Ma'an* 2011a, 2011b). It must be acknowledged that the Palestinian Authority, like the Polisario Front, has limited resources, as stressed by Nidhal Abu Dukhan (the Palestinian military intelligence director) to *Ma'an* News Agency, which reports that '[he] added that the Palestinians did not have the capabilities to evacuate its nationals, as other countries have done' (2011a).

While all Sahrawi refugees were eventually evacuated by the Algerian government to the Algerian-based Sahrawi refugee camps, precisely where Palestinian refugees should, could or might have wanted to be safely evacuated to, and by whom, was a much more complex issue, especially in light of the protracted humanitarian crises and degrading living conditions across Gaza, the refugee camps in Lebanon and the increasingly explosive situation in Syria, where even during the earliest stages of the Syrian conflict, Syrian forces had attacked the Palestinian refugee camps in Yarmouk (June 2011), Hama (July 2011) and Latakia (August 2011), with the latter displacing over 5,000 Palestinians (Dar Al-Hayat 2011; *The Guardian* 2011; also see Fiddian-Qasmiyeh 2012).[33]

Indeed, the Syrian forces' use of violence against Palestinian refugees in that country reflects the extent to which Palestinians in the region have often been subjected not only to 'general violence' and 'mass displacement' alongside other conflict affected populations, but have often been purposefully targeted for their imputed political opinions and affiliations. In March 2012, the *World Tribune* reported: 'Syrian regime said to target Palestinians *who won't fight uprising*' (emphasis added).

In the context of the 2011 Libyan conflict, Sahrawis and Palestinians were both reportedly targeted by both pro- and anti-Gaddafi supporters alike. As such, although all of the 104 Palestinian scholarship holders had been evacuated from Libya by early March 2011, at least one Palestinian scholarship holder (a young man from Khan Younis in the Gaza Strip who had been studying engineering in Misrata University) is reported to have been killed in Libya during the violence. The particular vulnerability of this cohort of young refugees was highlighted by his sister (cited in IMEMC 2011): 'there is a dangerous level of incitement against the Palestinians in Libya ... the mercenaries of the Qaddafi regime are responsible for several attacks against the Palestinians in the country'.

Other news reports also asserted that Gaddafi's forces had 'detained Palestinians studying at a military college in the northwestern city [of Misrata] after they refused to join the pro-regime forces' (Ma'an 2011a). In turn, these and other examples of Palestinians' refusal to join pro-Gaddafi forces strengthened anti-Gaddafi supporters' assumption that Palestinians were themselves Gaddafi's mercenaries (*murtazaqa*) precisely due to the support which he had offered them – including military scholarships – throughout the preceding decades.[34]

The Arab Spring, therefore, affected Sahrawis and Palestinians studying – and working – in Libya in numerous ways: they experienced the generalised violence but also, at times, were targeted precisely because of the close political relationship with Gaddafi which had facilitated the allocation of scholarships to begin with.

Furthermore, although the 2011 crisis was not orchestrated by Gaddafi in the way that the mass expulsions of 1995 were, it was equally characterised by thousands of Palestinians being forcibly displaced, while thousands of others were unable to cross the Libyan borders to Tunisia or Egypt, even when holding valid travel documents; these experiences visibly demonstrate the ongoing vulnerability faced in particular by Palestinians in the region, for whom the parallel processes of conflict-induced displacement and conflict-induced immobility, whilst characterised by an unprecedented degree of violence in 2011, may have been experienced as an instance of history repeating itself, yet again.

Conclusion

Thousands of Sahrawi refugee children who would otherwise have been unable to complete their basic education in their desert-based home-camps, accessed primary and secondary level schools in Libya through a structured scholarship programme which laid the foundations for their onward migration to pursue their tertiary studies elsewhere in the region (or, indeed, in Cuba), or for their return to the camps. Developed via a bilateral agreement between Libya and the Polisario/SADR which echoed Cuba's scholarship system for Sahrawi refugees, this highly institutionalised mode of support differed extensively from Palestinians' experiences of engaging in what I have referred to in this chapter as 'self-service' in Libya. Palestinians' ability to 'help themselves' to an education or to maintain their families in Libya (through their salaries) and in the camps in Lebanon (via remittances) may have been facilitated by Gaddafi's policies at times, and yet did not result from comprehensively designed policies per se. As such, although a small number of Palestinians received scholarships to attend military college, most post-adolescent Palestinians journeyed to Libya knowing that few bureaucratic barriers existed to their entrance to the country, its labour market, and educational establishments, while a new generation of Palestinians was born in Libya to Palestinian migrant families, with these children inheriting not only their parents' refugee status, but also the very education system which benefited from their parents' pedagogical contributions.

The combination of Palestinians' family-based and individual migration provided the opportunity for Palestinian students to form part of a broader community throughout the course of their studies, while young Sahrawi children (until 1983–1984) and adolescents (especially from the 1990s) were isolated from their families and community, with the concomitant difficulties this invariably entailed. In spite of the differences in accessing education and living in Libya, it is notable that in both the Sahrawi and Palestinian cases, large proportions of girls and young women attended schools and universities there, in dramatic contrast with the gender imbalance of access to and participation in the Cuban education programme on the one hand, and of the lower female enrolment and attendance rates, and the early withdrawal of girls from Sahrawi schools in the camps on the other.[35] While the high number of Palestinian girls may have been accidental – dependent upon the gender of the children born to migrant families – Sahrawi girls were reportedly prioritised as recipients of Libyan scholarships, at least partly due to perceptions of the Sahrawis' proximity with Libya, and the conceptualisation of Libya as a 'fraternal' space.

Paralleling many interviewees' accounts of being treated 'like brothers', or even 'like Libyans' throughout their studies in Libya, official declarations of 'fraternal' bonds with the Sahrawi and the Palestinians formed part of Gaddafi's

Pan-Arabist worldview, which simultaneously reflected his commitment to support oppressed and colonised Arab peoples in general, and the Palestinian cause in particular. It can be argued that the Libyan eduscape unintentionally promoted many Pan-Arabist aims, including by promoting students' knowledge of the Arabic language and culture, through close interactions between different groups of students and teachers from across the region, and by strengthening connections with other Palestinians and the Palestinian cause.[36]

Reflecting on the broader social, and political, benefits of having studied in Libya, Samira concluded that

> Studying and living in Libya made me a better person and widened my knowledge of the Arabic language. It enabled me to become more mature; more aware of other people's cultures. Collectively, it strengthened my relationship with fellow Palestinians. My time in Libya increased my national awareness and understanding of the Palestinian cause.

Anas (who was affiliated with Fatah) also identified Libya as a supportive arena in which to develop an active political commitment to the Palestinian cause:

> I was an active member of the Palestinian Student Union in Libya, but when I returned to [Baddawi] camp in Lebanon, I froze my political activities. There was a significant difference between the student environment in Libya and the political milieu of the camps, which are mainly led by uneducated figures.

Even after Gaddafi's discriminatory policies, and their experiences of violence and expulsion, many Palestinian interviewees nonetheless recalled the time that they spent living, studying and working in Libya with nostalgia and even a (measured) sense of longing: 'I felt very settled in Libya, and I miss the country. Although conditions are not suitable at the moment, I look forward to the day that I will be able to return' (Hakim).

While not all interviewees echoed Hakim's wish to return to Libya, or expressed such a sense of nostalgia,[37] and Sahrawi refugees have maintained their distance from Libya since the 2011–2012 evacuation, tens of thousands of Palestinians remain in Libya to date, in spite of the civil war which has engulfed the country since 2011.[38] It could be posited that this continued presence in – and even processes of return to – Libya, is precisely as a result of the harsh conditions which have led to the refugee camps in Lebanon being denominated 'insecurity islands', combined with the broader insecurity in the region, and the widespread nature of hostipitality witnessed in all of the countries which host Palestinians. Remaining in or returning to Libya in 2011 replicates the return of Palestinians who were forcibly expelled by Gaddafi in 1997–1998, and highlights the lack of viable alternatives which are available to Palestinians in the region.

The feeling of having been 'embraced by Gaddafi' whilst in Libya (Anas op. cit.) relates to one stage of a constantly fluctuating Libyan hostipitality towards

Sahrawis and Palestinians, who, on more than one occasion, were eventually to face the same forms of violence in Libya as their families and broader communities have experienced across the MENA region. It is precisely the regional context, and the political challenges and cleavages which have characterised this region throughout the postcolonial era, which lead us to continue asking not only how Sahrawi and Palestinian refugees can be most meaningfully supported in these protracted refugee situations, but also precisely what kind of self-sufficiency can be imagined, and ultimately achieved, by refugees such as the Sahrawi and the Palestinians.

Notes

1 This term was repeatedly used by the Palestinians interviewed for this component of the research.
2 There is also a 'historical' community of Palestinians in Cuba (effectively the descendants of Palestinians who travelled to the Americas via the Caribbean throughout the twentieth century – see Fiddian-Qasmiyeh forthcoming); in contrast, the Sahrawi presence in Libya (and, indeed, in Cuba) has been limited to the students and monitors participating in the scholarship programme.
3 Through these and other policies, approximately 5,000 Palestinians had migrated to work in Libya from their host countries across the Middle East – including from the Palestinian camps in Lebanon – in 1970 (Abu-Lughod 1973), a number which had increased to 23,759 by 1981 (Smith 1986: 90), and to 29,207 by the end of 1992 (Palestine Red Crescent Society 1994: 5). Following the mass expulsion of Palestinians from Libya in 1995–1996 (see below), the number of Palestinians decreased dramatically to approximately 17,000 in 1996 (Al-Majdal 2010). Although the figures are ultimately contested, it is calculated that between 50,000 and 70,000 Palestinians were resident in Libya at the beginning of 2011.
4 I am particularly grateful to Mohammed (Abu Iyad) and Mahmoud (Abu Ibrahim) for their research assistance in identifying interviewees for this chapter. Given the sensitivities surrounding the Libyan conflict, and the discrimination and violence faced as a result of Palestinians' multifaceted relationship with Gaddafi, many Libyan-educated Palestinians were wary of speaking to a researcher about their experiences of having lived and studied in Libya. This was especially the case amongst those interviewees who continue to have family members based in Libya. In spite of these sensitivities, and the increasing insecurity in Lebanon at the time of the research, Mohammed and Mahmoud persevered in their attempts to identify interviewees, travelling regularly between the refugee camps in North Lebanon and Beirut to do so. I am especially grateful to them for their dedication to identify potential female interviewees, especially in light of the difficulties experienced in finding Cuban-educated Palestinian women to participate in the research for Chapter 5.
5 In this chapter, the interviews conducted with Palestinians in Lebanon are in turn contextualised through insights garnered throughout my research in the Sahrawi camps and in Spain with and about Sahrawi refugees who were educated through full scholarships in Libya. In particular, see Crivello and Fiddian-Qasmiyeh (2010), Chatty et al. (2010) and Fiddian-Qasmiyeh (2012 and 2013a).
6 Furthermore, Palestinians' self-sufficiency in Libya has been repeatedly undermined, and at times directly destroyed, through fluctuating policies of exclusion and expulsion during Palestinians', and also Sahrawis', time in Libya, as explored in detail below.
7 UNRWA is not only the main employer of educated Palestinians, but can also be conceptualised as the Palestinians' 'better husband' (following Turner 2012: 72).

8 As discussed below, Gaddafi was able to utilise the Libyan education system to promote a particular political outcome, demonstrating the extent to which education 'always has political intention either for the domination of people or for their liberation' (Alzaroo and Lewando-Hundt 2003: 166, cited in Chapter 1).

9 With reference to the latter, Samira – a 41-year-old woman who was born in Libya and is currently an UNRWA teacher in Lebanon – noted that 'the Libyan state fully funded Indonesian students who were studying Arabic and Islamic Studies in Libya'.

10 The French terms and phrases cited in the original text have been excised from this quotation.

11 On the existence, and relevance, of Pan-Arabist discourses and practices of hospitality and discrimination alike throughout the region, and in particular vis-à-vis Iraqi refugees in Jordan, see Mason (2011).

12 These were reportedly confiscated at least once by Boumediene's regime (Damis 1983).

13 For a more detailed account of the conflicts pertaining to the SADR's membership of the OAU, see Hodges (1984).

14 This is after Algeria, which provides the largest number of full scholarships, and before Cuba – see Chatty, Fiddian-Qasmiyeh and Crivello (2010: 59).

15 Of the fifty households interviewed in the Sahrawi refugee camps by the research team funded by the Andrew Mellon Foundation as part of the University of Oxford's project, Children and Adolescents in Sahrawi and Afghani Refugee Households, 10 women aged between 33 and 41 and 4 men aged between 29 and 37 indicated that they had studied in Libya in the 1970s and 1980s; 5 interviewees referred to family members who had studied in Libya – primarily sisters and daughters (as discussed in Fiddian-Qasmiyeh 2012).

16 However, other interviewees highlighted their awareness of the *fluctuating* nature of the support offered by Gaddafi to the Sahrawi. Hence, fourteen of the young men whom I interviewed in Syria, Cuba and the Sahrawi refugee camps recognised the different, and fluctuating, types of Libya's support for the Sahrawi, with a science graduate whom I interviewed in Havana (November 2006) indicating that 'the Algerians have been our most steadfast supporters. [*Pause*] *It is true, I suppose, that Libya has given some fluctuant support to us*, and students have also received a few scholarships from Syria... *but that's all*' (emphasis added). As such, in spite of interviewees' personal and familial experiences of studying in Libya, it is notable that many of my interviewees did not present Libya as a particularly significant provider of assistance to the Sahrawi, typically prioritising the roles played by other state and non-state actors.

17 See Chapters 3, 4 and 5 and Fiddian-Qasmiyeh (2009, 2010a, 2012, 2013a, 2013b).

18 As a parting gift, this young man manually copied out sections of the Qur'an for me, to supplement the pamphlets about the Revelation and a tape of Qur'anic recitations which he had handed me following our first conversation in Arabic. As discussed below, while Cuban-educated Sahrawis rarely discussed religion during our interviews in Cuba or in the camps, this young man repeatedly highlighted the centrality of Islam in his life, and encouraged me to learn more about his religion.

19 The term Sahrawi was used by Palestinians such as Anas, but to refer to 'African Sahrawi refugees who came from the Niger–Libya border and were part of the Turka group'. This usage of the term 'Sahrawi' reflects its etymology, since the word literally means 'inhabitant of the desert' and has only relatively recently been 'monopolised' by the Polisario Front to refer to the current and former inhabitants of the Western Sahara.

20 Although individual Sahrawi children are fostered by European (especially Spanish) families and are therefore able to access schooling in the European Union, these are individualised opportunities, rather than group programmes providing an education to small cohorts of students as in the Cuban and Libyan initiatives.

21 The implications of these intersecting forms of migration are many, including the extent to which family migration itself ensured the relatively high proportion of Palestinian girls and women present in Libya – for instance, in 1980/1981 there were approximately 14,600 Palestinian males and 9,100 Palestinian females in Libya (Tahir 1985: 42) – and the intergenerational nature of Palestinians' participation in Libya's education system – Palestinian boys and girls attended Libyan primary and secondary schools precisely because of their parents' own presence in Libya as teachers.

22 For a detailed account of the complex relationship between Gaddafi and these and other Palestinian factions in the 1970s and 1980s, see Sayigh (1997: especially pp. 486–487).

23 The well-versed feminist adage, 'the personal is political', reveals, and rejects, the artificiality of such a distinction.

24 The Arabic verb *yaṣtathni* was used repeatedly by Anas in his interview, in particular with reference to the notion *'istithnaa' al-filisṭiniyiin'* – 'with the exception of Palestinians'. I return to the relevance of this concept in Chapter 7.

25 It can be argued that the Sahrawi were also subjected to a paradoxical, and intrinsically conditional, notion of protection, oscillating between Gaddafi's desire to protect individual Sahrawis and promote their cause (to secure their 'best interests') through the provision of scholarships whilst applying pressure on Morocco, and the expulsion of Sahrawi refugees and the rejection of any further solidarity with the quest for Sahrawi self-determination when the possibility of a Maghrebian alliance approached fruition.

26 Telephone interview, Benghazi resident, April 2011; telephone interview, Benghazi resident, September 2011; personal communication, relative of Palestinian refugee in Tripoli, April 2011. See Fiddian-Qasmiyeh (2012).

27 Inter alia, the invisibility of Sahrawis in the English media, and their centrality in the Spanish press, demonstrates the extent to which different actors have prioritised the protection needs of different migrant and refugee populations, in this case in part due to former colonial ties and broader Sahrawi–Spanish solidarity networks revolving around refugee children (see Fiddian-Qasmiyeh 2010b, 2013a and 2013b, 2014a).

28 See Fiddian-Qasmiyeh (2012) for an analysis of the term 'repatriation' to refer to the 'return' of Sahrawi children to their refugee home-camps.

29 Quoted on www.publico.es, author's translation.

30 Quoted on www.publico.es, author's translation.

31 Whether pressure applied by Spanish civil society played a role in securing this outcome, and precisely how Polisario and Algeria negotiated this 'solution', remains to be explored.

32 No further details are available to confirm which of the two numbers of Sahrawi evacuees reported by Polisario (916) or to/by UNHCR (753) is correct.

33 By August 2014, an estimated 270,000 Palestinian refugees had been internally displaced by the ongoing conflict in Syria, over 70,000 had fled to neighbouring countries, and all nine Palestinian refugee camps in Syria had been affected by the violence (latest figures available from www.unrwa.org, accessed 25/10/2014).

34 Numerous reports, which remain unsubstantiated to date and have been vehemently refuted by Polisario representatives, have claimed that Sahrawi mercenaries were contracted by Gaddafi in 2011 (i.e. see Coughlin 2011; SPS 2011).

35 In contrast, UNRWA reports gender parity in access to primary, intermediate and secondary schooling (UNGA 2004: 11), while Daoud and Dgheim (2009) examine the reasons for lower enrolment rates amongst *boys* in secondary level schooling, in spite of the uneven impacts of early marriage on girls (also see Al-Hroub 2009: 16).

36 As noted above, while Sahrawi students reflected an awareness of the Palestinian cause, and of the presence of Palestinian students and teachers in Libya, no reference was made to the presence of Sahrawi refugees by Palestinian interviewees, or to the Sahrawi quest for self-determination.

37 Kasim, for instance, asserted that 'I came to know more about the Palestinian cause and Palestinian factions and their principles *when I returned to the camps*' (emphasis added). A similar ambiguity emerged in the context of Cuban-educated Palestinians interviewed in Lebanon (Chapter 5).

38 As I write (21 July 2014), Tripoli airport is under attack in Libya, forcing 'hundreds of families' to flee 'as militias fighting for control of the area engaged in their fiercest battles since the 2011 revolution in Libya' (Stephen 2014), a week after the UN withdrew its staff from the country due to the worsening security situation there (AFP 2014).

References

Abu-Lughod, I. (1973) 'Educating a Community in Exile: The Palestinian Experience', *Journal of Palestine Studies*, 2(3): 94–111.

AFP (2014) 'Libya Considers Call for Help after Rocket Attacks Close Tripoli airport', *The Guardian*, 15 July. Available at http://www.theguardian.com/world/2014/jul/15/libya-tripoli-airport-closed-rocket-attacks, last accessed 21/07/2014.

Al-Hroub, A. (2009) UNRWA *School Dropouts in Palestinian Refugee Camps in Lebanon: A Qualitative Study*. Program on Policy and Governance in Palestinian Refugee Camps in the Middle East Research Report, November. Beirut: American University of Beirut.

Al-Majdal (2010) 'The Palestinian Crisis in Libya 1994–1996: Interview with Professor Bassem Sirhan', *Al-Majdal*, Issue No. 45: Forced Secondary Displacement: Palestinian Refugees in the Gaza Strip, Iraq, Jordan, and Libya, http://www.badil.org/en/al-majdal/item/1571-art-02, last accessed 09/09/2014.

Alzaroo, S. and Lewando-Hundt, G. (2003) 'Education in the Context of Conflict and Instability: The Palestinian Case', *Social Policy and Administration*, 37(2): 165–180.

Amnesty International (2010) Libya – *Amnesty International Report 2010. Human Rights in Socialist People's Libyan Arab Jamahiriya*. London: Amnesty International.

Badwan, A. (2011) 'Al-qalaq al-mutazayid wa haal al-filisṭiniyin fi libia' [Growing Concern for the Situation of Palestinians in Libya]', *Al-Quds*, 28 March.

Barbier, M. (1982). *Le Conflit du Sahara Occidental*. Paris: L'Harmattan.

Brand, L.A. (1988) *Palestinians in the Arab World: Institution Building and the Search for State*. New York: Columbia University Press.

Breidlid, A. (2013) *Indigenous Knowledge and Development in the Global South*. London: Routledge.

Chatelard, G., El-Abed, O. and Washington, K. (2009) *Protection, mobility and livelihood challenges of displaced Iraqis in urban settings in Jordan*, ICMC report. Geneva: International Catholic Migration Committee.

Chatty, D., Fiddian-Qasmiyeh, E. and Crivello, G. (2010) 'Identity With/out Territory: Sahrawi Refugee Youth in Transnational Space', in D. Chatty (ed.) *Deterritorialised Youth: Sahrawi and Afghan Refugees at the Margins of the Middle East*. Oxford: Berghahn Books, 37–84.

Choueiri, Y.M. (2000) *Arab Nationalism: A History*. Oxford: Blackwell.

Coughlin, C. (2011) 'Libya: Col Gaddafi "has spent £2.1m on mercenaries"', *The Telegraph*, 20 April.

Crivello, G. and Fiddian-Qasmiyeh, E. (2010) 'The Ties that Bind: Sahrawi Children and the Mediation of Aid in Exile', in D. Chatty (ed.) *Deterritorialised Youth: Sahrawi and Afghan Refugees at the Margins of the Middle East*. Oxford: Berghahn Books, 85–118.

Damis, J.J. (1983) *Conflict in Northwest Africa: The Western Sahara dispute*. Stanford, CA: Hoover Institution Press.

Daoud, T. and Dgheim, K. (2009). *Reasons for Lower Enrolment of Boys Than Girls in the Secondary Cycle*. Beirut: UNRWA-Lebanon Education Program.

Dar Al-Hayat (2011) 'Munazamat al-tahrir tudin fi shidda iqtiham mukhayyam al-Raml wa tahjir sukanihi [The PLO Strongly Denounces the al-Raml Camp Incursion and the Displacement of Its People]', *Dar Al-Hayat*, 16 August.

Derrida, J. (2000a) 'Hostipitality', *Angelaki: Journal of the Theoretical Humanities*, 5(3): 3–18.

Derrida, J. (2000b) *Of Hospitality*. Palo Alto, CA: Stanford University Press.

El-Hafed, S. (2011) 'Return to Sahrawi Refugee Camps of Sahrawi Students in Libya', *Sahrawi Press Service*, 7 March.

El País (2011) 'Testimonios desde Libya', *El País*, 23 February.

Fiddian-Qasmiyeh, E. (forthcoming) 'Embracing Transculturalism and Footnoting Islam in Accounts of Arab Migration to Cuba', *Interventions: International Journal of Postcolonial Studies*.

Fiddian-Qasmiyeh, E. (2014a) *The Ideal Refugees: Gender, Islam and the Sahrawi Politics of Survival*. Syracuse NY: Syracuse University Press.

Fiddian-Qasmiyeh, E. (2014b) 'Transnational Abductions and Transnational Responsibilities? The Politics of 'Protecting' Female Muslim Refugees Abducted from Spain', *Gender, Place and Culture*, 21(2): 174–194.

Fiddian-Qasmiyeh, E. (2013a) 'The Inter-generational Politics of "Travelling Memories": Sahrawi Refugee Youth Remembering Home-land and Home-camp', *Journal of Intercultural Studies*, 34(6): 631–649.

Fiddian-Qasmiyeh, E. (2013b) 'Transnational Childhood and Adolescence: Mobilising Sahrawi Identity and Politics across Time and Space', *Journal of Ethnic and Racial Studies*, 36(5): 875–895.

Fiddian-Qasmiyeh, E. (2012) 'Invisible Refugees and/or Overlapping Refugeedom? Protecting Sahrawis and Palestinians Displaced by the 2011 Libyan Uprising', *International Journal of Refugee Law*, 24(2): 263–293.

Fiddian-Qasmiyeh, E. (2011) Protracted Sahrawi Displacement: Challenges and Opportunities Beyond Encampment, RSC Policy Briefing 7. Oxford: Refugee Studies Centre.

Fiddian-Qasmiyeh, E. (2010a) 'Education, Migration and Internationalism: Situating Muslim Middle Eastern and North African students in Cuba', *The Journal of North African Studies*, 15(2): 137–155.

Fiddian-Qasmiyeh, E. (2010b) 'When the Self becomes Other: Representations of Gender, Islam and the Politics of Survival in the Sahrawi Refugee Camps', in D. Chatty and B. Findlay (eds) *Dispossession and Displacement: Forced Migration in the Middle East and North Africa*. Oxford: Oxford University Press, 171–196.

Fiddian-Qasmiyeh, E. (2009) 'Representing Sahrawi Refugees' "Educational Displacement" to Cuba: Self-sufficient Agents or Manipulated Victims in Conflict?' *Journal of Refugee Studies*, 22(3): 323–350.

Germann Molz, J. and Gibson, S. (2007) 'Introduction: Mobilizing and Mooring Hospitality', in J. Germann Molz and S. Gibson (eds) *Mobilizing Hospitality: The Ethics of Social Relations in a Mobile World*. Aldershot: Ashgate, 1–25.

Gimeno-Martín, J.C. and Laman, M.A. (2005) *La Juventud Saharaui: Una Realidad. Preocupaciones y Expectativas*. Rabuni, Sahrawi Arab Democratic Republic: UJSARIO-CJE-UAM.

Goddard, B. (2009) 'UNHCR and the International Protection of Palestinian Refugees', *Refugee Survey Quarterly*, 28 (2/3): 475–510.

The Guardian (2011) 'Syria Assault on Latakia Drives 5,000 Palestinians from Refugee Camp', *The Guardian*, 15 August.

Hernández Moreno, A. (1988) *Economía y Sociedad del Sahara Occidental en el Siglo XIX*. Murcia: Universidad de Murcia.

Hickling-Hudson, A., Corona González, J. and Preston, R. (eds) (2012) *The Capacity to Share: A Study of Cuba's International Cooperation in Educational Development*. New York: Palgrave Macmillan.

Hodges, T. (1984) 'The Western Sahara File', *Third World Quarterly*, 6(1): 74–111.

Hulieras, A. (2001) 'Qadhafi's Comeback: Libya and Sub-Saharan Africa in the 1990s', *African Affairs*, 100: 5–25.

IMEMC (2011) 'Palestinian Student Killed by Mercenaries in Libya', International Middle East Media Centre, 26 February.

Khalidi, R., Anderson, L., Muslih, M. and Simon, R.S. (eds) (1991) *The Origins of Arab Nationalism*. New York: Columbia University Press.

Lesch, A.M. (1991) 'Palestinians in Kuwait', *Journal of Palestine Studies*, 20(4): 42–54.

Lynn Price, D. (1981) *The Western Sahara*. Beverley Hills, CA: SAGE Publications.

Ma'an (2011a) 'Gadhafi Forces Detain Palestinian Students', *Ma'an News Agency*, 2 March.

Ma'an (2011b) 'Last Group of Palestinian Students Leave Libya', *Ma'an News Agency*, 7 March.

Madge, C., Raghuram, P. and Noxolo, P. (2014) 'Conceptualizing international education: From international student to international study,' *Progress in Human Geography*, 31 March 2014, doi:10.1177/0309132514526442.

Mason, V. (2011) 'The Im/mobilities of Iraqi Refugees in Jordan: Pan-Arabism, "Hospitality" and the Figure of the "Refugee"', *Mobilities*, 6(3): 353–373.

Miské, A.-B. (1978) *Front Polisario: L'âme d'un peuple*. Paris: Éditions Rupture.

Muñoz, A. (2011) '"Las abandonaron a su suerte" Mas de 7.000 estudiantes saharauis viven las revueltas atrapados en los dos internados libios que tienen el RASD en Trípoli y Bengasi', *El País*, 4 March.

Nahmias, R. (2007) 'Libya Threatens to Deport Palestinian Refugees to Gaza', *YNet*, 17 March.

OHCHR (2006) Report of the OHCHR Mission to Western Sahara and the Refugee Camps in Tindouf – 15/23 May and 19 June 2006, 8 September.

Otman, W.A. and Karlberg, E. (2007) *The Libyan Economy: Economic Diversification and International Repositioning*. New York: Springer.

Palestine Red Crescent Society (1994) *The Situation of the Palestine Refugees in Diaspora: Demographic, Socio-Economic Characteristics and Health Status*. Rome: PRCS.

Pazzanita, A.G. and Hodges, T. (1994) *Historical Dictionary of Western Sahara*. Metuchen, NJ: Scarecrow Press.

Sayigh, Y. (1997) *Armed Struggle and the Search for State: The Palestinian National Movement, 1949–1993*. Oxford: Oxford University Press.

Shiblak, A. (1996) 'Residency Status and Civil Rights of Palestinian Refugees in Arab Countries', *Journal of Palestine Studies*, 25(3): 36–45.

Smith, P.A. (1986) 'The Palestinian Diaspora, 1948-1985', *Journal of Palestine Studies*, 15(3): 90–108.

SPS (2011) '"It is Neither the Tradition nor the National Interest of the POLISARIO Front to Get Involved in the Sad Situation in Libya", says Sahrawi diplomat', *Sahrawi Press Service*, 12 March.

SPS (2001) 'Libya', *Sahara Press Service*, 17 October. Available at http://arso.org/01-e01-4245.htm, last accessed 23/09/2006.

Stephen, C. (2014) 'Libyan Militias' Battle for Tripoli Airport Forces Hundreds of Families to Flee', *The Guardian*, 20 July. Available at http://www.theguardian.com/world/2014/jul/20/libyan-militas-battle-tripoli-hundreds-families-flee-fight, last accessed 21/07/2014.

Tahir, J. (1985) 'An Assessment of Palestinian Human Resources: Higher Education and Manpower', *Journal of Palestine Studies*, 14(3): 32–53.

Turner, S. (2012) *Politics of Innocence: Hutu Identity, Conflict and Camp Life*. Oxford: Berghahn Books.

UNGA (2004) Report of the Commissioner General of the United Nations Relief and Works Agency for Palestine Refugees in the Near East: 1 July 2003-30 June 2004. UNGA Official Records, 59th Session, Supplement No. 13 (A/59/13).

UNHCR (2011a) *Update # 25. Humanitarian Situation in Libya and the Neighbouring Countries*. 18 May. Geneva: UNCHR.

UNHCR (2011b) *Update # 27. Humanitarian Situation in Libya and the Neighbouring Countries*. 3 June. Geneva: UNCHR.

UNHCR EXCOM (2011) *Update on UNHCR's operations in the Middle East and North Africa (MENA)*. Geneva: United Nations High Commissioner for Refugees Executive Committee.

Velloso de Santisteban, A. (1993) *La educación en el Sahara Occidental*. Madrid: UNED.

WFP (2004) *Protracted Relief and Recovery Operation – Algeria 10172.1. Assistance to Western Saharan Refugees*. Rome: World Food Programme.

World Tribune (2012) 'Syrian Regime Said to Target Palestinians Who Won't Fight Uprising', *World Tribune*, 4 March.

Yara, A. O. (2003). *L'insurrection sahraouie: de la guerre à l'Etat, 1973–2003*. Paris: L'Harmattan.

7 A reflection on exceptional margins and spaces of/for solidarity

Marginal exceptions – transcending expectations

The Cuban and Libyan approaches to cooperation explored in this book are 'exceptional' in many regards:[1] they embody a clear 'alternative' to Northern-led humanitarian 'rules', explicitly positioning themselves outside traditional conceptualisations of 'donor states' and officially aiming, in that process, to disrupt the power imbalances which characterise post-colonial and neocolonial North–South/donor–recipient relations. Both systems have thus aimed to 'share what they have, rather than give what is left over' (to paraphrase José Martí, cited in Chapter 3), whether through Cuba's solidarity with and carefully designed internationalist scholarships for citizens and refugees from around the world, or via Libya's targeted scholarship programme for selected students from the Arab region and broader policy of facilitating the migration of Arab brothers and sisters, including in particular Palestinians, as part of a broader policy of supporting the development of sovereign and independent Arab peoples and nations which would, in turn, constitute a coherent Arab *Ummah*. In so doing, it can be argued that Cuba and Libya alike historically (re)constituted themselves respectively as internationalist and Pan-Arabist 'sharers' – as opposed to 'donors' or 'providers' – as states which have simultaneously distributed humanitarian assistance to/in the Sahrawi and Palestinian refugee camps and (re)created a central margin for refugees' education and development.

The Cuban and Libyan approaches to hospitality for refugees have included Cuba's stated commitment to 'sharing' between citizens and refugees as equals (even during periods of acute crisis, such as at the pinnacle of the *Periodo Especial*) and working to bring refugees' educational and professional levels in line with Cubans', while Libya's bifurcated system has supported certain 'marginal' brothers and sisters (including Sahrawis and Palestinians) in ways which have led refugees to help one another (for instance, as refugee-teachers for other refugees) while they simultaneously help themselves (through refugee teachers' salaries and remittances to their home-camps). The presence of thousands of Palestinians as teachers in Libya also demonstrates the extent to which this alternative model of cooperation was multi-directional: Libya may have developed a form of 'reverse self-sufficiency' given the extent to which refugee-teachers maintained and strengthened Libya's national educational infrastructure, with Palestinian (and also Iraqi) refugee-teachers sharing their knowledge and skills with other refugees in Libya, but also with Libyan citizens.[2]

Palestinian and Sahrawi exceptions

The position of Palestinian refugees as 'sharers' within Libya is a further example of the relevance of the notion of 'the exception' in the intersecting case studies examined in this book – the roles which refugee-teachers have played in Libya in support of other refugees and in support of their hosts transcend mainstream expectations vis-à-vis 'the refugee'. Far from the archetypal dependent refugee awaiting externally provided aid, Palestinians have actively participated in the Libyan 'self-service' space, sharing with the wider Palestinian Self (family, relatives and broader community), but also with Others: citizens and refugees from across the MENA region.

More broadly, Northern academics, policymakers and practitioners have repeatedly, if differently, denominated Palestinians and Sahrawis as 'exceptions' to the refugee norm. As indicated in Chapter 1, Palestinians have historically often been overlooked by mainstream refugee studies and policies by virtue of claims of Palestinian exceptionalism, claims which are substantiated, for instance, through reference to Palestinians being under the responsibility of UNRWA (which has no protection mandate) while all other refugees around the world are under the remit of UNHCR (with protection at its institutional core). If Palestinians have been relegated to the margins of refugee studies, in spite of having been – in many regards – at the core of Libya's education system, external observers have long represented the Sahrawi as 'the most unusual refugees'[3] through the cumulative usage of superlative, and inherently comparative, terms.

By constituting the Sahrawi as 'ideal' refugees – self-sufficient, democratic, secular and gender-equal – the Sahrawi camps have been labeled a 'success story' amidst a failing humanitarian system which creates 'dependency syndrome' amongst refugees (Harrell-Bond 1986; Fiddian-Qasmiyeh 2014), and even invoked as 'the best run refugee camps in the world' (Brazier 1997, cited in Chapter 4). This discursive strategy has taken place precisely by asserting the Sahrawis' positional superiority (following Nader 1989: 324) over Other, supposedly non-ideal, refugees, thereby potentially inducing antagonisms and solidifying hierarchies between refugees, rather than encouraging refugees and observers alike to contest such processes (Fiddian-Qasmiyeh 2014: 266). The South–South educational migration system examined in this book is particularly significant in this regard given its role in helping maintain this image of the Sahrawi as uniquely 'successful' refugees: it is arguably the Sahrawis' access to basic and higher education in countries such as Cuba which has facilitated the Polisario/SADR's self-management in and of their desert-based refugee camps.

The superlatives used to describe Sahrawi refugees in their home-camps also resonate with interviewees' accounts of the ways in which Cuban and Libyan policies 'made an exception' for specific refugee-migrants. Palestinian and

Sahrawi refugees in Cuba and Libya, for instance, recalled having received 'special treatment' at specific points of time during their studies: in Cuba, Palestinians were reportedly treated as '*real* citizens', '*more than* citizens', as '*first class* citizens' and as '*complete* citizens' (Chapter 5), Sahrawi children were the last group of international students able to access secondary schooling on La Isla de la Juventud, and they enjoyed 'slightly more advantageous treatment' than Cuban citizens (UNHCR 2005 – see Chapter 4). In turn, in Libya, Palestinians were not only treated like 'brothers' and 'like Libyan citizens', but were concretely framed as exceptional through a rhetoric of similarity and equality with Libyans: Libyan decrees which were designed to differentiate between Libyans and non-Libyans were thus qualified through reference to '*bi istithnaa' al-filisṭiniyyiin*' – 'with the exception of Palestinians'. This exceptional treatment positioned Palestinians as part of the Libyan Self by creating a distinction between Palestinians and other Arab visiting students, but also through the allocation of 'special privileges' and 'favours' precisely because of their overlapping identities as refugees and as Arabs (Chapter 6).

However, while Gaddafi's Libya itself became the Sahrawis' and Palestinians' brother – welcoming and rewarding these refugees with a free education – it also became their ultimate Other – punishing them when their presence threatened to undermine Gaddafi's strategic objectives. The Libyan policies which were designed to 'make an exception' for refugees thus fluctuated between the allocation of special privileges for refugees, and the re-establishment of 'the national order of things' (to quote Malkki 1995): Sahrawis and Palestinians were offered special opportunities to maximise their inclusion in the education system, and yet they were also excluded, or taken out (the root of the term 'exception' in Latin, '*excipere*') from the national equation – prevented, at times, from competing equally with Libyan citizens for prestigious courses of study such as medicine and engineering, and barred from completing the first term of university.

In addition to being perceived as a threat to the Libyan national body, Gaddafi also 'took exception to' the Sahrawis and Palestinians in the 1980s and 1990s, expelling Sahrawi students and disowning the 'Arab Sahara' in order to pursue his aim of Maghrebian unity in 1983–1984, and punishing all Palestinians in Libya when he believed that Arafat had relinquished the Palestinians' right to return by signing the Oslo Accords. This third interpretation thus ties back to the first point made above: many external analysts have 'taken exception' to the usage of the epithet 'humanitarianism' to describe the initiatives developed by the Cuban and Libyan states – demoting/denominating these as ideologically and politically driven modes of action, whilst/by maintaining the assumption that Northern-led humanitarian institutions and states are apolitical and neutral. Neither Cuba nor Libya are conceptualised as 'traditional' donors nor have they been expected to be, or have they been accepted as, members of the international humanitarian community.

By noting these, and many other forms of 'exceptionalism', my aim has not been to idealise these alternative modes of responding to refugees, but rather to take one critical step towards writing the Other into the history of humanitarianism, as theory, policy and practice. The Cuban and Libyan approaches to peoples affected by conflict and occupation have often been relegated to the margins of political and academic analysis, and yet so too have beneficiaries' own embodied understandings of the motivations, nature and implications of these Southern-led initiatives and spaces of engagement. Just as Harrell-Bond poignantly critiqued the hegemonic humanitarian system which has historically 'imposed aid', and analytical categories, upon refugees (1986), we must also pursue a nuanced analysis of how different actors, including beneficiaries, 'define aid' and understand and value the diverse modes of response which have purportedly been designed and implemented on their behalf.

Examining the Cuban and Libyan programmes from a range of vantage points has thus enabled us to explore not only the extent to which different actors consider these initiatives to be 'humanitarian', 'ideological', 'political' and/or 'politicised', but also to prioritise the identification and interrogation of a variety of paradoxes which are inherent within these intersecting case studies. Perhaps the foremost paradox pertains to the multifaceted dynamics of inclusion and exclusion, centralisation and marginalisation, which themselves conceptually frame this study.

Inclusions and exclusions: South–South cooperation for whom?

The Cuban and Libyan paradigms of cooperation for refugees include trans-national education systems which have been created by, and in, the margins for other marginal(ised) populations: through such programmes, education has been provided by the Other for the Other, with providers and recipients alike being from and of the periphery. Concurrently, however, refugees' journeys from their respective positions of geopolitical marginality have arguably simultaneously created a new educational central margin in Cuba, a new periphery in Libya, and uneven processes of centrality and marginality in graduates' home-camps. Furthermore, in the Cuban context, it can also be argued that the Cuban margin may have provided support to the Sahrawi refugee/margin, and yet the Spanish core (Cuba's and the Sahrawis' former coloniser) has benefited through Cubaraui doctors' onward migration to work in Spanish hospitals.

The peripheral nature of Libya's education system for Sahrawi and Palestinian students is reflected, for instance, in the uneven hierarchies of value and worth assigned to education from Cuba and Libya upon graduates' return to their home-camps: Cuban-educated graduates have been highly valued professionally in the Sahrawi and Palestinian refugee camps alike, whilst Libyan-educated Sahrawis and Palestinians have remained underemployed and on their respective camps' margins, and have, in the Palestinian case, even faced difficulties in having their Libyan studies recognised by Lebanese universities.[4]

While Cubarauis have been particularly hyper-visible and hyper-audible to Sahrawi refugees and foreign visitors in their home-camps, Palestinian graduates have blurred their bonds with Cuba to maximise their employment with UNRWA. Nonetheless, even when the Polisario/SADR has been heralded for running the camps with little external intervention, in the Sahrawi case a subsequent resurgence of dependence upon Spanish doctors has arisen when (primarily male) Cubaraui graduates have prioritised their professional, and financial, development through migrating to Spain to send remittances to relatives in their home-camps. Although Cubaraui women and Cuban-educated Palestinians have also often wished to leave their home-camps to seek a 'better future' outside the region, their opportunities for onward migration have been restricted for a variety of structural reasons. In the case of the latter, these experiences of immobility have nonetheless ensured that Palestinian refugees in the camps continue to benefit from the medical care and services of these graduates through what I have referred to as an overarching process of circumstantial humanitarianism.

(Im)mobility: in whose best interests?

These experiences of immobility are intimately related to broader processes of inclusion and exclusion. Indeed,

> ... developing approaches that can envisage that international study is simultaneously as much about multi-scalar circularity and mobility from historically contingent multiple locations as it is about place-based immobilities is important because the latter can produce exclusions and marginalizations which have consequences on the ground for people in different places at different times.
>
> (Madge et al. 2014: 15)

By tracing the narratives of MENA students who were based in Cuba, and complementing these with the accounts of Sahrawi and Palestinian refugees who have returned to their home-camps after years, or decades, of studying and working abroad in Cuba and Libya, the immobility, exclusion and marginalisation of different students (and non-students) have arisen throughout this book. As such, in addition to asking who has been prevented from accessing these educational migration programmes, and why, an equally poignant question arising in this book is: who has been excluded and subjected to different forms of discrimination and abuse *precisely as a result of* their access to and participation in these migratory processes.

In effect, although migration to Cuba and Libya may have offered different degrees of self-sufficiency to Sahrawi and Palestinian individuals, families and collectives, such processes have offered little if any protection to students when they have been at heightened risk during their studies or upon their return to their home-camps. UNHCR monitored Sahrawi children's well-being in Cuba, and the Cuban state reportedly prioritised, rather than penalised, Sahrawis who remained in Cuba during the *Periodo Especial* (Chapter 3), and yet the cases of Cubaraui women who were subjected to personal, familial and collective violence upon their return to the camps for carrying a physical legacy of their participation in the scholarship programme highlight the dangers which certain students/graduates have faced precisely by virtue of having left their families to study abroad (Chapter 4). If women were targeted over and above Cubaraui men who might have also had 'productive' relationships during their time studying in Cuba, men and women, children and adults alike faced discrimination and violence in Libya during periods of political turmoil and civil unrest. The expulsion of Sahrawi and Palestinian refugee-students, and indeed Palestinian refugee-migrants, and the difficulties faced by refugees attempting to escape from the 2011 Libyan uprising, demonstrates the existence of a major protection gap with regards to these students. In essence, while UNHCR and UNRWA worked together to address some of the protection needs of Palestinians expelled by Gaddafi in the 1990s, in 2011 UNHCR was not aware of, or responsible for, the evacuation of Sahrawi children and adolescents from Libya, and neither the Polisario/SADR nor the PLO had the capacity to evacuate 'their' refugees.

Although migration to Cuba and Libya has been conceptualised as helping Sahrawi and Palestinian refugees alike achieve a better future – whether through accessing their right to an education per se, or enhancing their prospects to professional self-sufficiency with a view to providing the infrastructure necessary for an independent state – migration has itself at times increased, rather than mitigated or erased, processes of marginalisation and oppression amongst students and graduates.

These case studies, therefore, prompt the broader question of whether refugees who 'voluntarily' migrate for educational and/or economic purposes are conceptualised by different actors as being 'worthy' of international protection (also see Fiddian-Qasmiyeh 2012). Indeed, as researchers and policymakers increasingly focus on the blurred nature of categories such as 'forced' and 'voluntary' migration (Fiddian-Qasmiyeh et al. 2014: 4), these refugees embody the overlaps of being legally recognised as refugees under international definitions, and simultaneously being educational/economic migrants who have travelled outside their country of habitual residence or first country of asylum. The Palestinian and Sahrawi children, adolescents and adults referred to in this book thereby reflect the potential simultaneity of being a 'voluntary' and an 'involuntary migrant', and of the specific protection needs of refugee-students and refugee-migrants. Recognising the specificities of these protection concerns is particularly important in light of increasing policy interest in, and support for, migration and mobility as a 'fourth durable solution'. Whilst seen as a way to complement the three traditional durable solutions available to refugees – local integration in their hosting context, resettlement to a third country or voluntary repatriation to their country of origin – this book has highlighted that 'voluntary migration' may lead to increased risk, rather than being an effective and durable solution per se.

Prompted both due to the recognition that challenges can arise as a result of transnational educational migration, and also as a result of the end of the Cuban scholarship programme, one practical response is currently being proposed in the Sahrawi refugee camps: with financial and practical support from the Cuban state, South Africa and Spanish universities (amongst others), plans are underway to develop a 'University in the Sahara' in the vicinity of the Sahrawi refugee camps themselves, rather than relying upon transnational scholarship programmes as has been the case to date (Fiddian-Qasmiyeh 2011).

It remains unclear whether this University in the Sahara will be established or not, and yet it is evident that Sahrawi and Palestinian refugees are facing a major challenge, in light of the simultaneous loss of Cuba[5] and Libya[6] as educational hosting contexts, if they are to continue accessing a tertiary education. Moreover, the proposal to establish such a university near the camps suggests that the aim is to strengthen Sahrawi refugees' capacity for *proximate self-sufficiency* and *self-management*, rather than the overarching aim ostensibly guiding Cuba's and Libya's support for the Sahrawi and Palestinians as peoples pending *self-determination*: to secure the establishment of an independent Western Sahara and a free Palestine.

A 'better future' for South–South cooperation?

Given the ongoing instability, and hostipitality, faced by these and other refugee groups in the region[7] and the geopolitical shifts taking place across the Global South, this leads us to conclude by considering whether there is, or should be, a future for South–South models of cooperation for refugees.

Whilst this book has focused in particular on Cuba's international scholarship programme for children and adolescents, and on Libya's free education programme for youth and young adults, these programmes are exceptional and yet not unique. In effect, educational migration forms a highly significant role in many states' models for international cooperation – including countries such as Venezuela, South Africa and China which effectively unsettle the notion of 'the' Global South. Exploring refugee-students' experiences of studying in and returning 'home' from Cuba is especially significant given the extent to which Cuba's internationalist approach to South–South cooperation has inspired other countries to fund international scholarships and to become educational providers in their own right, including through programmes for refugees from around the world. For instance, although Cuba offered thousands of scholarships to Venezuelan students in the 1990s and Venezuela was therefore a 'student-sending' country during that decade, by the 2000s it had become a key funder of Bolivian students' educational migration to Cuba, and had established itself as the principal co-funder and leader of regional literacy and higher education programmes (Fiddian-Qasmiyeh 2010; Muhr 2010). In this way, Cuba and Libya can be seen as nodes within a much more complex transnational system, having expanded their own roles, but having also contributed to regional development initiatives both within and outside Latin America, reaching as far as the Middle East and North Africa.

By identifying South–South scholarship programmes as part of an alternative *discursive* model vis-à-vis migration, development and humanitarianism, it can, therefore, be argued that concepts such as 'self-sufficiency' and 'South–South cooperation' have a long history of 'travelling' over time and space (following Said 1983). As such, even if the Cuban and Libyan era of internationalist and

Pan-Arabist support for long-standing refugees from MENA has drawn to a close, elements of each of these models have travelled to, and been welcomed by, Others. It remains to be seen whether such elements will ultimately be reconfigured to establish cooperation mechanisms and processes of recognition which are founded upon meaningful reciprocity and solidarity with refugees, thereby potentially constituting an alternative to *the* alternative, or, to paraphrase Derrida (2000: 3), whether such elements will be 'parasitised' by the self-contradictions harboured within the global bodies of the North and the South alike.

Notes

1　The multifaceted, and multi-directional notions of 'exception' which have emerged throughout the course of this book themselves offer an alternative to the predominant application, or critique, of Agamben's notion of 'the state of exception' in analyses of refugee situations. Agamben conceptualises refugee camps as quintessential spaces of exception characterised by the suspension of the rule of law and refugees' reduction to 'bare life' (1998, 2005), with the Palestinian refugee camps in Lebanon having, in particular, been extensively analysed via this framework (i.e. Ramadan 2009; Hanafi and Long 2010; Knudsen 2010). Amongst others, Agamben has been extensively critiqued for discursively reproducing – rather than resisting – the depiction of refugees as non-agentic bodies which are the subject of diverse forms of governmentality, and for dismissing, a priori, the multiple meanings and sense of (be)longing(s) which may be developed, negotiated and contested by the inhabitants of protracted refugee camps. Relevant critiques and alternative readings include Puggioni (2006), Le Cour Grandmaison et al. (2007), Huysmans (2008) and Qasmiyeh and Fiddian-Qasmiyeh (2013).

2　In contrast, Sahrawis and Palestinians were prohibited from entering the Cuban labour market and were therefore dependent upon allowances provided by the Cuban government and their respective political representatives throughout their time in the Caribbean. Nevertheless, this period of economic dependence was paralleled by intensive work experience throughout their studies in Cuba, which may itself be conceptualised as a way in which Sahrawi and Palestinian medical students supported Cuba's national medical system through the provision of gratis/inexpensive medical care during their medical training.

3　Lippert (1987) and San-Martín (2005) cite a Red Cross field representative who described the Sahrawi as 'the most unusual refugees' in the 1980s.

4　Although many Palestinians interviewed in Lebanon announced that they would have preferred to complete their studies in Lebanon rather than in Cuba, in the Sahrawi context, this hierarchy of value could be summarised as follows: a Cuban education over a Libya one; a European/North American education over a Cuban one; and a Libyan education over a camp-based one.

5　Although the final Cubaraui doctor has now reportedly graduated from Cuba, embodying the end of Sahrawi refugee youths' participation in Cuba's South–South educational migration programme, it is possible that the intergenerational nature of Palestinian–Cuban students' access to scholarships will survive the wide array of transitions taking place in Cuba.

6　The 2011 uprising in Libya led to the end of a long era of Pan-Arabist educational cooperation, with the indefinite termination of the Libya scholarship programme for Sahrawis and Palestinians alike following Gaddafi's death. Whether a similar scholarship initiative will develop in due course remains to be seen, with interviewees divided on this matter.

7　For instance, see Mason (2011) on hostipitality towards Iraqi refugees in Jordan.

References

Agamben, G. (2005) *State of Exception*. Chicago, IL: University of Chicago Press.

Agamben, G. (1998) *Homo Sacer: Sovereign Power and Bare Life*. Stanford, CA: Stanford University Press. (Trans. D. Heller-Roazen.)

Brazier, C. (1997) 'Special Edition: War and Peace in Western Sahara', *The New Internationalist*, 297.

Le Cour Grandmaison, O., Lhuilier, G. and Valluy, J. (eds) (2007) *Le Retour des Camps? Sangatte, Lampedusa, Guantanamo…* Paris: Autrement.

Derrida, J. (2000) 'Hostipitality', *Angelaki: Journal of the Theoretical Humanities*, 5(3): 3–18.

Fiddian-Qasmiyeh, E. (2014) *The Ideal Refugees: Gender, Islam and the Sahrawi Politics of Survival*. Syracuse NY: Syracuse University Press.

Fiddian-Qasmiyeh, E. (2012) 'Invisible Refugees and/or Overlapping Refugeedom? Protecting Sahrawis and Palestinians Displaced by the 2011 Libyan Uprising', *International Journal of Refugee Law*, 24(2): 263–293.

Fiddian-Qasmiyeh, E. (2011) Protracted Sahrawi Displacement: Challenges and Opportunities Beyond Encampment, RSC Policy Brief, No. 7. Oxford: Refugee Studies Centre.

Fiddian-Qasmiyeh, E. (2010) 'Education, Migration and Internationalism: Situating Muslim Middle Eastern and North African Students in Cuba', *The Journal of North African Studies*, 15(2): 137–155.

Fiddian-Qasmiyeh, E., Loescher, G., Long, K. and Sigona, N. (2014) 'Introduction: Refugee and Forced Migration Studies in Transition', in E. Fiddian-Qasmiyeh, G. Loescher, K. Long and N. Sigona (eds) *The Oxford Handbook of Refugee and Forced Migration Studies*. Oxford: Oxford University Press, 1–19.

Hanafi, S. and Long, T. (2010) 'Governance, Governmentalities, and the State of Exception in the Palestinian Refugee Camps of Lebanon', *Journal of Refugee Studies*, 23(2): 134–159.

Harrell-Bond, B.E. (1986) *Imposing Aid: Emergency Assistance to Refugees*. Oxford: Oxford University Press.

Huysmans, J. (2008) 'The Jargon of Exception – On Schmitt, Agamben and the Absence of Political Society', *International Political Sociology*, 2: 165–183.

Knudsen, A. (2010) '(In-)Security in a Space of Exception: The Destruction of the Nahr el-Bared Refugee Camp in Lebanon', in J.-A. McNeish and J.H. Sande (eds) *Security and Development*. Oxford: Berghahn Books, 99–112.

Lippert, A. (1987) 'The Sahrawi Refugees: Origins and Organization, 1975– 1985', in R. Lawless and L. Monahan (eds) *War and Refugees: The Western Sahara Conflict*. London: Pinter.

Malkki, L. (1995) 'Refugees and Exile: From "Refugee Studies" to the National Order of Things', *Annual Review of Anthropology*, 24: 495–523.

Mason, V. (2011) 'The Im/mobilities of Iraqi Refugees in Jordan: Pan-Arabism, "Hospitality" and the Figure of the "Refugee"', *Mobilities*, 6(3): 353–373.

Muhr, T. (2010) 'Counter-hegemonic Regionalism and Higher Education for All: Venezuela and the ALBA', *Globalisation, Societies and Education*, 8(1): 39–57.

Nader, L. (1989) 'Orientalism, Occidentalism and the Control of Women', *Cultural Dynamics*, 2(3): 323–355.

Puggioni, R (2006) 'Resisting Sovereign Power: Camps in-Between Exception and Dissent', in J. Huysmans, A. Dobson and R. Prokhovnik (eds) *The Politics of Protection. Sites of Insecurity and Political Agency*. London: Routledge, 68–83.

Qasmiyeh, Y.M. and Fiddian-Qasmiyeh, E. (2013) 'Refugee Camps and Cities in Conversation', in J. Garnett and A. Harris (eds) *Migration and Religious Identity in the Modern Metropolis*. Farnham: Ashgate, 131–143.

Ramadan, A. (2009) 'Destroying Nahr el-Bared: Sovereignty and Urbicide in the Space of Exception', *Political Geography*, 28(3): 153–163.

Said, E.W. (1983) *The World, the Text, and the Critic*. London: Vintage.

San-Martín, P. (2005) 'Nationalism, Identity and Citizenship in the Western Sahara', *Journal of North African Studies*, 10(3): 565–592.

UNHCR (2005) *Information Note: Western Saharan Refugee Students in Cuba*. Geneva: UNHCR.

Index